RESOURCE REVOLUTION

RESOURCE REVOLUTION

HOW TO CAPTURE THE BIGGEST BUSINESS OPPORTUNITY IN A CENTURY

Stefan Heck and Matt Rogers
with Paul Carroll

New Harvest
Houghton Mifflin Harcourt
Boston New York

MELCHER
MEDIA

Produced by Melcher Media

Library of Congress Cataloging-in-Publication Data is available.
ISBN 978-0-544-11456-2

Produced by Melcher Media
124 West 13th Street
New York, NY 10011
www.melcher.com

Founder and CEO: Charles Melcher
VP, Operations: Bonnie Eldon
VP, Editorial Director: Duncan Bock
VP, Global Sourcing, Supply Chain,
and Logistics: Kurt Andrews
Assistant Editor: Lynne Ciccaglione

Designed by Downey Drouin

Printed in the United States of America
DOC 10 9 8 7 6 5 4 3

Matt dedicates this book to his wife, the Honorable Yvonne Gonzalez Rogers, without whom this book would not have been possible, and to his children, Christopher, Maria, and Josh, whose lives and careers will be shaped by how the resource revolution develops.

Stefan dedicates this book to his wife, Phoenicia Vuong, whose stories and tai chi practice showed the way, and to his daughter, Celine, who has already started her own resource revolution.

CONTENTS

LIST OF EXHIBITS

ACKNOWLEDGMENTS

This book reflects our personal experience across the last two decades, helping private-sector clients, governments, and nonprofit clients handle the challenges and opportunities arising from a world facing resource scarcity. We have benefited tremendously from the in-depth research done by the McKinsey Global Institute, Richard Dobbs, James Manyika, Jaana Remes, Diana Farrell, McKinsey's Sustainability and Resource Productivity Practice, Jeremy Oppenheim, Scott Nyquist, Martin Stuchtey, Tomas Naucler, Alberto Marchi, Giorgi Busnelli, Krister Aanesen, Per-Anders Enkvist, Ken Sommers, Dickon Pinner, Scott Jacobs, Fraser Thompson, Nikhil Krishnan, Kyungyeol Song, Jonathan Woetzel, Stefan Knupfer, McKinsey's Global Energy and Materials Practice, Ken Ostrowski, Harry Robinson, Claude Genereaux, Humayun Tai, McKinsey's Advanced Industrials Practice, Andre Andonian, Martin Hirt, Bill Wiseman, Sakae Suzuki, Daniel Pacthod, and Yasushi Sawada. Over many years, the McKinsey Global Institute has shaped the way companies and governments think about how productivity drives wealth creation.

The resource revolution theme comes from an important collaboration between the Sustainable Resource Productivity Practice and the McKinsey Global Institute, which looked at the roots of resource scarcity. To explain the opportunities for companies to win in this environment, we have relied heavily on our energy and advanced industrial partners for support and counsel.

Duncan Bock and Charlie Melcher from Melcher Media taught us to write for a general audience. Paul Carroll has been a remarkable collaborator, turning our turgid prose into a clear and, we hope, engaging text for the general reader. Rik Kirkland helped us frame this project up front and guided us through the vicissitudes of the publishing process with patience and grace. Nils Grimm provided much of the research support required to deliver this manuscript, with assistance from David Frankel, Alex Buell, Helga Vanthournout and Sean Kane. Downey Drouin lent her craft to the cover, layout, and exhibits.

Many other colleagues have contributed to this book, providing great examples of how productivity innovations can shape markets. The best ideas in this book have many parents; the errors and omissions are the responsibility of the authors alone.

INTRODUCTION

WE ARE STANDING AT THE THRESHOLD of the biggest business opportunity in a century.

That's the surprising conclusion we came to in 2006, after years of working as counselors to some of the world's leading technology, industrial, and energy companies.

It was not a popular conclusion at the time. Because of concern about natural resources, conventional wisdom had taken on a "we're all going to die" tone. The environmental community was certain that pollution and climate change had doomed the planet. Numerous books and published reports argued that copper, iron, and other materials, including the rare earth metals used in so many electronic devices, were on the same "we're going to run out" trajectory that was projected for oil. The economic community worried about the devastation that could occur when oil hit $200/barrel. Silver at $30/ounce, gold at $1,500/ounce, copper at $3.50/pound, aluminum at $2,000/ton, steel at $900/ton, corn at $6/bushel, wheat at $7/bushel—all compounded the fear in the market. Far from being optimistic, many in business wondered: How much could the global economy take?

The surge in wealth in China, India, and other developing countries heightened the worries, because billions of people would soon have the income to consume far more than they ever had before. The world's population was going to place unprecedented demand on natural resources just as they were petering out.

We had, however, come to different conclusions. Looking at the opportunities that came with adding 2.5 billion people to the middle class and at how the integration of industrial technology and information technology was changing all aspects of resource use, we saw opportunities for transformational changes. Radical improvements in productivity will come to the worlds of energy (both in terms of increasing production and reducing consumption), transport, buildings, water, agriculture, metals, and every other major commodity. These changes matter not just for major commodity producers but for any company that makes heavy use of electricity, fuels, or natural resources or that provides products and services to resource-intensive businesses—in other words, to a high percentage of all the businesses in all the countries of the world.

Rather than facing a crisis because of resource scarcity, we confront an opportunity that will reframe the world's economy and create opportunities for trillions of dollars in profits.

The next industrial revolution has, in fact, already begun, and it will dwarf the previous industrial revolutions in both size and speed. Managing businesses in this revolution will be hard. Revolutions are always hard. But managers who can adopt the necessary new methods will achieve breakthroughs in efficient use of resources, seize tomorrow's biggest growth opportunities, and create the companies that lead the global economy for the next century.

Our argument is relatively simple:

- Combining information technology, nanoscale materials science, and detailed understanding of biology with industrial technology and infrastructure yields substantial productivity increases.
- Embedding high-productivity economic growth in the developing world to support the 2.5 billion new members of the middle class presents the largest wealth creation opportunity in a century.
- Capturing these opportunities requires a new approach to management.

We recognize the challenges ahead. On its current course, the world sees stagnating economic growth, accelerating commodity price inflation, increasing pollution, political gridlock, and the return of the frictions among powerful nations like the United States, China, Russia, India, and Germany.

Accommodating the new members of the middle class will require so much construction that commodity prices will increase and supply chains will be challenged. The increasing rate of change has driven a number of companies into bankruptcy, leading some to believe that we are moving backward, not forward. Pollution levels, especially in the developing world, are reaching choking levels.

Many people, companies, and even nations will try to resist the new industrial revolution. People always resist revolutions. The Luddites tried to kill the first industrial revolution by destroying the steam engines, even though the new machines took Europe out of grinding poverty by delivering productivity that drove unprecedented economic growth. Political gridlock and two world wars tried to kill the second industrial revolution, which eventually defined the dramatic improvements in economic outcomes in the twentieth century.

Doomsayers will always be with us, repeating their dispiriting chant. At the start of the first industrial revolution, Thomas Malthus predicted that the end was nigh. At the end of the nineteenth century, the Royal Society echoed Malthus, even as the second industrial revolution was starting to kick in. Most recently, the Club of Rome issued a dire forecast toward the end of the twentieth century.

From an economic and technological perspective, the doomsayers are wrong. The resource productivity that comes out of this revolution should enable the next 2.5 billion members of the middle class in the developing markets to enjoy the prosperity, the clean air and water, and clean cities that only the OECD countries enjoyed for the last one hundred years—while creating breathtaking economic opportunities for those sharp enough to find them.

∽

Although we had never worked together and arrived separately at our optimistic conclusion in 2006, we knew each other through the partnership at McKinsey. We joined forces—the energy guy with the background in oil, gas, and other heavy industries and the tech guy with the long-held belief in innovation and renewable energy—and helped to form what has now grown into the global Sustainability and Resource Productivity Practice (SRP).

Together with our colleagues, we began with the sort of heavy-duty analysis that characterizes McKinsey—looking at learning curves and cost curves for all relevant technologies and for important natural resources; studying the possible effects on every conceivable industry; and understanding how change would take hold in cities, nations, and regions around the world. The first knowledge piece was a major McKinsey Global Institute Report on Energy Productivity (produced by Matt, with our director colleagues Scott Nyquist and Diana Farrell) that argued that there was an opportunity to reduce energy use 25 percent globally with known technologies and that peak demand would come well before peak oil—in other words, while many worried that oil production had peaked or was about to do so, demand for oil was going to hit its peak and start to decline before oil production started to fall. This piece was followed by the now iconic McKinsey Greenhouse Gas Abatement curve work (Jeremy Oppenheim and Per-Anders Enkvist), the U.S. Greenhouse Gas Abatement curve work (Ken Ostrowski and Anton Derkach), and the U.S. Energy Efficiency Opportunity (Ken Ostrowski, Hannah Granade, Scott Nyquist, and Stefan). More recently, Jeremy Oppenheim, Richard Dobbs, and Fraser Thompson wrote the seminal report on the resource revolution ahead that laid the economic foundation for this book. We concluded that the economic case for change was clear and that, once the markets realized that change was coming, the shift in thinking about resource productivity would be revolutionary.

We also realized that to win in these rapidly restructuring markets, management practices had to change. Managers had driven capital productivity and labor productivity hard for decades but had been lulled into a false sense of security about resources because of almost a century of declining commodity prices—resource productivity had languished while capital and labor productivity flourished. The resource revolution required a new approach to management.

Yet it seemed that no one else saw this once-in-a-century opportunity. Those who wrote about the new possibilities took a limited approach, focusing on renewable energy sources, crop yields, or other narrow fields. No one took a comprehensive look at all the threats—and the opportunities—that the resource revolution is bringing.

So, our analysis moved to book writing in the fall of 2010. The timing was auspicious. The economy was recovering, albeit tentatively, so companies had begun thinking about opportunities again. The rise in commodity prices had been going on for more than ten years, so it couldn't be dismissed as a blip; rather, it was becoming clear that the climb was part of a decades-long, fundamental shift in supply and demand.

Meanwhile, the rapid development of shale gas and shale oil was providing the first great example of the principles of the resource revolution in action. For decades, people had known that there were enormous deposits of oil and gas in shale formations, but extracting them was prohibitively difficult. By the mid-2000s, advances in technology were making it possible to finally tap the oil and gas in shale at an affordable price, largely through horizontal drilling and hydraulic fracturing, often jointly referred to as "fracking."

Because of the integration of information technology, drilling would no longer be primarily about roughnecks slinging heavy equipment around on platforms amid large volumes of mud and sulfurous fumes; drilling would be about quiet rooms with high-resolution screens at remote locations, where experts used joysticks to maneuver drill bits through geological formations to tap every bit of available oil and gas, using the same Nvidia chips for rapid image processing that had been developed for the video game industry. Of course, the reality in the field is more complicated—unconventional oil and gas still depends on safe drilling protocols, effective well casings, quality water management, and efficient land use—but economically, geologically, and environmentally, unconventional oil and gas resources proved much less risky than other oil and gas production technologies.

As the effects of the United States' suddenly abundant natural gas supply rippled through markets and global politics, we quickly came to an insight that made us feel even more confident about the importance and timeliness of this book. Adam Smith's classical work on economics, *Wealth of Nations* (1776), defined three major inputs for business: labor, capital, and land. The two industrial revolutions the world has seen thus far focused primarily on labor and capital rather than land, which can be thought of broadly as resources such as food, water, and wood that can be produced from that land, mined from it, or disposed of on it. The Watt steam engine produced radical improvement in labor productivity in the late 1700s and early 1800s—one person

Defining characteristics of resource revolutions

Economic growth drives resource scarcity and price volatility and increases environmental, and/or social pressures

Innovation creates new technologies to enable either step-change more efficient use of those resources or substitution away

Resource prices stabilize, reflecting the new, higher productivity economic structure

Multi-decade economic transition from one set of primary resources to another: unleashing substantial economic growth and productivity improvements, enabling millions to enter the middle class, and giving birth to new industries and business models

New business models and management tools develop to deploy new technologies at scale, driving a step change in resource productivity across the economy

The economic shift across industries disrupts employment patterns, but accelerating productivity eventually supports **higher wages and expanding middle class**

The overall economy begins to evolve as new industries replace less productive incumbents, enabling accelerating growth and wealth creation

could operate numerous machines spinning cotton into thread at high speed, rather than having hundreds of people manually producing thread at spinning wheels. The first industrial revolution also gave us the limited liability corporation to drive this growth at scale. The second industrial revolution, from the late 1800s into the early 1900s, gave the world oil and the electric grid, cars and roads, skyscrapers with elevators and air-conditioning, and a host of other developments that required a massive deployment of capital. Not so coincidentally, the capital-based revolution also gave us scientific management practices, global corporations, and the modern banking system. But neither of the first two revolutions focused on Smith's third input: land and nat-ural resources. That is precisely what we see happening now, and we believe the benefits to businesses and their customers will be every bit as great as the benefits accompanying the first two revolutions.[1]

Before Watt and his steam engine came along, productivity improvement had been so slow that the average European was only about two times as well off as a Roman in the time of Julius Caesar, nearly two millennia earlier. But that first industrial revolution put the world on a path of such rapid improvement that the average European today is some thirteen times as well off as his counterpart in 1750. The principles we describe in this book will provide the next leg in the remarkable progress that Watt started.

The principles of this next industrial revolution are still a work in progress. They have to be. No one can predict how business will look in twenty or thirty years, any more than Watt could have foreseen how his steam engine would transform the world. But we've already seen enough success that we can say, with confidence, both that resources are the right area of focus and that the opportunities are extraordinary.

Already, Boeing has the potential to reduce its buy-to-fly ratio for titanium parts from 30:1 to 3:1 or even 1:1, using laser welding, additive manufacturing, and closed-loop recycling. Dow and DuPont have sys-tematically translated waste streams into high-value products over the last decade. The best refineries, including GS Caltex and SK Refining, both in Korea, use 20 to 30 percent less energy than their competitors and also translate waste streams into high-value products. Walmart has gone to great lengths to eliminate all forms of waste—energy, CO_2, packaging—across its supply chain to reduce costs and risk and to increase long-term competitiveness. Zero-waste manufacturing is becoming the norm among major U.S. automakers.

---

1   We aren't saying that the first industrial revolution produced only improvement in labor productivity and that the second industrial revolution led only to more productive use of capital. In fact, all revolutions affect all three of the inputs that Smith described. In the first industrial revolution, for instance, the use of coal became far more efficient. Until Watt's steam engine came along, roughly half the coal that was dug from an underground mine had to be used to power the earlier type of engine that pumped water from underground and made it possible to mine the coal in the first place. Watt's engine drastically reduced the amount of coal that had to be used to allow mining. But because steam power became so widespread, the aggregate demand for coal rose dramatically.

Those examples are just the start. It's easy to imagine that in fifteen or twenty years radically new types of companies will dominate the landscape. Perhaps one company will mine waste streams to recover gold and silver from consumer electronics, or lithium from geothermal effluent. Maybe another will handle all travel services: The passenger will just type in where he or she wants to go, and the company will lay out the optimal way to get there; perhaps the company would provide a car that drives itself. Rental cars may no longer even be "rental" cars in the classic sense. Already, with Zipcar, drivers can rent cars on a cheap, subscription basis rather than buy a capital-intensive asset that is parked the vast majority of the time. The capital requirements for our transportation systems could drop by 80 percent.

Meanwhile, there will be nearly limitless opportunities for companies—new and old, big and small—to provide the equipment and services that make established companies and emergent behemoths operate more efficiently.

To help start the process of thinking about how to get to that bright future, we begin the book by showing how the two prior industrial revolutions played out and by framing the challenges and opportunities that businesses face as they head into the third revolution. We then go into the five principles that can be applied to make any company, any supplier community, and any customer segment drastically more efficient in using resources, making resource productivity sustainable. We show how to apply these principles and how they will lead to far different products and services—those that deliver more performance with fewer resources.[2] In other words, we aren't talking about skimping or doing less with less. We're going to describe how to do more with less. This is the opposite of the conventional thinking about what so many see as a coming age of scarcity.

In subsequent chapters, we explain how to get the timing right and how to bring an idea to scale—a tricky problem when markets are changing rapidly. Because of the importance of management discipline, we also

---

2   The dramatic upshift in resource productivity will have substantial environmental and pollution benefits, but these will come as a by-product of a higher-performing, more efficient technology and business model, rather than as the primary focus.

explore how management structures and metrics will have to change to focus more on resource productivity, a transformation that will require new types of talent recruited from new places, organized and trained in new ways. Finally, we explain how to make the resource revolution a permanent one, rather than just achieving one breakthrough and declaring victory.

As we'll show in chapter one, the challenges facing businesses—indeed, the whole planet—are formidable. But the opportunities are unprecedented. We intend to help you find them.

CAPTURING THE GREATEST BUSINESS OPPORTUNITY IN A CENTURY

THE KEY FACT FOR BUSINESS for at least the next two decades is this: More than 2.5 billion people in China, India, and other developing countries are moving out of poverty and will urbanize and move into industrial and service occupations by 2030.

That 2.5 billion is on top of the 1.5 billion people who have already moved into cities and into the middle class.

That 2.5 billion is eight times the current population of the United States. Three and a half times the population of Europe. More than the populations of Africa, North America, and South America combined.

Standing shoulder to shoulder at the equator, those urbanizing and industrializing would circle the globe forty times.

To accommodate all these people urbanizing, industrializing, and moving into the middle class, China alone will build two and a half cities the population of Chicago every year for the foreseeable future. India will build one new Chicago each year. The United States took more than a hundred years to build twenty-five metro markets of more than a million people; China will have 221 cities that size by 2025. Just building this infrastructure will create massive demand for energy and raw materials. Think of the amount of concrete, iron, and steel in a bridge or skyscraper; the amount of copper in a power grid and the energy required to power the cranes, bulldozers, and other machines that build it—and multiply those amounts by tens of thousands.

What's more, China, India, and the other countries where much of this building will happen do not yet use resources with the same efficiency as the industrialized countries. In the United States, for example, 55 percent of the copper supply comes from recycled sources; in China, that figure is only 5 percent, because copper has to go into new infrastructure first, before it can be recycled. (We will see in chapter four how this massive infrastructure buildout creates enormous business opportunities for those who can do it more efficiently.)

Accelerated expansion of the middle class

GDP per capita in 1990 U.S. dollars purchasing power parity

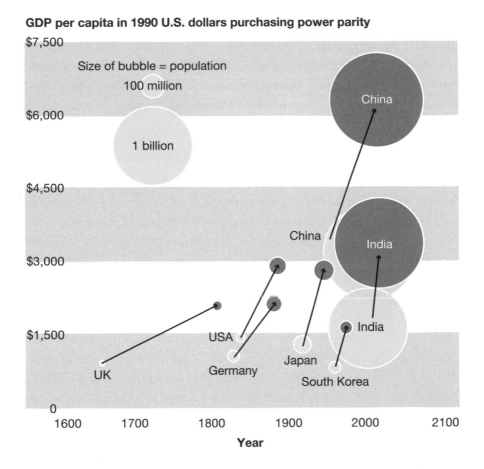

After the infrastructure is built, the new members of the urban middle class will want to drive to work, heat their homes in winter and cool them in summer, eat meat most days of the week, wash their clothes at home in clean water, and play with their smartphones while lounging in front of their flat-screen TVs and eating microwaved snacks. These people will drive hundreds of millions of cars, consuming billions of gallons of gasoline and diesel each year.

The economic power that comes with all this new demand for access to energy, water, and protein could drive economic growth for generations. But this growth is in danger of being cut short because so much stress will be placed on natural resources, much more even than accompanied the first and second industrial revolutions.

In the first industrial revolution, which began with the steam engine and ran from the late 1700s through the mid-1800s, 13 percent of the world's population industrialized (Western Europe). In the second industrial revolution, 16 percent of the world industrialized for the first time (the United States, Canada, Australia, Russia, and Japan). This time, 37 percent of the world's population will industrialize for the first time (mostly China and India and other parts of Asia and South America). Roughly 130 million people benefited from the first industrial revolution. This time, the number will be 2.5 billion. That's almost twenty times as many people—meaning twenty times the stress on resources.

Yet that figure is just the beginning. Before the first industrial revolution, the daily energy usage of someone in the middle class pretty much consisted of the food he consumed, or some 2,000 kcalories. Today, a member of the middle class uses more than 200,000 kcalories of energy a day, including gasoline for cars, electricity for lighting, natural gas for heating, and so on. That's a one hundred times increase.

Do the math: With twenty times as many people demanding one hundred times as much energy and resources, a smart manager can argue that the new demands about to be placed on the world's resources dwarf those from the first industrial revolution by a factor of 2,000.

Change is happening far faster, too. The U.K. needed 150 years for its GDP per capita to double in the first industrial revolution. The United States needed fifty years in the second industrial revolution. China's GDP per capita has doubled in less than fifteen years.

The phenomenal gains in income in China and India, along with similar improvements in Brazil, Indonesia, and other developing economies, mean that the demand for steel is expected to rise 80 percent by 2030. Other metals and construction materials will see similar increases in demand. The need for energy will climb by a third—a rise that will require adding more energy output than is currently consumed by the United States and Europe combined.

The newly middle class will consume massive amounts of additional water. People will shower more and increase other personal uses. A new member of the middle class will use a lot more water if they have indoor plumbing than if they have to walk a mile to a well and carry any water that they use.

Agriculture will require more water, land, and energy. A third of the world's arable land is already used to produce crops, and much of the rest

The land, water, and energy content of food

	Land required m² per kg	Water required m³ per kg	Energy required Oil barrels per kg
Tomato	▮	◗	◖
Corn	▮	◗	◖
Rice	▮	◗	◖
Milk	▮▮▮	◗	◗◗◗
Farmed fish	▮▮	◗	◗◗◗◗◗◗ ◗◗◗◗◗
Poultry meat	▮▮	◗◗	◗◗◗◗◗◗◗ ◗◗◗◗◗
Beef	▮▮▮▮▮▮ ▮▮▮▮▮▮ ▮▮▮▮▮▮	◗◗◗◗◗◗ ◗◗◗◗◗◗	◗◗◗◗◗◗◗ ◗◗◗◗

is used for grazing animals, so there isn't much room for expansion. Stress on resources will also rise because increasing income usually corresponds with a rapidly growing demand for protein, and a pound of beef takes fifteen times as much water to produce as a pound of rice. A calorie of beef requires 160 times more energy to produce than a calorie of corn. Animal protein requires around six times more land than plant-based proteins, with beef around eighteen times more. So, meeting the rising expectations of the new middle class for protein will require either a major increase in land, water, and energy productivity or a sharp dietary shift away from animal proteins that we have not seen with previous increases in income.

As daunting as the surge in demand will be, it's only half the problem when it comes to resources. In fact, we face a double dilemma. Resources are also becoming more difficult to find and extract, and thus more expensive. Energy prices have already increased 450 percent over the past twelve years.

Take oil. When oil first began to be used as a fuel, in the mid-1800s, it was literally lying on the ground. That's why Titusville, in northwestern Pennsylvania, was the site of the first commercial oil well in 1859—so much petroleum had seeped to the surface there that businessmen expected they could find bountiful supplies just beneath it. The first well struck oil at sixty-nine feet. After World War II, the deserts of the Middle East yielded the same bounty—petroleum lying on the ground pointed the Saudis in 1948 to the world's largest oil field, Ghawar, which has generated 65 billion barrels of oil and is still producing 5 million barrels a day.

In the ensuing sixty-five years, though, as oil went from use in kerosene lamps to providing the fuel for most of the modern transportation system, drillers have had to go deeper and deeper and spread into less accessible territories as the easy pickings were used up. We've gone from scooping ready-to-burn oil off the ground to running giant offshore rigs that pull oil to the surface from 25,000 feet below the Gulf of Mexico, from high-pressure, high-temperature reservoirs—a remarkable engineering feat, but a lot more difficult and expensive than the original wells in Titusville. We've gone from drilling a couple of hundred miles from major population centers to drilling in the Arctic. The cost of bringing each new oil well online has more than tripled over the past decade.

In 2007, Petrobras announced the discovery of the biggest find of the last thirty years, but it is in the Atlantic Ocean, 180 miles off Rio de Janeiro (and is only one-fifth the size of Ghawar). Petrobras will have to drill miles below the surface of the ocean and build a pipeline that safely delivers the oil to the coast of Brazil. Just developing the field will cost Petrobras $50 billion to $100 billion.

What is true for oil is true for just about every other traditional natural resource: The amounts being discovered each year have leveled off, while the money being spent on exploration has significantly increased. When copper was first used, big nuggets could be found lying on the ground. Those nuggets were 95 percent pure. Today, copper typically accounts for just 0.4 to 1 percent of the rock that is mined for ore, and the purity is in steady decline. Copper is so expensive that thieves sometimes tear down electrical transmission wires, strip them, and sell the copper. Gold is even more extreme—many mining companies are so starved for ore that they are reprocessing tailings of old gold mines that had been discarded as waste. (This is an example of turning former waste into new raw materials, which we will see more of in chapter three.)

Freshwater is typically thought of as a God-given "right"—or simply taken for granted—but natural sources of sweet water are limited, as well. Rivers such as the Colorado in the United States and the Yellow River in China often dry up before they reach the ocean because of overuse of their water. In some areas, it will be necessary to drill deep for water as groundwater aquifers are depleted. In other areas, it may become necessary to turn to capital-intensive desalination. Singapore already gets 25 percent of its water from desalination and expects that figure to reach 80 percent by 2030. In San Diego, a $1 billion desalination plant is under construction.

In addition to the problems of individual resources, there are increasing links among energy, food, and water. As a result, problems in one area can spread to another, creating a destructive cycle of dependence. For instance, Uganda experienced a prolonged drought in 2004 and 2005, threatening the food supply. The country was using so much water from massive Lake Victoria that the water level fell by a full meter, and Uganda cut back on hydroelectric power generation at the lake. Electricity prices nearly doubled, so Ugandans began to use

Reserves are getting more expensive to extract

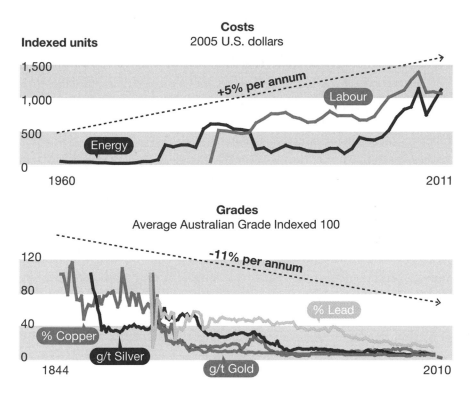

Costs
2005 U.S. dollars

Indexed units

1,500

+5% per annum

1,000

Labour

500

Energy

0

1960   2011

Grades
Average Australian Grade Indexed 100

-11% per annum

120

80

% Lead

40

% Copper

g/t Silver

0

1844   g/t Gold   2010

more wood for fuel. People cut heavily into forests, which degraded the soil. The drought that began as a threat to food sources became an electricity problem and, eventually, an even more profound food problem. Cycles like these can end in political unrest and disasters for whole populations.

The other major challenge is pollution. While this is a business book, not a treatise on the environment, current trends are worrisome. Industrial growth has driven high pollution levels in the cities of China and India, similar to those seen in previous industrial revolutions in London or New York. Extrapolating current economic growth and pollution would point toward incalculable social costs—fouled water-ways, choking air-pollution levels, widespread famine or illness from contaminated food, and accelerated global warming. Yet, a growing middle class worldwide will demand significantly cleaner air, water, and open space. Just as the United States and Europe demanded and built an economy wherein clean air, clean water, and clean cities accelerated economic growth, so, too, the Chinese and Indian middle classes have the right to argue that cleaning up wasteful, uneconomic, and corrupt high-pollution industries will accelerate rather than slow economic growth.

Trends have already created enough concern that businesses need to focus on increasing productivity as a core element in reducing pollution. Indeed, as soon as pollution has a price, businesses find remarkably low-cost, high-productivity approaches to slash pollution.[3] Businesses must be prepared for the possibility of regulation, such as more government pricing of carbon emissions as a revenue opportunity and as a way to reduce pollution; these regulations could change the game. Just as businesses address the increased incidents of disruptive weather, which could cause problems for supply chains, many businesses have the opportunity to reduce risk by increasing resource productivity across the company.

ço

The good news is that the world has faced crises before—and, not only are we still here, but each crisis and the revolution it spurred created tremendous opportunity and wealth for the innovators and entrepreneurs who unleashed the productivity that overcame the crisis and vastly improved standards of living.

The tension between the bad news and good news today resembles what the world has faced before, at the onset of both the first and second industrial revolutions. That tension boils down to the worldviews of two scholars, Thomas Robert Malthus and Adam Smith, both of whom wrote in the late 1700s.

---

3   Specifying the approaches required to reduce pollution can have very high costs and significant unintended consequences, but setting a price on pollution tends to deliver significant results at a low cost. We saw examples of this in the Montreal protocol to prevent ozone depletion: Coal plant sulfur emissions standards were met with the use of new scrubber technology that came in at less than a tenth of the originally estimated compliance costs.

Thomas Robert Malthus (1766–1834), English cleric and economist who wrote An Essay on the Principle of Population *in 1798.*

Malthus argued that the growing population would overwhelm the world, leading to widespread famine. Smith argued that businessmen could adapt and innovate rapidly enough that productivity could increase faster than consumption. Where Malthus saw disaster, Smith saw opportunity. While over time there have been eruptions of famine and shortage in different parts of the world, Smith was right. As the first and second industrial revolutions unfolded, opportunity has trumped scarcity. We believe that history is repeating itself and that Smith will be right again.

Smith's seminal work, *The Wealth of Nations,* described economic advancement in terms of three factors of productivity: labor, capital goods, and land or natural resources. During each previous industrial revolution, all three factors of productivity changed—but in each, one factor changed most dramatically.

The first industrial revolution radically improved labor productivity, as workers moved from the fields to the factories and as the steam engine allowed a factory worker to perform the work of many men. Emphasis on increasing labor productivity has continued ever since.

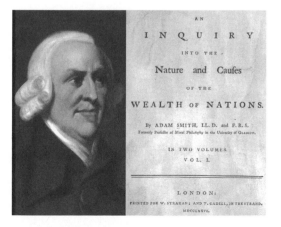

Scottish philosopher and economist Adam Smith (1723–1790) and the title page from the first edition of his seminal work, Wealth of Nations, *published in 1776.*

In the second industrial revolution, massive amounts of capital were invested in manufacturing facilities, skyscrapers, mechanized machinery, railroads and bridges, and so on. In fact, the largest banks, such as J. P. Morgan, emerged to fund these investments. Today,

Wealth creation in industrial revolutions

Total wealth in billions of 2013 U.S. dollars

MECHANIZATION 1770–1840

John Jacob Astor (1848) American Fur Company	Furs/land	$146
Stephen Girard (1831) Girard Bank	Banking	$104
Stephen Van Rensselaer (1839) Rensselaerswyck Manor	Land	$80
Richard Arkwright Jr. (1834) Richard Arkwright & Company	Banking	$79

URBANIZATION 1880–1920

John D. Rockefeller (1937) Standard Oil Company	Oil	$241
Cornelius Vanderbilt (1877) New York Central Railroad	Shipping	$180
Andrew Carnegie (1919) Carnegie Steel Company	Steel	$94
Alexander T. Stewart (1876) A.T. Stewart Department Store	Retail	$88
Frederick Weyerhaeuser (1914) Weyerhaeuser Company	Lumber	$86
Jay Gould (1892) Union Pacific	Railroad	$84
Henry Ford (1947) The Ford Motor Company	Autos	$67
J. P. Morgan (1913) J. P. Morgan & Company	Banking	$57

RESOURCE REVOLUTION 1990–2030

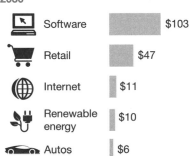

Bill Gates (2006) Microsoft	Software	$103
Sam Walton (1992) Walmart	Retail	$47
Robin Li (2013) Baidu	Internet	$11
Li Hejun (2013) Hanergy Holding Group	Renewable energy	$10
Elon Musk (2013) Tesla	Autos	$6

after more than a hundred years of improvements, capital markets allocate capital with exceptional efficiency. Most companies have developed highly efficient capital allocation processes and tools. Every good manager now knows how to calculate net present value and return on capital employed.

What has not yet been optimized is the third of Smith's inputs to businesses: land or natural resources. Adam Smith wrote about land in an era when the greatest part of production was still agricultural and most resources were still directly derived from land. But we are using this term in an expanded sense that reflects the large number of resources we now get from land—the metals, minerals, oil, gas, coal, etc., we get from the earth; the food and fertilizer necessary for modern agriculture; the water rights that are now codified like property ownership; fishing rights in a particular area; air rights or regulations that residents find in many cities; and even the right to dump and dispose of materials.

All of these are land and natural resources, in a modern sense. Natural resources represent the inputs that the third industrial revolution must use wisely in the face of extraordinary demand by the new middle class. Yet very few managers regularly measure or report their return on energy or water or steel "employed." Nor have they mastered the basic analytical tools to drive resource productivity consistently. The coming resource revolution will change everything about the way we manage businesses in the twenty-first century.

Industrial revolutions are crucibles. They forge companies that dominate for decades; but revolutions also ruin many companies. While the first industrial revolution led to giant factories that spun cotton, it savaged the leather-tanning business. Before the arrival of finance on Wall Street, much of lower Manhattan was organized around leather tanning. Cotton clothing also put an end to one of the largest fortunes ever amassed by one man: John Jacob Astor, who earned the equivalent of $146 billion in today's dollars from the fur trade in the American West. The first industrial revolution gave us the great textile, shipping, and railroad companies of the nineteenth century, but the need for lumber as a primary fuel disappeared. The second industrial revolution helped kill the whaling industry, which had produced oil for lamps, but gave us General Electric (GE) and Siemens, Ford and General Motors (GM)—the companies that defined the twentieth century. It also displaced railroads and telegraph companies from the Dow Jones Index and replaced them with chemicals, automotive, and oil companies. In both revolutions, thousands of companies competed to define economic leadership for the new era; hundreds went bankrupt in the transition between eras; and, only a few survived to prosper for a century.

The same is true for individual workers. Many observers worry that increasing productivity will usher in an extended period of unemployment. Indeed, the late nineteenth century saw decades of hardship and discontent as the market shifted from a largely agrarian to a largely urban economy. Individuals who could not keep up with the productivity changes in the broader economy struggled. The social upheaval from this massive economic shift led to great social unrest. Only when Henry Ford figured out how to engage the assembly line to dramatically increase labor productivity, while simultaneously expanding the middle class market for new automobiles, did the market begin to define the social compact that made the second industrial revolution sustainable. This book is not a social history and cannot adequately address the social challenges coming from the resource revolution; however, we are encouraged that the next round of innovations, from 3-D printing to distributed solar, building controls via iPhones, and shale oil and gas innovations, have much lower capital costs per unit and are significantly more accessible to many more individuals, enabling individual productivity growth to accelerate over time. We are moving away from the era where large corporate or government balance sheets are required to fund power generation, manufacturing, and transportation. Increasingly, specialized companies and even individual entrepreneurs can combine information technology with industrial technology and insight to invent new business models like Airbnb or Zipcar. This dynamic will enable more people to participate in the productivity revolution, both in the United States and increasingly in emerging economies. Indeed, many of these innovations are being pioneered in parts of the world where the classical centralized power grid or transportation infrastructure have not yet been established.

Adapting isn't easy. Game-changing technologies take time to develop. Their course can be hard to predict, and they can proceed in fits and starts; so timing is tricky. They require new management skills—in particular, system integration capabilities—and even new structures. (The factory didn't exist before the first industrial revolution, and firms bore almost no resemblance to those of today until the second industrial revolution.) Market leaders often strain to preserve their old markets rather than develop new ones, then get swept aside when the new prevails.

A look at the first two industrial revolutions helps us understand what is in store this time around.

THE FIRST INDUSTRIAL REVOLUTION: STEAM SUPPLANTS SWEAT

The 1700s had created grim prospects in Europe. Population growth had accelerated so much that Malthus published his gloomy predictions. Jonathan Swift wrote his satirical essay, "A Modest Proposal," which said poor children might as well be fed to rich people—the children were just going to die anyway, and the rich deserved to eat. Animal power was so scarce that the black market for Europe's 14 million horses and 24 million oxen made horse thieves and dealers in stolen horses their own social class in England.

Then, on a Sunday afternoon walk on the Glasgow Green in May 1765, James Watt figured out how to radically improve the productivity of the steam engine. His insight changed the course of the world.

Watt's modification was deceptively simple. He had been thinking about the Newcomen engine, one of which was owned by the University

A painting of young James Watt (1736–1819) working on a prototype of his steam engine.

of Glasgow, where he repaired astronomical instruments. The Newcomen engine heated steam that drove a piston, then injected cold water to condense the steam, allowing the piston to return to its original position to begin another stroke. As the steam condensed, the piston and cylinder cooled. The engine reheated them, as well as the water, at each stroke. The design was inefficient and had barely changed in the more than fifty years since it was invented. On his walk, Watt figured out how to vent the steam at the end of each piston stroke, allowing a new stroke to begin without cooling the piston and cylinder.

Watt's small change made the steam engine so efficient that it could economically produce the power of many horses for days and weeks and months on end—as long as the supply of coal lasted. When Watt took his stroll, only about seventy-five steam engines were in operation in all of Britain. His new engine soon spread across the landscape and pushed manufacturing into a frenzy of productivity. Commonly known as *the* Industrial Revolution, that revolution, which would move from Britain to the United States and continental Europe, generated a tenfold increase in productivity that reshaped the global economy, created untold wealth, and redefined the basics of business.

This first industrial revolution freed many people from reliance on water wheels, firewood, animals, and other traditional forms of energy. Inexpensive power became available in cities, far from riverbanks, and by 1870 fossil fuel power exceeded usage of animal and water power. Watt's engine led to abundant new sources of energy, as well, by allowing the U.K. to mine vast quantities of coal below the water table for the first time. Mining, manufacturing, transportation, and agriculture all enjoyed accelerating growth and dramatic improvements in productivity. For example, in 1790, a farm worker could harvest about a quarter acre per day with a scythe, which then had to be flailed by hand. By 1890, a man could harvest ten acres with a threshing machine. Wages began an inexorable climb, too, because the investments in equipment made workers so much more productive. Growing wages pulled much of the developed world out of poverty and famine over the next two centuries.

Watt's steam engine also led to a new model for business: the limited liability corporation, which was developed specifically to support the capital formation necessary to deploy the steam engine and its progeny. Local guilds and feudal land grants gave way to the limited liability corporation as the primary engine for economic growth.

Watt's steam engine revolution did not always proceed smoothly—timing is tricky in revolutions. It took Watt more than ten years to perfect his design.[4] The new engine required higher-quality iron because the cylinder was under constant pressure, but such iron didn't become widely available until cannon makers innovated as part of the munitions buildup for the Revolutionary War between Britain and the United States. Even with better iron, early metal-machining techniques could not always guarantee a precise fit between pistons and cylinders; boilers were so liable to explode that Watt couldn't let inside pressure exceed standard atmospheric pressure.

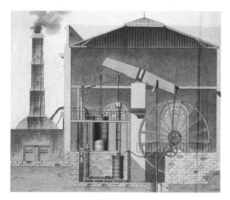

The real benefits of the improved steam engine didn't take hold until system integration skills were applied, allowing the engine to mesh with all aspects of production—just adding a steam engine on a water wheel was not enough. So, the full impact wasn't felt until the 1830s, more than a decade after Watt died, at age eighty-three.

A cross-section of Watt's steam engine, the machine that heralded the first industrial revolution.

When the revolution did kick in, it increased demand so much that there was a thirty-year surge in prices for commodities like iron, cotton, coal, and copper. Prices for fuel and lighting soared by more than a factor of five.

Though the Industrial Revolution helped create industries and fortunes, there were plenty of business casualties. The textile guilds couldn't come close to competing with the efficient new factories. Sailing ships gave way to steamships. The watermill that had dominated village flour production gave way to steam-powered flour milling at scale. The Luddites fought against

---

4   Watt had to give up two-thirds of his business in return for crucial capital, and, even then, had to take on work as a surveyor and civil engineer for eight years to support himself. Watt's partner, Matthew Boulton, gave up more than half of the remaining equity to commercialize the new technology. The two fought patent battles for decades. It took a long time for Watt to become wealthy.

the new, high-productivity machines, and Charles Dickens wrote about the pain of the displacement of traditional methods, but the economic and social benefits driving the Industrial Revolution were overwhelming and positive—longer lives, less hunger, and greater wealth for millions.

While the first industrial revolution wreaked havoc on weaker technologies and unprepared businesses, it also gave rise to some behemoths, probably none more important than Richard Arkwright's textile empire. Born in northwest England in 1732 as the youngest of a tailor's thirteen children, Arkwright never went to school. Apprenticed to a barber, he developed and patented a waterproof dye that could be used for men's wigs. He made enough money to be able to strike out on his own.

When he did, Arkwright tackled one of the major industrial problems of the day: how to turn raw cotton into thread in an efficient manner. Raw cotton first had to be cleaned of seeds, husks, and other debris. Then it had to be carded, which separated individual fibers and began straightening them. Finally, the short fibers needed to be spun together into thread, a process that historically used armies of women at spinning wheels. In the 1770s, Arkwright, with others, first came up with a patented way to make carding more efficient. Then, he turned his attention to the far more complicated issue of spinning.[5] Eventually, Arkwright patented what became known as a spinning frame. The complicated device used a system of precisely weighted wheels, each spinning

An engraving of Richard Arkwright (1732–1792) with his spinning frame, turning raw cotton into thread.

---

5 A better method for cleaning cotton would have to wait until 1793 and Eli Whitney's invention of the cotton gin.

faster than the previous one, to grab cotton fibers, straighten them, and combine them into thread. While many others had attempted similar devices, Arkwright's was the first to get the distance between the wheels exactly right—too close, and wheels spinning at different speeds would grab fibers at the same time and rip them apart; too far apart, and neither wheel would grab fibers, leaving many fibers loose and producing frizzy thread. Arkwright got the design so right that his approach is still the basis for spinning cotton into thread today.

Initially, Arkwright designed his spinning frame to be powered by two or three horses walking in a circle. Then the Watt steam engine came along, and Arkwright incorporated it into his system. More than 30,000 workers churned out cotton thread in mills based on his design—putting out of business all those who hadn't seen the move beyond spinning wheels. Arkwright became so rich that he could have paid off England's national debt out of his own pocket.

In the process of designing and running his mill, Arkwright made his most lasting and revolutionary contribution: He invented the modern factory. Arkwright came up with a very organized and structured approach to work that set aside the at-home, piecework approach that had been used for millennia.[6]

Multiple new technologies (including steam and Arkwright's spinning machine), when used together with the factory's standardized work scheme, made output jump and the entire process scalable. A single technology like carding made relatively incremental difference in output. But combine it with spinning, a governor, and direct-drive steam power and the market enjoys a "step change." Adding standardized piecework, multiple shifts, and large factories with multiple machines began to produce order-of-magnitude changes in output and productivity. In the days of a guild, the limiting factor was availability of skilled labor: Apprenticeships

---

6   In many ways, Arkwright was the stereotypical plutocrat of the Industrial Age. He initially employed children as young as seven. He increased the lower limit on age by the time he retired, but only to age ten. He employed whole families, many of whom lived in cottages he built on mill property. He granted a week of vacation a year, but only if those taking it didn't leave the village. Arkwright even looked the part. He was described as corpulent, with heavy jowls and pasty skin. For good measure, he had a red, bulbous nose—at least, that's how he's shown in a portrait he commissioned. On the plus side, Arkwright did establish a school to educate the children who worked in his mill. In his later years, he taught classes at the school.

ran five to seven years. But a factory could be set up in less than a year and new workers trained in weeks, not years.

Arkwright and Watt showed that revolutions are messy and demand considerable persistence and agility. Wholly new ways of thinking, including new management techniques, are the way to win. And extraordinary opportunities don't necessarily go to the incumbents. In class-conscious eighteenth-century England, the two men who defined the first industrial revolution were a repairman and a barber's apprentice.

THE SECOND INDUSTRIAL REVOLUTION: URBAN GRIDS

By the late 1800s, the first industrial revolution had transformed Europe and the United States. Cities sprang up around factories as millions of people left farms. Industrialization was powerful, but urbanization had created a mess.

Tenements sprawled across the city landscape. People sickened and died young because contaminated drinking water and inadequate sewage systems spread infectious diseases. Pollution from factories left a haze over cities; and smoke from fireplaces, lanterns, and candles made the home a dangerous (and often noxious) place. With the population exploding and food production not keeping up, many were again predicting widespread famine. Steaming mounds of horse manure piled up on street corners; the *Times* of London estimated that horse manure would bury that city nine feet deep by 1950.

This time, the solution required more than a walk on the town green. The second industrial revolution sprang most directly from the widespread availability of electricity, oil, and steel, but required a raft of inventions that produced the modern city and transportation network.

This revolution, in fact, allowed cities to grow substantially larger and more dense, an outcome that would have surprised most observers. New York had just over 800,000 people in 1860, and Philadelphia was the only other city in the United States with over half a million. By 1925, New York had overtaken London as the largest city in the world, with seven and a half million inhabitants.

But additional population growth is only one part of the massive change in infrastructure that overtook cities. Building materials changed from wood, which had caused massive fires in 1835 and 1845, to low-cost, high-strength steel by the end of the century. The shift allowed buildings to grow taller than the four to five stories that wood and masonry allowed. Steel also allowed the development of low-friction bearings for machinery and enabled lower rolling resistance for trains running on steel rails, compared with wooden cart wheels running over bumpy roads. These efficiencies contributed substantially to the twenty-eight-fold improvement in transport costs from 24.5 cents per ton mile by wagon in 1890 to 0.875 cents per ton mile by railroad. Goods also moved faster as the travel time from New York to Chicago fell from six weeks to two days. Sewage was captured and sewers were put underground. Freshwater (in New York's case, from the Adirondacks upstate) was brought in. All buildings got access to running water, and dangerous cesspools were filled in.

Lighting changed from wood, kerosene, and candles to electric lights, making homes safer and extending productive time for everyone by hours. Electricity spread to appliances, air-conditioning, and elevators, giving the average family access to amazing amounts of power. Electricity also enabled the development of the assembly line, as Henry Ford took his experience at Detroit Edison, where he had worked for Thomas Edison, and applied it to making a production line move.

The development of low-cost oil and the internal combustion engine helped free cities from manure, and, later, enabled suburban communities to grow. The high density of energy in petroleum allowed trucks to move goods great distances, permitting the development of businesses not directly on rail lines.

As stunning as these technology changes were by themselves, this second industrial revolution also brought significant changes to management principles, corporate entities, and capital formation, irrevocably changing the balance of power between people, governments, and corporations.

The second industrial revolution created trusts, the first national corporations and then multinational ones, and corporate banks. The scale of investments required to lay track across the United States, to finance a skyscraper, to build a subway system, or to build a huge factory went far beyond what a family business could fund. These investments required stockholder capital and the ability to raise money through corporate debt. Trading and shipping products internationally required the

Changes in infrastructure in New York City from 1850 (left) to 2013 (right).

development of letters of guarantee. In some cases, such as the railroad's, the initial development also depended on government land grants and loans. Railroad builders received 127 million acres of land from Congress, nearly half of all land granted through the Homestead Act. By 1856, railroads made up 341 of the top 500 companies—though more than a quarter of them had failed by 1893, demonstrating how dynamic these times of rapid infrastructure change can be.[7]

Just as cities were growing, companies were expanding by leaps and bounds. By 1900, U.S. Steel had become the first corporation to attain a billion dollars in revenue. Otis was one of the first companies to not be limited to a charter in one state, as it bought elevator companies across the country. Standard Oil, Carnegie Steel, and many other trusts followed and became national leaders.

As companies grew larger, they needed to adopt formal, scientific approaches to management. Accounting standards were developed. Frederick Taylor conducted his famous time-and-motion studies to optimize manufacturing processes. Alfred Sloan laid down the principles of managing a large multibusiness corporation to make it possible to run a company the size of General Motors. Corporate R&D became a focus for the first time, because companies could now surpass what individuals could do on their own. The holding company was invented. In broad terms, the second industrial revolution and the massive, capital-intensive businesses it produced led to the command-and-control structure that defines the modern corporation.

The period of 1850–1920 saw the formation of not only the leading American global corporations but the establishment of the very notion of "business" and the American model of entrepreneurship. (We will argue in chapters seven and eight that the third industrial revolution will unleash a similar wave of new business processes, structures, and market mechanisms.)

Companies that adopted the new approaches to management thrived. Siemens, which began as a telegraph company in the mid-1800s, became

---

7   Given the tight linkage between financing and infrastructure in those days, it's not surprising that several companies were both railroads and banks in one firm. The phenomenon was not unlike the *keiretsu* during the Japanese industrialization boom after the Meiji restoration, when each family of companies included a bank, a steel company, and a chemicals company.

a major maker of electrical equipment. IBM took a technology that was used to control looms and made it the basis for tabulating machines for businesses, on its way to a computer empire. The big steel companies emerged. So did GM and Ford. General Electric—originally called Edison General Electric—became ascendant.

In the early 1900s, Fritz Haber and Carl Bosch established the basis for an industrial giant by figuring out how to resolve, once again, the fear of famine. That fear, voiced by Malthus and others before the first industrial revolution, had returned, but what has become known as the Haber-Bosch process allowed for the production of synthetic fertilizer in vast quantities; until the advent of their process, nations were scrounging so hard for natural fertilizer that Chile, Bolivia, and Peru fought a five-year war over bird guano. That's right, bird poop.

The process has become so important that it consumes 1 percent of the world's electricity and generates fertilizer that is responsible for sustaining a third of the world's population. Agriculture yields improved so much that we could produce corn not just for ourselves but could feed it to chickens, pigs, and cattle in large quantities, making meat affordable on a regular basis for the middle class. The process also allowed for the high-fructose corn syrup that makes food taste better by making it sweeter (while expanding waistlines). About half of the protein in our bodies contains nitrogen that comes from fertilizer produced using the process.

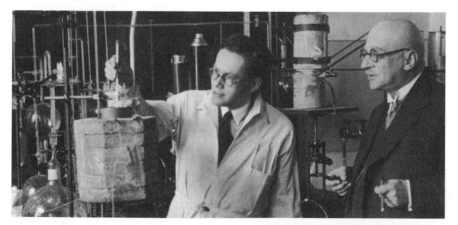

German chemists Carl Bosch (1874–1940, left) and Fritz Haber (1868–1934, right), inventors of modern nitrogen fertilizer.

BASF, the company that employed both Haber and Bosch, became wildly successful and is still the world's largest chemicals company.[8]

Just as in the first industrial revolution, plenty of companies fell by the wayside. Andrew Carnegie put hundreds of steel companies out of business. Hundreds of car companies disappeared after Henry Ford beat them to the possibilities of a mechanized assembly line by leveraging massive capital and the electric grid. Today, people are surprised when most of the world's 300 solar-energy companies go bankrupt as the technology matures and scale becomes more important, but that's only because we forget that most of the world's auto companies also failed early; more than 1,800 American car companies were reduced to three in the first decades of the twentieth century. The companies that provoked the war over bird guano lost when Haber and Bosch provided more bountiful sources of nitrogen for fertilizer. Chile, the major source of bird guano, went into the doldrums when its economic engine disappeared.

As with the first industrial revolution, broadly based increases in income caused such a surge in consumption that resources were strained. There was another thirty-year rise in commodity prices, from 1890 to 1920. Again, energy and oil prices increased by more than a factor of five, and metals prices doubled. Food prices rose 50 percent. Again, there were major disruptions. Competition over precious materials (in this case, diamonds and gold) led to the First Boer War in South Africa in 1868 and the Second Boer War in 1886. The Spanish–American War broke out in 1898 over sugar production in Cuba. The "banana wars" broke out in Central America to protect the agricultural interests of the United Fruit Company (now known as Chiquita Brands).

---

8   There were ugly twists and turns along the way. Haber assisted in the German war effort during World War I, became the father of chemical weapons, and personally supervised their use on the battlefield. His first wife, a chemist herself, was so ashamed of his work that she killed herself; decades later, their son also committed suicide out of shame. Haber rejected requests for help by the Nazis and fled the country in 1933. Bosch, a vocal critic of the Nazis, lapsed into alcoholism as they consolidated their power and died in 1940, at age sixty-five. BASF combined with Bayer, Hoechst, and three other companies to form IG Farben in 1925, and the company was later coopted by the Nazis. Among other things, it produced the poison gas used in concentration camps. Dow and DuPont used patented research by BASF to develop explosives and incendiaries that were used to firebomb Tokyo, the single most destructive aerial bombardment in history. The Allies liquidated IG Farben after the war—after sentencing thirteen of the twenty-four directors to prison terms of one to eight years—and BASF was reestablished as a separate company.

But once again, dark predictions succumbed to innovations in technology and management disciplines. Instead of famines, steaming piles of horse manure in low-rise tenements, and nights dimly lit only by the smelly kerosene lantern, the second industrial revolution gave us the modern world.

The urbanization crisis was largely solved, doubling life expectancy while allowing for huge improvements in levels of education and raising the standard of living to heights that would have been unimaginable to even the wealthiest people in the 1870s. The founding of many of the major American universities, concert halls, and museums dates from this period.

A NEW RESOURCE CRISIS—AND OPPORTUNITY

Now we're in crisis mode again.

Warnings have been issued since the early 1970s, when the Club of Rome returned to the Malthusian thesis in its report, "The Limits to Growth." The global think tank, composed of scientists, politicians, and business leaders from around the world, started with the premise that the world has finite resources, then argued that resources would soon run out. Oil, for instance, was to last only into the early 1990s.

The Club of Rome's 1972 publication, The Limits to Growth.

As it happens, "The Limits to Growth" came out just as the integrated circuit, invented in 1958, really began to come into widespread commercial use. By now, the computer chip in the standard personal computer or smartphone has so many transistors on it that manufacturers have pretty much stopped counting. Intel's flagship processor has billions of transistors today, versus the few thousand that were on the most advanced mainstream chip when the Club of Rome published its dire forecast. The forecast assumed that technological progress would be linear and that only pollution, population, and resource use

Inventors Jack Kilby (1923–2005) with the first integrated circuit, inside a glass case (left) and Robert Noyce (1927–1990) with a microchip diagram (right).

would grow exponentially. In fact, over the past forty years the power of computers has grown exponentially, while population growth has not even been linear. Some current projections are for population growth to stop altogether by 2050 at around 9.6 billion. Local pollution has declined in developed countries, though it is still rising in emerging countries. Innovations that companies built on top of the transistor, coupled with new business models and regulatory changes, have transformed many industries to dramatically improve productivity and output. Since "The Limits to Growth" was published, food production has tripled, while population has little more than doubled. Productivity has risen so fast that world GDP per person is more than double what it was when the Club of Rome said the end was nigh.

Still, the demands of the emerging middle class have become so great that we are already twelve years into a surge in commodity prices. Prices for oil and energy have more than quintupled since 1998. Metals prices have tripled. Food prices have risen 75 percent. Just since the beginning of the twenty-first century, an index of commodity prices has risen almost 150 percent. Those prices are now 50 percent higher than they were in 1900. Battles over oil, water, and food are the inevitable consequences.

The cost of resources, having remained steady or declined slightly in inflation-adjusted terms for nearly a century, has now become an economic headwind. The pressures are affecting every business, not just builders that use steel, aluminum smelters that consume vast quantities of electricity, or agricultural producers that depend heavily on diesel fuel

Commodity price evolution during industrial revolutions

Wholesale commodity prices in the United States
Index value (5-year moving average)

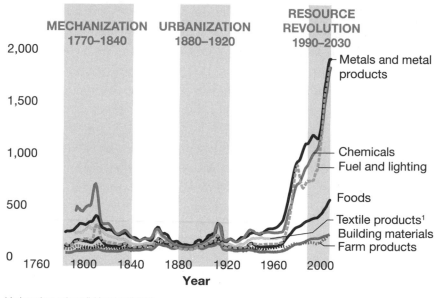

1 Index values only available up until 1970

and fertilizers derived from oil and natural gas. Rapid commodity price inflation acts as a regressive tax, increasing income disparity and slowing economic growth. And, while both earlier industrial revolutions saw the surge in commodity prices end after three decades, the current surge, if not addressed effectively, could well last longer, given the unprecedented scope of the demand being created by the expanding middle class.

Even companies that seem to consume almost no resources will need to operate differently. At Google, it may appear that all the energy consumed is the brainpower that goes into coding. In fact, the IT industry as a whole is already on a path to exceed the emissions of the airline industry, with all those enormous data centers running millions of servers 24 hours a day, 365 days a year—worldwide, data centers consume the output of about 30 nuclear power plants. In the near future, as we detail in chapter four, there will be huge opportunities to provide software and services that help others cope with increasingly scarce resources.

THE THIRD INDUSTRIAL REVOLUTION: RESOURCE REVOLUTION

Producing a third industrial revolution that focuses on how we use resources will require a rethinking of the way companies operate, and managers will have to adapt quickly to profit from the once-in-a-century opportunities that are in front of us. Just as the Watt steam engine and other technologies provided a tenfold improvement in productivity, the current revolution needs to deliver the same dramatic results by addressing natural-resource productivity.

Many are skeptical about our ability to innovate fast enough to keep pace with soaring demand. For instance, in an opinion piece in the *Wall Street Journal* titled, "Why Innovation Won't Save Us," Northwestern University professor Robert Gordon wrote that "the evidence suggests to me that future economic growth will achieve at best half [the] historic rate" of 2 percent a year that was present from 1891 to 2007. He said that just about all important inventions have already appeared and he warned, "The old rate allowed the American standard of living to double every 35 years; for most people in the future that doubling may take a century or more."

But we believe that this next revolution will follow the rough paths of the first two. Its seeds have already been planted and are sprouting all around us—as William Gibson noted, the future is here, it's just not evenly distributed.

Although lots of companies will fall by the wayside, the revolution will also allow for the creation of the next group of international giants that will dominate for the foreseeable future, as well as nimble specialists that facilitate resource revolutions. Those that win will be the companies that not only take advantage of emerging technologies but that combine them with managerial innovations that follow in the tradition of the factory, the assembly line, and other breakthroughs from the first two revolutions. Far from being overwhelmed by rising prices and the scarcity of resources, successful companies will benefit from the dramatic increase in demand for high-productivity goods and services while ushering all of us into a new era of prosperity.

The challenges we face may be unprecedented, but, simply put, any bet that we will succumb to a global economic crisis is a bet against human ingenuity. No such bet has ever paid off.

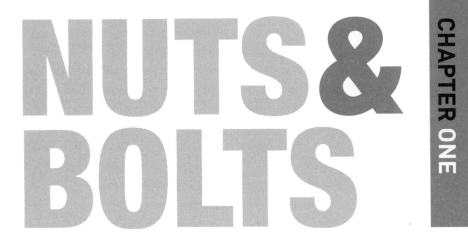

NUTS&
BOLTS

THE INDUSTRIAL REVOLUTION TRIGGERED BY THE STEAM ENGINE offered enormous business opportunities and potential for wealth creation, while also killing off companies and industries that could not keep up.

THE DRAMATIC IMPROVEMENT IN LABOR PRODUCTIVITY also brought increased power to capital owners and established the limited liability corporation.

THE WAVE OF URBANIZATION AND ELECTRIFICATION at the turn of the twentieth century created equally large productivity opportunities.

THESE INNOVATIONS HELPED CREATE GLOBAL CORPORATIONS that have prospered for a century and banks to support and fund them, making capital deployment substantially more productive.

BOTH REVOLUTIONS UNFOLDED OVER SEVERAL DECADES and required many additional innovations in manufacturing, metallurgy, management systems, and selling approaches to ensure a business could scale.

BOTH REVOLUTIONS ALSO INITIALLY CAUSED A COMMODITY price spike, as demand for steel, copper, food, etc., outgrew traditional production methodologies, but eventually increased welfare as newer, higher-productivity automated methods took hold.

WE ARE NOW FACING A THIRD such commodity spike driven by the rise of cities and the number of middle-class citizens in emerging markets.

WE ARE CONFIDENT A STEP CHANGE in resource productivity will not only allow the economy to work its way through the resource challenges but deliver new opportunities for creating wealth and cementing the position of leading companies for the coming decades.

CHAPTER TWO

JOYSTICKS MEET DRILLING RIGS, LAUNCHING THE REVOLUTION

TO BEGIN TO UNDERSTAND HOW THE RESOURCE REVOLUTION unfolds and how big the impact can be, let's look at the story of Texas oilman George Mitchell. In the early 1980s, after decades of success as a wildcatter and as the head of an independent oil and gas company, Mitchell reached an impasse. The output of natural gas from his wells in Texas was approaching the end, but he had long-term contracts to deliver gas to a pipeline that carried the gas to Chicago. He needed more.

Mitchell knew that his previously tapped wells still contained plenty of natural gas, as did numerous untapped areas. The problem was that the gas was trapped in shale, and the industry had long ago decided that drilling for the gas was far too expensive.

In shale formations, vast quantities of gas (and oil) can be trapped in innumerable tiny cells permeating the rock. But an exploration company can't just run a drill down into the shale, declare victory, and withdraw gas for decades. The company has to fracture the shale, section by section, to release the gas. The company also has to keep the oil and gas flowing smoothly so it can travel up a pipe to the surface. A process had been developed in the 1940s and 1950s to inject mud into fissures in the shale and make it explode, releasing the gas, but the process was so inefficient that it was abandoned.

Whenever Mitchell drilled adjacent to the Dallas–Fort Worth metropolitan area (which extends underneath the airport), sensors reported a "show" of gas as the bit passed through a layer known as the Barnett Shale.

In 1981, Mitchell decided to explore the shale. His engineers told him he was nuts: The shale simply wouldn't yield its gas easily enough. But, without many options, Mitchell made a momentous decision: He would figure out how to make hydraulic fracturing work.

Mitchell was in his early sixties, nearing the age when many people think about retiring, but he was just embarking on the most important journey of his life. That journey turned the energy industry's economics upside down, and its impact has begun to ripple through just about every industry and country on the globe. His journey—together with that of a strange bedfellow, a start-up named Opower that we describe at the end of this chapter—shows how the resource revolution can come from attacking either a supply problem or a demand problem.

Mitchell's approach to the problems he faced in the 1980s and 1990s turns out to have valuable lessons for anyone who wants to turn today's resource crisis into opportunity.

George Phydias Mitchell was born in Galveston, Texas, in 1919, the son of Greek immigrants. His father, a goatherd back in Greece, shined shoes for a living in the United States. Galveston, a town of only about 60,000 at the time, had good public schools, and Mitchell excelled as a student. He graduated from high school at fifteen. One summer, he went to work with his brother Johnny, ten years his senior, at some oil fields in Louisiana and fell in love with the business. Mitchell enrolled at Texas A&M to study petroleum engineering, with an emphasis in geology. Putting himself through school by, among other things, tailoring clothing for his classmates, Mitchell graduated first in his class.

He went to work for Amoco (originally Standard Oil of Indiana; now, BP), then enlisted in the army at the beginning of World War II. The army had the good sense to keep him in the States, where he used his engineering skills to help design facilities to store ordnance, work on new methods to make the barrels for guns, and lay out dozens of airfields. While Johnny Mitchell was racing across France as part of General George Patton's Third Army in 1944, George Mitchell was working with the U.S. Army Corps of Engineers on equipment and methods that could deliver gasoline and diesel fuel to Patton faster and keep him moving.

After the war, the Mitchell brothers and a partner formed a small exploration company. The war had consumed all available steel, severely curbing oil drilling, and there was a lot of pent-up interest in exploration. George Mitchell lined up six financial backers, each of whom paid him

$50 a month so he could support himself, his wife, and their first child. (They eventually had ten children.) He and his two partners hired a secretary and piled on top of each other in an office in Houston that he described as being slightly bigger than a closet. They couldn't afford to buy the geological reports that helped drillers choose targets, but Mitchell had a friend at a company that produced such reports. He worked out a deal that let him collect reports at the end of the business day and return them first thing the following morning, having stayed up half the night to study them. Mitchell put together drilling plans, which Johnny and the other partner presented to the financial backers and other prospects—their office was over a drugstore that was a hub for oil and gas brokers. Johnny and the third partner hung out at the counter to pick up scuttlebutt and prospect for deals.

Hydraulic fracturing pioneer George Mitchell (1919–2013) in his office in 1979.

Just a few dry wells in a row would have killed the fledgling business, but they hit oil early and often. As they built an enviable track record, they drew hundreds of additional investors and financed bigger and bigger projects. The company grew to more than 2,000 employees. Along the way, during various downturns, George Mitchell bought out all the investors and partners, including his brother.

Belying the stereotypical conflict between oilmen and environmentalists, Mitchell became concerned enough about ecological issues in the 1960s that he financed one of the principal researchers who contributed to the Club of Rome's report, "The Limits to Growth." Despite being in the oil and gas business, Mitchell long favored a tax on fossil fuels. He had also become concerned about issues related to race and urban development. After visiting Brooklyn's Bedford-Stuyvesant neighborhood and Los Angeles's Watts neighborhood, with its simmering racial tensions, in the 1960s, he decided to try his hand at a better form of urban development. He bought 50,000 acres near Houston and turned half of them into the

Hydraulic fracturing

Conventional gas not associated with oil

Sandstone

Seal

Light tight oil

Light tight oil

Horizontal drilling

Fractures

Oil-rich shale

Truck volume by payload
(one-way trips)

Truck transportation of water requires
600-900 one-way truck trips per well,
or 67% of total trucks trips, creating
noise, air and pollution problems.

Water	Other	Total
600-900	295-450	895-1,350
300	155	455
600	295	895

FMC Technologies

Coalbed methane

Conventional gas
found with oil

Conventional oil

Tight sand gas ⟶

Light tight oil

Tight sand gas

Oil-rich shale

Gas-rich shale

Woodlands, an upscale suburban master-planned community with about 95,000 residents and numerous corporate campuses that is often cited as a premier example of environmental responsibility.

By 1981, when Mitchell started working on fracturing the Barnett Shale, the federal government had conducted considerable research on shale in response to the energy crisis created by OPEC in the 1970s. Indeed, a government/industry partnership had produced detailed maps for most of the shale geology in the United States. The Department of Energy had also built on industry efforts in 3-D seismic imaging, which is important for working a drill through a shale formation, and the Bureau of Economic Geology had provided images that helped show how porous the rock was. In addition, the federal government provided tax credits for unconventional oil and gas wells, such as Mitchell's, creating an incentive to experiment.

That said, the breakthrough was all George Mitchell. "George always pushed technology," says Dan Steward, a geologist who worked with Mitchell. Everyone knew where the resource was, but no one thought it was economically feasible. Only Mitchell found the key.

It took eighteen years to crack the code. Along the way, Mitchell's board began to doubt him. He spent almost $1 billion to develop the process, roughly the net worth of the company. Deciding that he needed more capital in the late 1990s, when the price of natural gas was languishing, he tried to sell the company but got no takers. The industry ignored Mitchell so completely that a National Petroleum Council survey on gas reserves in the late '90s didn't even mention the Barnett Shale. The best minds in the oil industry, government, and academia concluded in the study that natural gas was running short, even though Mitchell was already working on turning the Barnett into one of the most productive fields in the world that would deliver decades' worth of natural gas to the United States.

Associates say that, despite all the adversity, Mitchell was remarkably disciplined about the process. He methodically tried large numbers of permutations of fluids, chemicals, and other materials to see what worked best. One of Mitchell's staffers once suggested that they try injecting horse manure into the shale—after all, they'd tried everything else.

The breakthrough came when Mitchell tried something that contradicted conventional wisdom. The accumulated expertise in the oil patch said water would be a bad fluid to inject into the wells because the shale would absorb it and expand, closing the fissures rather than opening them up so much and so fast that the rock exploded. But the methodical Mitchell tried injecting water. It worked.

In 2002, Mitchell sold his company to Devon Energy for $3.5 billion. He could have waited for the market to really believe in the value of fracking, but he was in his eighties and decided that he'd had enough. Forbes calculated his personal net worth at $1.6 billion, at age ninety-three, even though he had given away at least $150 million to Texas A&M and other organizations. (Mitchell, who died in 2013 at ninety-four, had signed the Giving Pledge, promising to donate half his net worth to charity, whether during his lifetime or in his will.)

Devon took the technology to the next level. It had expertise in horizontal drilling—drilling thousands of feet underground, then having the drill bit head off at an angle as sharp as ninety degrees. Devon experimented with fracturing shale formations by going into them sideways and found that the method surpassed even the seemingly miraculous results that Mitchell had produced in formations that had historically been viewed as useless. Probing sideways into a horizontal shale formation is much more efficient than drilling a bunch of holes vertically through it, and Devon is expert in using sensors to provide information to joystick-wielding operators who guide the fracking fluids to the spots that will produce maximum yield.

The markets remained leery until 2008, when the price of oil hit $140 a barrel and gas hit $12 per thousand cubic feet—each a generational high. Oil and gas is a boom-and-bust world. Just because someone has a big strike today doesn't mean there will be another one tomorrow. But the evidence that Mitchell had unlocked a secret that would change the dynamics of the market finally became overwhelming. Others began to copy Devon's techniques in shale formations in other parts of Texas, plus Louisiana, Oklahoma, North Dakota, British Columbia, Alberta, and "the mighty Marcellus," an enormous formation underlying parts of New York, Pennsylvania, Ohio, and West Virginia.

Industry estimates now see gas from shale accounting for more than 20 percent of U.S. gas production, up by almost a factor of twenty from the year 2000, and that figure could reach 46 percent soon. While many

North American unconventional oil and gas reserves

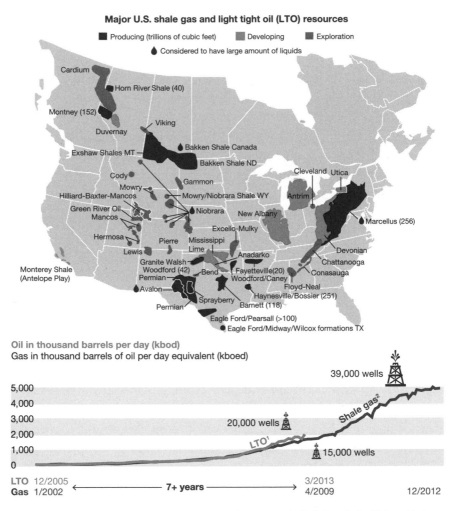

Major U.S. shale gas and light tight oil (LTO) resources

Oil in thousand barrels per day (kbod)
Gas in thousand barrels of oil per day equivalent (kboed)

1 Bakken, Eagleford, Granite Wash, Avalon, Mississippi Lime, Spraberry, Austin Chalk, Bone Spring, Niobrara, Monterey, Woodford—only liquids included; Wells with production after Jan. 2000 (production data through March 2013)
2 Barnett, Eagleford, Fayetteville, Haynesville, Marcellus, Woodford—only gas included (production data through Dec. 2012 due to Marcellus lag time in reporting)

had feared that gas was running out, U.S. reserves are now seen as abundant enough to last at least a century. As a result, prices for natural gas in the United States have plunged more than two-thirds since 2000.

Leveraging the same technology, unconventional "light tight oil" production is growing at an even faster rate than shale gas. The United States is now producing more than 2 million barrels a day and adding 75,000 barrels per day to production each month. This is on top of the 6 million barrels per day of current oil production. The United States is on a path potentially to pass Saudi Arabia as the world's largest oil producer within a decade and is now exporting refined petroleum products for the first time since World War II. Rather than import natural gas, the United States is on pace to export 10 billion cubic feet each day—at a value of some $15 billion a year. On current course, the United States will not need to import crude oil after 2020 from outside North America. This unconventional oil growth will reshape global trade patterns, almost eliminating energy trade across the Atlantic. Because 60 percent of the U.S. trade deficit is oil imports, the United States is on a path to dramatically improve the national trade balance and energy security.

That's just the first part of the story. What happens as the consequences of a resource revolution ripple outward through the world?

Many utilities, which build plants that last some fifty years, were caught with a fleet of coal-fired power plants that were uneconomical in the face of cheap natural gas. Even some old nuclear units are turning out to be too expensive to operate and maintain. The restructuring in economics has left utilities scrambling to switch to cheap gas as quickly as possible.

Chemicals companies rely on gas and associated liquids as raw material for a huge percentage of their products; American companies, with access to cheap gas, immediately gained a cost advantage on competitors overseas. A recent study found that gas prices in the United States have dropped 66 percent since 2008, while prices have risen 35 percent in Europe. Companies that still use by-products from crude oil in their chemicals processes are having a hard time keeping up with those that use gas. Energy-intensive manufacturing of steel, glass, aluminum, etc., which had been fleeing the United States because of cheap inputs and cheap labor overseas, may start to move back to North America to take advantage of inexpensive gas and power.

The geological formations the United States is tapping have been identified throughout the world, and global commodity markets tend to con-
verge, so while the United States doesn't have a permanent leg up, it has a
huge first-mover advantage, and this could last for some time. Other countries typically bar landowners from owning the resources below ground,
have less gas-distribution infrastructure, and have less of the technological
know-how for developing these resources, so tapping the new energy source
could take more time abroad. Additionally, expertise must be developed in
other countries before they can begin fracking their own sources.

The environmental community remains concerned, legitimately. Some
worry that the chemicals used in the process can contaminate the water
supply. Fracking typically takes place so far below the water table that more
than a mile of impermeable rock separates the chemicals from the water we
consume, so careful procedures should avoid problems, but there are still
uncertainties. Many are concerned that poor techniques and improperly
set well casings can release significant amounts of methane, exacerbating air
pollution and accelerating global warming—poor performers have, indeed,
failed to complete wells appropriately. Improper drilling and water disposal practices can cause earthquakes, though companies that adjust their
drilling patterns to avoid local seismic faults should make the phenomenon rare. The sheer volume of water used in fracking—5 million gallons
per well—has raised concerns, especially in areas like China, Poland, and
parts of Texas where water supplies are lacking. Even if no contamination
occurs, some environmentalists contend that fracking will extend the
world's reliance on fossil fuels. Gas may burn much more cleanly than coal,
but its emissions are not as clean as solar, wind, or hydropower.

Still, the use of natural gas is reducing pollution at a rapid pace
and is much safer, cleaner, and more economic than the alternatives
today. In addition, as fracking continues to innovate, the techniques will
reduce land use, water requirements, and airshed impact. Companies
are already working to reduce land use per well by 90 percent. The
company that develops high-productivity, waterless fracking will score
a huge win.

Whatever the case, fracking demonstrates the huge curveballs that
resource revolutions deliver—and not just because fracking turned the
son of an immigrant goatherd and shoeshine man into a billionaire. For

an industry rooted in gradual change, fracking rapidly redefined the land-scape of extraction and consumption of fossil fuels. The change started with gas exploration companies but, as we've seen, went far beyond those just involved in extracting a resource.

Mitchell's innovation highlights some of the core principles we are going to explore in this book. He focused on a big opportunity—small opportunities need not apply. He innovated rapidly and repeatedly—all companies need to start behaving like Silicon Valley tech companies, mak-ing continuous research and development a central mission, a challenge that we discuss in chapter nine.

Mitchell and his team integrated software and other information technology with traditional tools, producing an enormous increase in pro-ductivity. The mash-up of IT and heavy industry is one of the hallmarks of resource revolutions, as we will see in chapter four. Mitchell and then Devon showed the power of borrowing technology when they took sensor and even joystick technology from the world of video games and used them to optimize oil drilling. How to borrow technology is the subject of chapter seven, where, among other examples, we'll see how Cree borrowed crucial technology from semiconductors and helped transform the world of lighting. Crucial technologies are already out there—fracking had been around for decades before Mitchell figured out how to make it work for shale—if only we can learn how to see them.

Demonstrating the importance of getting the timing right, Mitchell found a significantly more cost-effective substitute when energy prices were reaching all-time highs. Mitchell and his team acquired large acreage blocks at pennies on the dollar before the market realized the massive scale of the opportunity. And Mitchell handed the company off to a manage-ment team at Devon at a time when his ability to innovate with fracking was slowing; Devon's horizontal techniques were necessary to take frack-ing to the next level.

Note that, despite Mitchell's breakthrough, Devon had to continue the process of reinvention to stay relevant and profitable, moving to include extraction of shale oil as well as natural gas. In the third industrial revolution, rapid change is a constant; upheavals happen quickly and fre-quently. Companies that make continuous reinvention into a core mission will stay ahead of the curve.

If these targets seem either too remote or specialized, let's think again. It doesn't take government policy makers or titans of industry to move the earth. Let's look at Mitchell's strange bedfellows, a couple of college friends who have built a burgeoning business by targeting a very specific problem that is so familiar and everyday it seems almost impossible to change: people who forget to turn off their lights.

Resource revolutions occur in two familiar categories: supply and demand. Both have the potential to drive exponential growth. Fracking and horizontal drilling used technology to increase natural-resource supply, in effect converting unusable shale formations into a valuable resource. The company founded by the college friends, Dan Yates and Alex Laskey, addresses the other half of the equation: resource demand. To do this, their company, Opower, has utilized the latest cloud infrastructure technology, "big data" software tools, and cutting-edge consumer psychology to convince customers to use less power.

Yates and Laskey met at an ice-cream social on their first day at Harvard in 1995. This was just at the start of the Internet boom, and Yates caught the fever. After completing his degree in computer science, he headed to Silicon Valley—just in time for the bursting of the bubble. But he rebounded, cofounded a company that made educational testing software, and sold it to Houghton Mifflin for $40 million in 2003. He went from having a few hundred dollars in a checking account to being set for life. He and his girlfriend (now wife) bought a Toyota 4Runner and shipped it to Anchorage, Alaska. They strapped gasoline cans to the roof and spent a year driving down the Pan-American Highway to Ushuaia, Argentina, often camping by the side of the road. Yates came home depressed by the ecological damage he and his girlfriend saw.

Meanwhile, after earning a degree in history, Laskey had become involved in managing political campaigns. "I was very good at coming in second and third," he says with a chuckle, "but I did not win." Deciding to look for a new field, he reconnected with Yates.

They both wanted to do something to help sustain the environment, and they methodically considered any number of possibilities, staring at a whiteboard of ideas. They even looked into the possibility of using Mylar balloons—basically, big versions of shiny birthday balloons—to concentrate light on solar panels. Finally, they came across some research from a professor at Arizona State University that looked into how to motivate people to use less electricity. He had hung flyers on people's doors in San Diego encouraging them to use a fan rather than air-conditioning at night. None of the messages worked—except for this one: "Did you know that most of your neighbors choose to use a fan at night?"

Yates and Laskey decided they could build on that idea, encouraging people to use less electricity by comparing their energy-using habits with the neighbors'. They initially thought of pursuing the idea as a nonprofit but quickly realized that utilities, at the urging of regulators, would gladly provide access to customer data and pay to pursue conservation. Drawing on two of the key early lessons of the resource revolution—the need to apply heavy doses of IT to heavy industry and the need to explore new business models—they launched Opower.

They had a hill to climb: Because kilowatt hours are so cheap, people just don't pay much attention to their electricity usage. The two like to say that people spend only about six minutes a year thinking about their electricity usage, so most people think about pop singer Justin Bieber more than they think about their consumption of electricity.

But, drawing from the professor's insight into behavioral economics and applying information technology to the problem, Yates and Laskey began to build a sophisticated model of energy usage. They don't just look at the size of a house and make comparisons with similar homes in an area. Drawing on the second-by-second information available from smart meters, they can infer how many people live in a particular house and whether anyone is in the house during the day. They can even account for variations in the weather when evaluating energy usage. Combining all the information, they provide a sophisticated ranking that the utility includes in monthly statements, which shows consumers how their electricity usage compares with that of people in similar circumstances—and when a customer finds he's in the forty-third percentile among his neighbors, he reacts.

Opower finds that it can get consumers to cut electricity consumption by more than 2 percent just by giving them feedback using available data and providing a few suggestions on how to make saving energy easy. This may sound less consequential than the shale gas revolution, but a 2 percent reduction nationwide would eliminate the need for some 130 power plants. Even more broadly, Opower shows how information technology can make a broad impact with negligible expenditure of resources. A small intervention can create quantum results quickly.

Getting going took some time. Opower was lucky—just as the company entered the market in 2007, the price of natural gas hit a multidecade high, passing through $8 per thousand cubic feet, heading to $12; the rise sent the price of power up around the country and sent utilities (and their regulators) on the hunt for new approaches to save energy. The company quickly got positive feedback from some regulators and utilities and lined up venture capital, but it took years to turn the feedback into contracts. Casting as wide a net as possible, Laskey used some political connections to get a hearing with state officials in Texas, even though they didn't expect Texas under Governor Rick Perry to spend a lot of time focusing on energy conservation. Yates and Laskey were invited to testify before a committee of the state legislature, only to be strung along for so many hours that they didn't make their appearance until three in the morning. But they got language into a bill that eventually helped make Texas a marquee market for Opower.

Persistence paid off, and the company started getting contracts in 2010, both in the United States and in Europe. Opower now reports on electricity usage to more than 10 million households, just in the United States. They say they have motivated people to save some 2 billion kilowatt hours of electricity, or about $250 millions' worth. The company is up to about $100 million of annual revenue and continues to grow rapidly.

Rather than creating and marketing hardware to consumers of energy, Opower's business model focuses instead on marketing software to utility companies, the producers of energy. Opower has been able to scale quickly through a lean-operations approach by avoiding expensive hardware, instead utilizing less-capital-intensive software. Traditionally, utility companies reach out to customers with dollars-and-cents arguments, whereas Opower's approach pulls on our competitive nature through behavioral psychology. Opower is a business-to-business company that succeeds because of its business-to-consumer capabilities.

Laskey says he got an insight into how far their reach has extended when he and his wife rented a vacation home for a week in a remote area in the Catskills. As the owner unlocked the house and showed them around, she asked what kind of work Laskey did. He said something vague about helping utilities be more energy efficient, and she perked up. She complained that her utility sent her a rating every month that said she and her husband were way below average in energy efficiency. As she went on about how bad she felt, Laskey's wife couldn't contain a smile. Finally, she told the woman that this was all Laskey's doing, that he was the one who got the utility to ding her every month.

While that woman and the millions of others touched by Opower are only making small changes, in the aggregate those small changes may have a huge effect. Merely having consumers turn those lights off and cut electricity consumption by a few percentage points would save billions of dollars a year and remove the need for scores of power plants just in the United States. By leveraging cloud computing and applying information technology to an industry that has not changed since the time of Thomas Edison and George Westinghouse, Opower has shown great progress in minimizing energy consumption.

Opower describes its ability to reduce energy consumption and generate revenues as a "double bottom line"—making money while helping the environment. And the employees of Opower are described as being at the "intersection of true (sustainability) believers and business people." Opower believes this mentality of "doing good" while making a profit can benefit other industries, as well: "Our minds go to things and industries such as healthcare," Laskey says. "Our product and our business model are very replicable. There are many industries that can benefit from being able to help the customer and the company."

By zeroing in on a truly minute potential for savings on a customer-by-customer basis, Yates and Laskey used the exponential possibilities of the digital age to reduce demand on resources—and make a fortune.

Opower exemplifies three of the fundamental principles of resource productivity: virtualization, optimization, and waste reduction, about which we learn more in the next chapter. Clever approaches like these will yield hundreds of similar successes—larger ones, too.

Chapter three lays out the formula for success for companies that intend to lead through the next two decades and beyond.

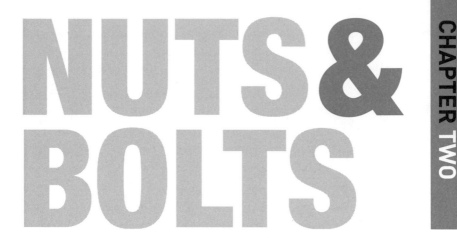

NUTS & BOLTS

MITCHELL ENERGY SHOWS THE GREAT OPPORTUNITY TO EXPAND SUPPLY.

OPOWER DEMONSTRATES THE ECONOMIC ATTRACTIVENESS OF DEMAND REDUCTION. The consumer benefits from both expanded supplies and reduced demand.

TODAY, INNOVATIONS OFTEN INVOLVE COMBINING traditional industrial technologies with new software tools that can scale rapidly.

THESE INNOVATIONS OFTEN REQUIRE NEW BUSINESS MODELS to work at scale.

THE RESTRUCTURING COSTS ARE HIGH when the market gets surprised by a major innovation that changes the economics of a process by a factor of five to ten—those who don't see the new wave coming can go bankrupt quickly.

CHAPTER THREE

THE RECIPE FOR TENFOLD RESOURCE PRODUCTIVITY IMPROVEMENT

THE CAR IS SUCH A MATURE TECHNOLOGY that we are approaching the 250th anniversary of the first auto accident. In 1771, a Frenchman used an early, coal-fired steam engine to haul cannons but lost control and crashed into a wall. Since that first auto-related shout of *Sacre bleu!* (or whatever French equivalent he used for "We're all gonna die!"), the auto industry has offered an instructive look at how things can go right—and then wrong—and then right again—when it comes to major industrial shifts.

The car industry also shows the power of the five principles that we'll cover in this chapter and that are the first areas a company should look at when thinking through how to win the resource revolution. Those five principles are:

1. Finding opportunities to substitute away from scarce resources.
2. Eliminating waste throughout the system, from production through end use.
3. Increasing "circularity"—upgrading, reusing, or recycling products.
4. Optimizing efficiency, convenience, safety, and reliability.
5. Moving products, services, and the processes that develop or deliver them out of the physical world and into the virtual realm.

After motorized travel showed early promise in the mid-1800s, a backlash developed. Cars were classified as "road locomotives," and speeds were restricted to 4 mph in the country and 2 mph in towns and cities—

where, for good measure, a man carrying a red flag had to walk in front of each car.

There were incorrect assumptions about how the technology would develop. Many worried, for instance, that the adoption of cars would be limited because, after all, at some point the world would run out of chauffeurs to drive them. Many also initially assumed that cars would be electric, if only so that a driver didn't have to turn a crank to provide the compression that would start a gasoline engine—while risking a kick from the crank that broke many an arm.

Finally, in the late 1800s and early 1900s, the second industrial revolution turned the car into a raging success. Rudolf Diesel invented the internal combustion engine. New forms of "cracking" petroleum provided wide access to gasoline. Henry Ford's automated assembly line made cars available to the mass market.

Cars spread across the landscape, as did roads and the cities they enabled. The development of the oil industry and the automobile saved New York and London from being buried in manure, saved whale populations worldwide, allowed suburbs to develop, allowed fresh produce to be delivered to cities, and opened a new era of dramatic economic growth.

Although many observers argue that the world will soon have to spend more capital and get less of a product or service in return, the history of the automobile in the early twentieth century highlights the fact that resource revolutions are actually about providing far more capability at sharply lower cost. Where steam-powered cars had 2 or 3 horsepower (hp), a 30-mile range, and a top speed of 12 mph, the Model T generated 20 hp, had a 250-mile range (getting 25 mpg) and had a top speed of 45 mph. Yet Ford's cars cost a fraction of what steam-powered vehicles cost. The technologies and business models that win will deliver dramatically better performance—more output for less input—just as the lightbulb was invented as a way to reduce whale oil use and won by delivering remarkable improvements in health and working hours, making it possible to work after dark at low cost without soot, noxious fumes, and fire hazard.

In terms of the three economic inputs laid out by Adam Smith, automakers have invested huge amounts of capital and have pushed hard on labor productivity in the decades since Ford. Companies have focused on

Henry Ford (1863–1947) with one of his company's Model T automobiles, c. 1920.

speeding up the assembly line and employing fewer workers, leading to innovations such as the lean production system pioneered by Toyota and necessitating the increased use of robotics in manufacturing. But the pendulum has swung back in the other direction. Having been a paragon of efficiency for so long, cars now have obvious problems that can only be solved by paying attention to Smith's third input: land and natural resources.

Henry Ford defined the current model of car ownership in the early twentieth century. Owning a car became a status symbol. A car represented suburban freedom, adventure, and achievement. The car has evolved into a basic necessity to get around, given the nearly complete lack of mass transit infrastructure in the United States. But, even though the quality of cars and their efficiency have continued to improve, some aspects of car usage have become much less efficient.

Though most cars still have five seats, average occupancy has dropped to 1.6 people per vehicle. American cars have more than tripled in weight from the 1,200 pounds of the Model T to more than 4,000 pounds today. As physicist and environmentalist Amory Lovins has pointed out, less than 1 percent of the energy in a tank of gas really goes toward moving the passenger from point A to point B; the rest is lost in heat, tire wear, and moving hunks of metal and air.

Even worse, most of us own a car mainly to park it 96 percent of the time. Cars are typically the second biggest capital expenditure we make[9]—the first is buying a house—yet they spend almost their entire lives sitting at home or in parking lots. While car companies have innovated in finance—they now lease the car to an individual to park rather than selling it to an individual to park—the basic productivity equation has not changed. The driver still gets precious little use out of the car.

Roads are likewise extremely inefficient. A freeway operating at peak throughput of 2,000 cars per lane per hour is less than 10 percent covered by cars. Add more cars, and congestion drops speeds and reduces throughput. Freeways take up anywhere from 2 to 6 lanes in each direction, 24 hours a day, 365 days a year, even if that full capacity is used only for a few rush-hour periods five days of the week, and sometimes only in one direction. This translates to 4 to 5 percent of the time that roads reach peak throughput if there are no traffic jams. What if we could move 20 times the volume on existing roads or reduce the highway requirements by 90 percent?

These problems aren't the kind that can be solved by investing in new equipment or making workers more productive. These problems require that car makers truly rethink their product for the first time in a century.

In the process, they may wind up without internal combustion engines, without individual owners, and potentially even without drivers, while providing breakthroughs in convenience and safety and radical reductions in costs for both consumers and manufacturers.

---

9 Americans devote 17% of their annual spending to transportation, including 5% on gas and 6.1% to buy the vehicle. They also spend 1.4% of GDP of roads at all levels of government, lose 1.6% of GDP sitting in congested traffic, and lose $1,522 per person annually to traffic accidents, which are also the ninth leading cause of death globally.

Waste in fuel, cars, and roads caused by automobile transportation

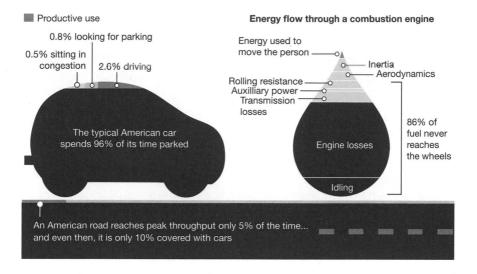

Companies are already starting to seize the opportunities to optimize car usage. Mobile apps are making it easier to arrange car pools. Zipcar, acquired by Avis in early 2013 for $500 million, offers memberships that let people rent cars cheaply by the hour in major cities; each Zipcar is estimated to replace twenty-one cars in its subscriber base. Uber smoothes out inefficiencies in cab and limo systems by letting people summon a car and driver via a smartphone app. Going even further, RelayRides and Getaround provide marketplaces where individuals can rent their cars to others, rather than just have the cars sit idle. GM is working with RelayRides so renters can receive a code to type into their smartphones that will unlock a car via GM's OnStar; that way, owners can simply leave the keys in the car and avoid having to arrange a meeting to hand them over. BMW and Daimler have started car-sharing programs and publicly said they are transportation companies, not car manufacturers.

Soon enough, roads and other infrastructure will adapt to make cars more efficient, too. Cars will be able to communicate with traffic lights, so they'll know whether they're going to make it before a light turns red and can either maintain speed or slow down and save fuel. Pilot tests by the Department of Transportation found fuel savings as high as 15 percent in urban settings from this sort of communication. Local governments will notify drivers of the nearest empty parking spot via an app on their phones, and drivers will be able to reserve a spot by paying for it even before getting there—30 percent of the emissions from cars in cities come from people circling the block while trying to find a parking space, so savings on fuel and emissions will be significant. A start-up, Sensity, says it will take advantage of the upgrade of incandescent streetlights to more efficient and longer-lasting LED, and will offer municipalities the opportunity to include sensors in the new streetlights that will monitor and report on the availability of parking spots on streets.

Inrix gathers location information from tens of millions of mobile devices in forty countries, combines the data with all kinds of other information—about concerts, sporting events, impending snowstorms, etc.—and feeds information on traffic flow and optimal routes to drivers through in-car navigation systems, smartphone apps, radio stations, and other devices. Inrix reports that levels of traffic congestion it measures in the United States have been declining steadily since 2010.

Inrix came about because of the sort of simple but profound insight that often fuels a resource revolution. At the time it was founded, municipalities measured traffic flow mostly by digging up roads and installing induction coils, and news organizations paid for helicopters to monitor rush-hour traffic. But Bryan Mistele, the president and CEO of Inrix, and Craig Chapman, CFO, realized they could crowd-source the data gathering and get information for free by drawing on all the sensors that people were already carrying with them. Mistele had a background in the car industry: His first job, at Ford, was building computers that handled the shipping of cars; he then went to work at Microsoft, where he created software for cars. He had seen rapid demand growth in software, but even he was surprised at how quickly the idea for Inrix resonated with people. In 2005, when the company had just six people, he made a presentation to the CEO of one of the two big digital map companies, to try to interest the company in using Inrix data. Half an hour into the presentation, the CEO slammed his hand on the table and stopped the meeting. "Uh-oh," Mistele thought, "we're going to get kicked out." In fact, the CEO of the mapmaker wanted to give Mistele the twelve people in his traffic department in return for certain rights to sell Inrix's data.

Technology will also reduce accidents greatly, cutting the need for repairs and new cars. At the moment, some 9.4 million cars a year are involved in accidents just in the United States. Simply getting adaptive cruise control into 20 percent of the cars on the road is expected to change the flow of traffic enough to cut the number of traffic accidents sharply. Other automated-driving technologies for parking and crash avoidance, which the big car companies are introducing steadily, will also cut accidents. A recent study in the United States found that 33 percent of drivers didn't even touch the brakes before their collision and that a further 99 percent didn't fully engage the brakes. There is lots of room for improvement by giving cars the capability to apply the brakes automatically in advance of a potential collision.

The path to optimization won't always be straightforward. Uber, for instance, found itself doing battle with the entrenched taxicab oligopolies—a medallion to operate a single taxi in New York City costs about $1 million, so incumbents will fight hard to prevent new types of competition. Taxi companies have had at least occasional success arguing that car services shouldn't be able to use GPS to meter the precise time and distance of a trip, to book a pickup less than thirty minutes ahead of time, or even to allow "electronic hails" at all—in the name of protecting consumers, of course. For instance, when Uber tried to launch in Austin, Texas, to provide free service during the South by Southwest gathering, the local taxi companies sued and launched a high-profile campaign to label Uber a risk to the community. But Uber has made steady progress as the public hooted down the self-serving claims by the taxi companies and the initial sympathetic actions by regulators.

Anti-collision technologies face their own hurdles, mostly because liability issues get tricky once control of a car is taken away from a driver. But, with millions of accidents a year and some 33,000 highway deaths just in the United States—about the same number as from lung cancer, guns, and suicides combined, and an order of magnitude more than war, poison, fires, and falls—the conclusion is inescapable: Good drivers are in a minority. Either the government will eventually intervene to mandate technology that can prevent collisions or someone—likely the insurance companies—will provide incentives that encourage adoption.

While the smart car companies currently focus on optimization, there are also plenty of opportunities to reduce waste. For instance, the adoption of 3-D printing will eventually slash waste. It will no longer be necessary to machine a sheet of steel for a door by "subtractive" manufacturing: punching out a hole for a window, thereby creating a piece of scrap. It will be possible to simply print the door panel in an "additive," or layering, process to produce its final shape. In fact, it will be possible to "print" the whole car body, creating all kinds of possibilities for waste reduction, both in terms of materials and of labor. All sorts of connections will no longer be needed, and material will only be used where it's needed—rather than have doors be of uniform thickness, because that's how sheet metal is produced, each part of the door can be made exactly as thick as required. (We explain the 3-D process and its implications in more depth a little later, in our discussion of waste reduction.)

Car dealer networks will be reinvented, cutting more waste. At the moment, in the United States, car makers take their best guess about what buyers want, and dealers place orders for cars that may then sit on lots for weeks or months. Car dealers are currently protected by state laws that require a car to be sold by an independent dealer who can set a price and make consumers haggle, but the writing is on the wall: When consumers realize how much more convenient it can be to order custom-configured cars on the Internet for home delivery, laws will change so that car makers will eventually be able to take orders directly from consumers and cut out a whole layer of inefficiency.

Although the scale of car manufacturing means that companies use materials that are manifestly available, there will still be opportunities for substitution. For instance, carbon fiber will be used instead of steel because it is far stronger and lighter, allowing longer driving range and better acceleration. The new BMW i3 already incorporates a carbon fiber body, just like the Boeing 787 Dreamliner. Electric motors may substitute for the internal combustion engine in massive quantities.

While much of the material in cars is already recycled, the use of "circularity"—the idea that technology and materials continually cycle through the economy the way nutrients cycle through a biological system—promises greater gains. Systems or components can be upgraded, refurbished, reused, or materials reclaimed and recycled, leading to multiple uses, longer life, and much higher productivity, because the same amount of natural resource generates much more functional use in an efficient economy. For cars, circularity can mean higher recycling rates for steel and glass, as Lexus and Ford and others have achieved, but can also mean software upgrades that add capability to the car. Car companies may not be the ones to think about virtualization—they want cars to be used, not circumvented—but plenty of other companies will find ways to avoid having people climb into cars and drive places. Amazon, for instance, is trying to crack the code on grocery deliveries with Amazon Fresh pilots in Seattle and Los Angeles, obviating all those quick trips to the store. Amazon leverages customer optimization technology to increase the density of deliveries on routes and improve margins.

Then there's Google, which is trying to take the driver out of driving. Its car already has a license to operate in California, Florida, and Nevada (with a driver behind the wheel, ready to take over if needed). The car has driven more than 500,000 miles without causing an accident. Even if Google doesn't try to commercialize the technology—and a $258 million investment in Uber, the car-hailing app company, suggests that Google is serious—the company has created an arms race in driverless cars. Nissan has already said it will have driverless cars on the market by 2020; Tesla and Daimler have also committed, and the new Mercedes S-Class is already close to driving on its own.

The cars are improving fast. In 2008, a state-of-the-art driverless car went two blocks on a closed course at 25 mph; today, a car can operate in real-world conditions while traveling at 75 mph. Because electronics are the key to the driverless car, improvement is expected to continue at the pace of Moore's Law, which says that advances in digital devices will occur at exponential rates. In fact, improvement will accelerate as more cars get on the road. Unlike humans, who learn primarily from their own experiences, the artificial intelligence software in the Google car learns from every experience of every car. If hundreds of thousands or millions are on the roads, they will generate a real-time map of road conditions, so every car that needs to know will be made aware of an oil spill that just happened or that there is black ice on a road at a certain spot.

Through virtualization, the driverless car could increase productivity in all facets of car use. Far fewer cars would be needed, because they would stay in constant use rather than being parked 96 percent of the time.

In an example of optimization, self-driving cars would get better mileage, because they could "platoon" on highways, driving a few feet apart—if the first car had to slow or stop, it could signal the cars behind it and have them all hit the brakes simultaneously. Platooning increases gas mileage by 30 to 40 percent because every car except the one in the lead drafts behind the car ahead.

If the cars demonstrate that they can greatly reduce crashes—Google predicts that accidents will drop 90 percent—then many of the safety systems and much of the weight can be taken out of cars. Cars could also generally be smaller. At the moment, people tend to buy the biggest car that they might possibly need, say for soccer car pools, but the optimal driverless car can be summoned for each trip. Most trips are one- or two-person journeys, so far fewer large cars would be needed.

As is often the case with a breakthrough in resource productivity, the ripples from a successful driverless car would spread far and wide. The biggest benefit would be the human one. If Google is right that its car can reduce accidents by 90 percent, that would mean more than 30,000 lives would be saved in the United States every year. More than 2 million people, just in the United States, wouldn't have to go to emergency rooms because of traffic accidents; and $260 billion would be saved, according to an American Automobile Association study. People would also gain ten additional "days" per year—the time we now waste in traffic jams.

Fewer roads would need to be built, because cars would travel more closely together. Today, optimal capacity on a freeway is about forty to fifty cars per mile. Once you get to around 200 cars per mile, we call it a severe traffic jam; speeds drop to below 15 mph. If Google cars coordinated, we could fit 320 cars per lane per mile at highway speed. That's the equivalent of making a four-lane highway into a thirty-two-lane super freeway. We can stop building new roads. We will also be able to reclaim most parking lots; they could be used for building or turned into green space. Many self-driving cars would just head off to pick up another passenger.

There would, of course, be losers, too. Companies that build cars and build and service roads would see business plunge. Many car insurance companies would go out of business. Who needs liability insurance if there aren't any accidents? And how do you steal a self-driving car? Similarly, many body shops would go out of business; the primary repairs would be for things like hailstorms and foul balls from baseball games. Governments, which are already losing revenue as vehicle miles traveled decline and reduce the taxes paid on gasoline, would lose more revenue, because traffic fines would disappear—all cars would obey all laws; at the same time, governments would also need fewer police officers on the road and would need less jail space, if only because drunk drivers would no longer be an issue.

Rather than having millions of drivers acting on their own, cars could be managed as a network, a change that would create all sorts of opportunities for new businesses. For instance, a company might offer consumers transportation that they would pay for by the mile. Studies suggest that a company could offer a consumer access to car transportation for 80 percent less than he currently pays, and still make a hefty profit. Today, telecom companies make 8.5 percent net margins selling minutes, while automotive companies make about 4 percent selling cars. Why not make 15 percent selling miles? In addition, if someone can crack the code and provide a sort of operating system for driverless cars, that company could become the Microsoft or, in fact, the Google of the car business.

Even if the driverless car doesn't fulfill the big dreams that are being laid out for it, it shows how inexpensive innovation is these days. The Google car is the work of just a dozen engineers and cost Google some $50 million.

ELON MUSK: THE REAL IRON MAN

The revolutionary potential for the auto industry is already apparent at Tesla, the brainchild of Elon Musk—though it's hard to imagine that any of us will ever be as cool as Musk, who was a model for the Tony Stark character in the *Iron Man* movies (and had a cameo in *Iron Man 2*). Musk's fundamental innovations and the opportunities these innovations open up for other application developers hold the potential to reshape the automobile industry.

Born in South Africa in 1971, Musk had his first business success by age twelve: He wrote and sold a space video game on a PC that his father, an engineer, had bought for him. As he neared college age, Musk and his parents decided he should avoid South Africa's mandatory military service, because apartheid was still in force; they didn't want Musk to play a role in supporting apartheid. His mother is Canadian by birth, so Musk enrolled at Queen's University in Ontario. After two years, he transferred to the University of Pennsylvania, where he earned bachelor's degrees in economics and physics. He was accepted into the PhD program in physics at Stanford University, but this was 1995 in Silicon Valley, just as the Internet boom was getting started. Musk lasted two days at Stanford before dropping out to start a business.

He and his brother, Kimbal, founded Zip2, which maintains consumer websites for media companies. Musk slept on a futon at his office and showered at the local YMCA to save money. The company ran short of cash and had to bring in investors, but Musk still came away with $22 million when Compaq bought Zip2 for more than $340 million just a few short years later in 1999.

That same year, Musk invested $10 million of his money to start a company called X.com, designed to be an online bank. X.com figured out how to securely send money to someone's e-mail address, then, in 2000, he bought a small company with a service designed to let users of personal digital assistants transfer money to each other. The service's name: PayPal.

Soon, Musk renamed the whole company PayPal and built it into the most used method for sending money online. In 2002, he sold PayPal to eBay for $1.5 billion. This time, Musk came away with $165 million.

He had already started his next business, SpaceX. Initially envisioned to reenergize interest in space exploration, SpaceX was set up, with Musk's investment of $100 million, to carry cargo such as satellites into space. To design from scratch a rocket and engine that would be reusable and cost far less than what NASA was spending, Musk and his team scrimped wherever possible, even buying parts on eBay. SpaceX's rockets are guided by computers that are essentially the core of ATMs and cost just a few thousand dollars. After three launch failures, and down to what he figured was his last chance before running out of money, Musk launched the fourth rocket on September 28, 2008. It worked. There have been tense moments since then, but SpaceX has established itself well enough that customers have booked fifty launches with SpaceX that represent $4 billion in fees.

Musk ventured into the clean-energy world when he gave an idea to brothers Peter and Lyndon Rive, and in 2007 he financed their initial development of SolarCity. SolarCity's market cap of more than $3 billion makes it one of the most successful solar energy companies to date. The company's innovation: Rather than ask customers to front the money for solar panel installations, SolarCity handled the financing. It charged an electric rate that was well below what customers had been paying but that covered the cost of the panels, installation, and financing, while providing a healthy profit.

So, although Musk is just forty-two, Tesla is his fifth start-up, and, as of this writing, it's looking like he's five for five.

Musk became interested in electric cars in the early 2000s out of environmental concerns but also because of a very cool prototype sports car made by AC Propulsion. He put up the initial money and, with four others, founded Tesla. Musk became chairman and chief product designer and, like Henry Ford with the Model T, took a systemic approach that let him deliver more performance from less input. To do so, he employed all five of the driving principles in a resource revolution.

Tesla began with the idea that inexpensive electricity could substitute for gasoline as the primary fuel for cars. That's a potentially important switch: At the current cost of electricity and gasoline, the cost to operate an electric car is about one-fifth as much as a gasoline-powered car per mile driven. That's the equivalent of paying—astonishingly—about 40 cents per gallon.

As is often the case, once Tesla started down the path of substitution, it found that the change could allow for important new features. For instance, electric motors reach full torque almost instantly and don't need to warm up, so Musk could provide sports-car-like acceleration even in his family sedan. While electric cars have an image of being glorified golf carts, Porsche has built two electric motors into its 918 Spyder plug-in hybrid; it can go from zero to 60 mph in a head-snapping 3.0 seconds.

Performance
Zero to 60 mph: 4.4–6.5 sec
¼-mile: 12.6–13.7 sec
Top speed: 110–130 mph
Braking, 70–0 mph: 147 ft
Motor Trends, 2013

Fuel economy
EPA city/highway driving:
88/90 MPGe
Motor Trends , 2013

Safety
Overall: ★ ★ ★ ★ ★ ✦ (5.4 stars, highest rating ever)
Frontal crash: ★ ★ ★ ★ ★
Side crash: ★ ★ ★ ★ ★
Rollover: ★ ★ ★ ★ ★
Model S, NHTSA testing 2013

Electric motors are 95 percent efficient (compared with 40 percent for the most advanced internal combustion engine). Electric motors are far quieter than internal combustion engines, and Musk designed a nearly silent ride. (Some state regulators insist that Tesla design noise into its cars so that pedestrians used to car noise don't step into the street and get hit. Musk rejects the proposals as the modern-day equivalent of making someone walk in front of a "street locomotive" with a red flag in the mid-1800s. The car's silence is a key part of the mystique for him.) With so much voltage on board, Musk provided an entertainment system with an exceptionally bright and clear 17-inch touch screen.

It's rarely possible to get the full benefit of a substitution just by taking out one piece of the puzzle and plunking in another, and Musk rethought his cars from the ground up. He put the batteries down low to get the center of gravity closer to the ground, improving handling and safety. He also improved handling by getting rid of the heavy engine up front—the disparity can throw a car off balance.

Far from producing a new golf cart notable only for its fuel efficiency, Musk came up with something that won *Motor Trend*'s Car of the Year award and received a score of 99 out of 100 from *Consumer Reports*, the highest score it has ever awarded. The Tesla earned the highest safety rating in the industry for its sedan, thanks to remarkable design innovation that could provide crumple zones and passenger protection without having to worry about where to fit the engine. The online headline on the *Wall Street Journal* review of the Model S read: "I Am Silent; Hear Me Roar: It Doesn't Snarl Like a Lamborghini, but Tesla's New Model S Is No Eat-Your-Broccoli All-Electric Car." When a *New York Times* reporter wrote a column saying the range of the Tesla wasn't as advertised, waves of passionate customers took to Twitter, Facebook, and other social media to rebut the story with detailed analyses and personal experiences.

Rethinking the design from the ground up enabled Musk to take advantage of the next principle on our list: waste reduction. The engines are physically smaller and generate less heat, meaning it's possible to cool them with air rather than requiring elaborate water cooling. Electric cars don't need a transmission or any mechanical device for transmitting the power from the front of the car to the wheels. So, replacing an internal combustion engine with electric motors can give the manufacturer a car without engine cooling, transmission, and most of what's under the hood, but with better acceleration, better handling, and better safety. Electric motors also require less maintenance; in fact, with no transmission, no clutch, no spark plugs, and almost no other parts that wear out, the Tesla is the first car that doesn't require maintenance to keep its warranty.

Building on the natural advantages of electric motors, Musk went to great lengths to reduce power consumption in his cars. He developed sophisticated software to control charging and discharging, battery pack temperatures, and charge levels to optimize efficiency and significantly extend the lifetime of the battery. Using eight years of road data to optimize performance, Musk is far ahead of the competition in terms of range. The EPA rates Tesla at 200 to 230 miles, depending on the model. Only 90 percent of that range is recommended for use, because using that last 10 percent diminishes battery life, so Teslas have a real range of 180 to 205 miles.

Tesla is also building a network of Supercharger stations around the country—using solar power whenever possible—that are free for Tesla owners. Musk's goal is that a Tesla driver will be able to travel from Los Angeles to New York and pay zero dollars for fuel. (The network is already active between Boston and Washington, D.C., and between San Francisco and Los Angeles.) As electric and hybrid technologies proliferate, electric charging infrastructure should be able to deliver electric transportation energy at approximately a $1 per gallon equivalency.[10] Talk about waste reduction.

Musk created a recycling program for Tesla's battery packages, allowing for much higher reuse. The program recaptures the cobalt and separates out the lithium for safe disposal.

Tesla's biggest innovations may be in its system and network optimization, whose effect on performance and waste reduction we've already described. While cars that just add a battery to an existing design find the new feature can degrade performance, Tesla's focus on optimizing the whole system has translated every element into an advantage that increases performance.

Tesla increased virtualization with a live cellular connection to each car that means Tesla can upgrade key software systems remotely. Tesla provides overnight software updates that work just like the updates on an iPhone to add applications like navigation options and entertainment channels or to adjust engine performance parameters. The maintenance network also receives data from the cars. The navigation and entertainment systems sync readily with personal devices without a physical connection.

Plenty of things can still go wrong for Tesla, and many surely will. In some states, car dealers are trying to use state and local laws that protect them to stop Tesla from selling directly to customers—either to end Tesla sales or force the company to sell through existing dealer networks. (In the tech world, what the dealers are doing is the equivalent of Best Buy's suing Apple for launching its own stores—an idea that would be laughed out of town.)

---

10 The cost of raw electricity amounts to 40 cents per gallon. We've added 60 cents to that figure to account for a projected increase in taxes. Today, electricity is taxed at much lower rates than gasoline. If large numbers of consumers switch to EVs, the government will need to make up for the lost revenue by raising electricity taxes.

95 percent improvement in cost and range of electric vehicles over 25 years

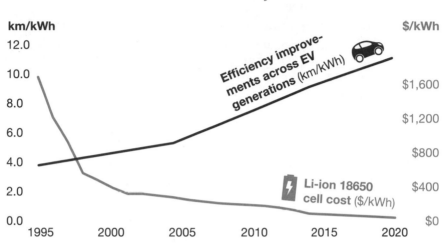

Illustrative models used: 1997 GM EVI, 2010 Chevy Volt, 2010 Nissan Leaf, 2011 Ford Focus EV, 2013 BMWi3, 2013 Smart fortwo. 2020 estimate based on forecasted improvements to battery costs and performance and vehicle efficiency.

Even when dealers can't win on the basic argument, they invoke legislation such as Indiana's requirement that a dealer have at least ten vehicles on hand. A small, innovative company like Tesla wants to be visible in high-traffic, urban areas where real estate is expensive and wants to just have a demo on hand to capture attention.

The real issue with electric cars, of course, is batteries. Their range is limited, and, as a brutal corollary, the cost to achieve the same range as a gasoline car is prohibitively high today. For an electric car with a range of 200 miles, the cost for the battery is about $20,000. In addition, batteries take far longer to recharge than the time it takes to fill up a gas tank—four to twelve hours on an AC charger or thirty minutes to two hours on a DC charger.

But the problems are already diminishing. Battery prices dropped from $1,000 per kilowatt-hour to $400 per kilowatt-hour between 2008 and 2013, and improvements in battery technology make it likely that the cost will be less than $150 per kilowatt-hour by the end of the decade. That $20,000 battery pack could come down to as little as $5,000; and then every car will want to have a battery for performance and efficiency. To address the issues with charging time, Tesla's Superchargers charge half the battery in thirty minutes.

Musk bought himself time to work out the kinks through an unconventional decision about how to enter the market. While cars have long been seen as a mass market, Musk decided to target the first cars at enthusiasts. He knew that his first model—the Tesla Roadster—would be expensive and that there would undoubtedly be issues with range and recharging time. These points would restrict mass appeal, but enthusiasts would be willing to pay the $100,000-plus list price for the car and tolerate inconveniences. Musk didn't need to sell a lot of cars initially, but he needed to turn buyers into zealots and try to develop a cult following for building great cars.

Since the first Roadster came off the production line in 2010, more than 10,000 Teslas have been sold, and the cars have become status symbols in Silicon Valley and other wealthy precincts. Now, having reported a profit for the first quarter of 2013 and having generated a market cap of more than $20 billion, Musk has turned his attention to a $60,000 model and a $40,000 model that is selling at a rate of 500 cars a week. Musk has unveiled a prototype of the SUV Model X and is designing the next-generation Tesla midsize passenger car, targeted at a price point of $35,000.

As the Musk story illustrates, looking at ways to use the five principles will help a company start to identify the opportunities that will enable that company to win in the resource revolution. The five aren't a series of steps that need to be followed in sequence. In fact, they typically overlap—the substitution led Musk to find ways to reduce waste, for instance. But the five principles are the way to categorize the opportunities ahead.

Let's look at each in more detail.

SUBSTITUTION

The guiding principle for substitution: Look at every single resource a company uses in its core products and every single resource that customers use or consume, then look for higher-performing, less expensive, or less-scarce materials that might work as substitutes. But, like Musk, don't think of the new resources as straight substitutes for the current bill of materials. Look at how substitutes can deliver superior overall performance—carbon fiber will not only save some weight but will let a company build a better car or airplane.

GE and Apple have actually gone through the periodic table, element by element, assessing which elements pose the biggest risks in terms of supply and regulation. They have developed substitution opportunities for each risky element. We recently completed a review for a major oil company looking at the resource risk embedded in its supply chain and found that lack of available water looked likely to cut its growth sharply below expectations over the next decade. Looking a decade ahead gives companies a time advantage in responding to potential constraints.

Beyond the carbon fiber used in car bodies, a slew of new materials have begun to reshape industrial and consumer products. A much richer understanding of materials science at the nanometer scale combined with advanced computer processing power has catalyzed a broad revolution in surface properties, absorption characteristics, and optical and electrical properties. Carbon in another form—activated carbon, typically made of nanoscale particles with custom-engineered pore size—is dramatically improving the efficiency of water filters, electrodes in batteries, and, potentially, even power-plant exhaust scrubbers. For the first time since the development of leaded crystal centuries ago, glass is being reinvented—from high-bandwidth optical networking fiber to Gorilla glass that Corning has developed to allow touch screens to capture the imagination in portable devices and, soon, on larger interactive screens. A company called View is even creating something it calls "dynamic glass," which can change its visible and infrared light transmission, enabling windows that can be programmed to block the sun on hot days but capture sunlight in the depth of winter, replacing heating and air-conditioning in Mediterranean climates where cool nights mix with hot days.

Another form of substitution is inspired by biology. Swiss engineer George de Mestral in 1941 invented the Velcro fastener when he decided to take a closer look at burrs he removed from his dog to see how they worked. Dermal denticles that mimic shark skin have produced quieter submarines and faster swimsuits. Inspired by the structure of the lotus flower, a German company, Ispo, has developed a paint that rejects dirt.

Possible resource shortages

■ Sustainable for now   ■ Some concern   ■ Significant risk/impact

	Potential for shortage					
	Global market size $ Billions	**Years of reserves** (reserves/annual production)	**Volatility** (2004-2009 standard deviation of price/mean price)	**Geographic concentration** (number of countries with significant reserves)	**Dependency** (mined only as by-product of another material)	**Recyclability** (classification and percent estimate for recycling)
Phosphorous				High	Low	Low
Potash	18	283	68%	High	Low	Low
Rare earth	11	846	42%	High	High	Low
Chromium	44.7	16	29%	High	Low	60%
Vanadium	1.2	243	45%	High	Medium	Medium
Coking coal	151	<50	34%	Medium	Low	Low
Iron ore	206	75	30%	Low	Low	61%
Germanium	0.1	N/A	34%	High	High	30%
Platinum group metals[1]	20[4]	174	24%	Medium	Medium	Medium
Indium	0.3	N/A	24%	High	High	60%-65%
Cobalt	3.0	83	38%	High	Medium	25%
Molybdenum	6.0	42	34%	Low	Low	30%
Gallium	0.1	N/A	10%	High	High	High
Tungsten	1.6	48	33%	High	Low	30%-40%
Bauxite/Aluminum[2]	72	133	18%	High	Low	48%
Nickel	29	49	42%	Low	Low	43%
Copper	144	00	00%	Medium	Low	02%
Zinc	28	21	45%	Low	Low	30%
Gold	104	20	40%	Low	Low	High
Lead	20	20	30%	Low	Low	77%
Tin	7	20	24%	Medium	Low	34%
Silver	14	23	29%	Low	Low	High
Lithium	0.1	514	8%	Medium	Medium	Medium

1 Platinum group metals includes ruthenium, rhodium, palladium, osmium, iridium, and platinum and are grouped together because of their similar physical and chemical properties as well as tendency to occur together in the same mineral.
2 Data for reserves and geographic risk pertain to Bauxite. Other data pertain to Aluminum.

Impact of shortage

Substitut- ability	Contribution to production processes	Resource linkages with food/ energy	Industrial uses
Difficult	High	High	Agriculture
Difficult	High	High	Energy, fertilizers, primary constituent of gunpowder
Difficult	High	Low	Energy, glass industry as coloring and polishing agents
Possible	High	High	Energy, autos, textiles, construction, electronics
Difficult	High	Medium	Energy, steels, chemical industry, ceramic manufacture
Challenges	High	High	Steel production
Difficult	High	High	Steel, construction, industrial applications
Challenges	Medium	Low	Energy, technology, plastics
Difficult	Medium	Low	Technology manufacturing, medicine, glass, oil and gas
Possible	High	Low	Energy, dental
Challenges	High	High	Energy, steel, medicine, agriculture
Possible	High	Medium	Energy, autos, plastics
Challenges	Medium	Medium	Energy, technology manufacturing, medicine
Possible	High	Medium	Energy, high intensity industrial processes
Challenges	High	Medium	Construction, manufacturing, aerospace
Difficult	High	Low	Construction, chemicals
Challenges	High	Medium	Energy, construction
Possible	High	Low	Automotive, building and construction
Challenges	Low	Low	Jewelry, electronics, medical, aerospace
Challenges	High	Low	Technology manufacturing, lubrication and heat transfer, paint
Possible	High	Low	Electronics manufacturing, construction, chemicals, glassware
Possible	Medium	Low	Energy, household goods, coinage, jewelry, dentistry
Challenges	Low	High	Energy, ceramics, pharmaceuticals, aerospace

3 Wherever possible, market size represents finished/refined metal e.g., market size is for Aluminum metal and not Alumina or Bauxite.
4 2009 data

In the Iraqi war, heavy steel plates in body armor have been replaced by ceramic composite plates that are lighter, more mobile, and stronger, like the shells of crustaceans—reducing fatalities despite the increase in improvised explosive devices. As we will see later in this chapter, nature can also inspire changes in production processes themselves, substituting room-temperature, water-based self assembly for energy-intensive smelting processes that operate at high temperature and high pressure. Natural processes are also typically reversible, meaning materials can be recovered or reused.

The potential for substitution extends even to food production. Hampton Creek Foods, for instance, is substituting away from using corn in producing eggs. Some 1.7 trillion hens' eggs are laid every year, but only about 6 percent are sold in stores. The rest are used to hold mayonnaise together, in baked goods, and to handle other behind-the-scenes tasks. Hampton Creek has developed "plant-based" eggs, a substitute called Beyond Eggs that uses peas, sorghum, beans, and other plants to make a product that tastes like, and has the same nutritional properties as, eggs. Basically, Hampton Creek thinks it can give us the nutrition directly from plants without having to pass them through a hen. The company says its process is already nearly 20 percent less expensive than the price of making eggs, and costs will fall as scale increases. Hampton Creek also says its product will suffer less from drought—at the moment, about 70 percent of the cost of an egg is corn, a crop that is susceptible to drought and is increasingly linked to the price of oil; Hampton Creek uses hardier crops and relies less on oil. So, Hampton Creek's egg substitute may offer lower cost and lower risk for major food producers.

The new types of food don't have to be just for humans, either: BASF has developed new strains of algae that National Prawn uses to feed shrimp on farms in Saudi Arabia.

Proterra, a manufacturer of buses, shows how substitution can add value across a number of dimensions. Proterra uses a light, carbon-composite body instead of a traditional metal one and substitutes an electric motor and battery for a combustion engine. Like a Prius-style hybrid car, the Proterra bus captures energy from braking and stores it in the battery for reuse, a big gain in stop-and-go city traffic. In all, the Proterra bus is five times more fuel efficient than traditional fossil-fuel buses on city routes. Proterra's form of substitution—tailoring a product specifically to its application—generates significant savings for companies.

The Proterra bus, like all electric vehicles, also creates an important option. A traditional gasoline-powered bus can only burn gasoline and a diesel vehicle can only burn diesel, but a vehicle powered from electricity can be powered by whatever fuel source is most cost-efficient at the time, whether that's natural gas, solar, or some other form of energy that generates electricity.

Sometimes, the option to substitute can add just as much value as the substitution itself. Technology that enables easy substitution will keep costs lower and more stable over time.

ELIMINATE WASTE

While labor productivity has improved almost 100 percent over the last two decades, resource productivity has increased only 5 to 10 percent—and it's not because there isn't room for improvement.

One of the biggest examples of waste in current industrial processes is energy, often in its industrial forms of steam or heat. One surfactant manufacturer we worked with found that only 10 percent of the energy it used actually went into making its products. The rest was wasted in heating, cooling, and reheating the same equipment.

The standard air-conditioning process today is incredibly inefficient: Air is cooled, partly by reducing humidity, but then has to be heated again before being released, to make it comfortable. In most manufacturing processes, it's standard to heat up something that was recently cooled or cool something that was recently heated.

Transforming iron ore into various types of specialty steel is a model of inefficiency. For instance, carbon is added in various steps, then removed in subsequent steps, only to be added and removed again later. Newer steelmaking technologies such as electric arc furnaces are less than one-fifth the capital cost of the traditional basic oxygen furnace and focus on using recycled steel as input, which requires less energy than making pig iron from iron ore. Technologies being pioneered by ULCOS (for ultra-low CO_2) such as Hlsarna and Ulcowin offer an additional 20 to 30 percent savings in energy by reusing heat to preprocess incoming material and remove oxygen and other impurities. The reduction in energy usage cuts costs considerably, because energy is the second-largest cost component in steel, after raw materials.

In our experience, manufacturers have the opportunity to reduce energy usage by 30 percent and materials used by a further 30 percent,

Fuel efficiency by country

Regional light-duty vehicle fuel efficiency in miles per gallon (MPG)

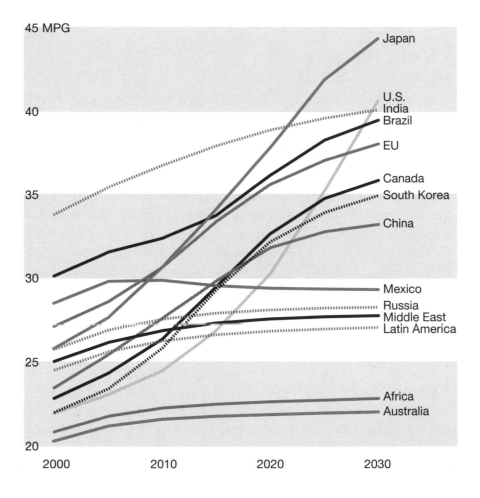

greatly improving economics. One refinery we worked with increased revenues by $2 million by converting fuel gas consistently into gasoline and diesel. The challenge was that the unit that was generating the fuel gas could not create the gasoline, and the cat cracker operators did not know that the extra feed stream was available and that the piping was already in place to deliver it. Other types of businesses will have varied experiences, partly depending on size and industry, but it's a rare company that can't find ways to reduce wasted energy and materials.

Many companies have already worked hard to reduce waste of the primary material they process because it often visibly accumulates as scrap and in many cases can be returned to an upstream supplier for recycling—thus the recycling of titanium in aerospace and steel in automotive. But energy and water and their combined form, steam, are more difficult to visualize and track. They have therefore received less focus, even though they can be just as significant in cost and can have even more impact on pollution.

In eliminating energy or water waste in production, the best approach involves assessing how much energy or water is used throughout the entire process versus the amount actually required at each step—often, the amount of energy used is more than twice what is technically required. One of the chemicals companies we serve made a change that allowed for some additional evaporation, immediately reducing by 10 percent the energy it had to use drying its products. At a much simpler level, just walking an assembly line with a heat-imaging gun can quickly identify where energy is leaking out of a system.

It's also important to think beyond production when coming up with ways to reduce waste. Products can be redesigned, sometimes at fundamental levels, to cut waste. And companies shouldn't just think about cutting their own waste—the best think about reaching upstream to their suppliers and downstream to their customers. Boeing reduces materials requirements and operating costs for their suppliers by adjusting parts specifications, as it reduces the operating costs of airline customers by reducing fuel consumption and equipment downtime. CostCo redesigns packaging so that its suppliers can reduce transportation costs and passes the savings on to its customers.

EcoMotors is trying to cut waste by reinventing the internal combustion engine. It has revived an old technology that has pistons opposing each other in the engine block, so that, as one fires, the opposed piston is falling back. The start-up's technology holds the prospect for a 20 to 50 percent increase in fuel efficiency while cutting the cost of an engine by 20 to 25 percent. The engines are about half the size and weight of traditional engines, creating the opportunity for further savings by designing them into a lighter car. In a lightweight, five-passenger vehicle, the engine could deliver 100 mpg. EcoMotors announced in early 2013 that a Chinese partner would spend $200 million to build a plant to make the engines, which should be on the market in 2014.

The aggregate benefits of waste reduction are dramatic. The implementation of the tighter corporate average fuel economy (CAFE) standards for vehicles in the United States will not only bring average efficiency to 54.5 miles per gallon but will save $1.7 trillon in fuel costs and eliminate the need for 12 billion barrels of oil imports over the twenty-year life of the program.[11]

Kaiima is going even further and trying to reengineer the very biology of food crops. One challenge is that, given current climate conditions, the world grows corn better than most grains. Corn has become so ubiquitous that, by some estimates, 60 percent of the packaged foods in grocery stores have some form of corn as an ingredient. Yet, from a nutritional standpoint, humans would be better off with a broader range of grains in their diet. The opportunity is to design wheat, rice, and grains that can grow as well as corn in relatively arid environments and on marginal land. Kaiima is also redesigning these other grains so they are polyploid. That means that they have additional pairs of chromosomes and, as a result, have more nutritional value. At the same time, polyploid grains are considered to be safer than genetically modified organisms, which have been altered through genetic engineering. If Kaiima succeeds, grains will require less water, land, and energy, while providing more variety and nutrition, all of

---

11 While adoption of new technologies to improve fuel efficiency, such as fuel injection, computerized engine control, lighter weight, and new materials will add to the upfront cost of the car (Energy Information Administration [EIA] estimates are about $3,000 per car), this is substantially less than the $8,200 in projected savings per car. In addition, experience suggests that the costs of the new technologies will decline rapidly as scale is achieved.

which will be vital in a world with so many more people consuming at middle-class rates.

Kaiima, an Israeli company whose name means "sustainability" in Aramaic, has already produced varieties of castor beans that increase the yield of feedstock per acre for biofuels by a factor of three to four. The company is aiming for a tenfold improvement.

At the other end of the food chain, companies like Winnow Solutions work with restaurants, hospitals, and food services to apply software, algorithms, and scales to track food usage and consumption in restaurants, and make adjustments to menus and portions to reduce food waste by half.

While we've already described the possibility for waste reduction in cars if so-called 3-D, or additive, printing can be widely used, the process has broad possibilities for all manufacturers. In 3-D printing, there is zero waste: Whatever material isn't used to print an object stays in the printer for later use.[12] Plus, parts don't have to be packaged and shipped; they can be printed right where they're used. Inventory never has to be written off or marked down as obsolete, because objects are only printed as needed.

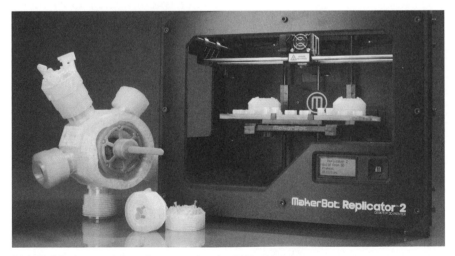

MakerBot's Replicator 2 desktop 3D printer, released in 2012.

---

12 In one version of the process, a laser shines onto a bed of material and binds that material together. That layer of material, which can be vanishingly thin, is then lowered, and the laser forms the next layer on top. The process repeats until the desired object is "printed."

The process was conceived in the 1980s as a way to "teleport" objects to nuclear submarines that spent months without surfacing—while nobody was going to ask Scotty to beam him up, the idea was that the navy could transmit a design to a sub where a printer would create the desired object. The process has come a long way and is ready for prime time in some applications.

While 3-D printers initially only worked with plastics, they can now "print" in steel, titanium, gold, and other metals. The process was initially just used for demos or design work, but 3-D printing is now being used in production processes for everything from hip replacements and braces to iPhone covers and jewelry. The 3-D printer eliminates so much resource waste and provides such opportunities for customization that growth opportunities are tremendous.

Virtually every industry will be affected, and not just for big production runs. Soon, for instance, every airport maintenance operation will have a 3-D printer that can spit out an exact replica of any piece on an airplane, reducing inventory requirements globally and keeping planes flying more each year.

The guiding principle for waste reduction was made famous by Toyota as "kaizen": to drain the swamp so the rocks become visible. This means measuring input materials and energy and water, comparing them to the delivered product, and understanding all the waste factors in between: scrap, idle machines, changeover time or other interruptions, and so on.

INCREASE CIRCULARITY

While waste reduction limits the use of natural resources in the creation of products, circularity looks to find value in products after their use.

Aluminum shows how powerful recycling can be—and how disruptive for those who aren't prepared. Starting in 1970, in just one decade, the industry went from using 20 percent recycled material to 70 percent. That change took some doing, because of all the cans and other garbage that had to be collected and processed, but it saves 95 percent of the energy required to make new aluminum from bauxite ore. To put it in fuel terms, each empty aluminum soda can that was thrown out wasted as much energy as is in the amount of oil that would fill half that can. The change to recycling caught some companies with excess production, as they had clung to the model that the only way to produce aluminum was to take bauxite and add a bunch of energy to it.

Reuse and recycling can create enormous profits. The processes typically are cheaper because of lower energy requirements and because recyclers can purchase scrap input at a fraction of the cost of new materials. Shipping costs also fall because scrap contains so much less waste than ore. In the case of aluminum, bauxite ore is only 15 to 25 percent aluminum, so, when ore is shipped, at least three-quarters of what is being transported is waste.

In the world of cars, parts are often refurbished and reused, and scrap metal can be recycled. Johnson Controls has made such a good business of recycling that the company is essentially renting the lead in car batteries. The company sells the batteries, then buys them back after they're used up—most consumers effectively subsidize the handling of the batteries by paying a disposal fee when they buy one. Johnson Controls extracts the lead and reuses it in the next set of batteries, thereby not only preventing the potential environmental liability of its product but also reducing the input cost of the most expensive single component of batteries so drastically that competitors have found it hard to enter the business and make a profit. (Beyond lead, a battery is mostly plastic, acid, and a bit of wiring.) It would not be a stretch to say that Johnson Controls has shifted from selling batteries to "renting" lead to people who need modest electrical storage.

Friedola Tech, a German company that started up in response to environmental concerns there in the 1980s, buys certain waste streams from industrial companies and turns them into plastic automotive parts, among other things. Its products are standard, but it has a competitive advantage because its materials costs are so low—companies don't have to pay much to buy things that were going into the garbage.

Caterpillar has started encouraging circularity by pricing its products at a significant percentage "below new" if a customer makes a deposit that will be refunded when a product is returned to Caterpillar at the end of its life. Caterpillar says the program lets it recycle 148 million pounds of iron a year and intends to get to the point where zero percent of its products wind up as waste in a landfill. Meanwhile, Caterpillar figures that circularity means it can use 85 to 95 percent less energy and material to produce a product than it would if it started from scratch.

While cars, as a mature market, have already worked through many of the opportunities for circularity, huge possibilities are appearing in newer markets, such as for consumer electronics. When an individual purchases a new car, the dealership offers to purchase the current car, or apply its value to the new purchase. This same approach can be applied to other products and has, recently, with cell phones. For instance, eRecyclingCorps works with cell phone carriers in the United States to offer customers a roughly $50 rebate on the purchase of a new phone or an accessory if they'll turn over their old phone. eRecycling wipes the data from the phones, refurbishes them, and sells them to low-cost U.S. carriers or to carriers in the developing world. The company quotes government statistics showing that Americans buy 150 million cell phones a year but only reuse 10 percent of them, so the potential supply is enormous. And the appetite in the developing world is voracious: In many countries, more people have cell phones than have electricity or running water. A McKinsey study found that $90 billion could be generated each year by refurbishing and reusing electronics.

Companies can participate at every step along the way, beginning with the designers, who should have the end of life of a product in mind from the very start and should make it easy to disassemble and reclaim valuable materials and reuse parts. The companies that create the design can then figure out multiple ways to collect some of the revenue from the circularity that they facilitate. Other companies can jump into the process wherever opportunities present themselves, as eRecycling has done.

For ATMI, a technology provider for semiconductors and life sciences, recycling electronics has been a gold mine—literally. The company recognized that e-waste contains 100 times as much gold as the best ore in the world in South Africa and developed a proprietary process to extract it. Historically, the process of extracting gold from e-waste has been either quite toxic, requiring acids that give off poisonous vapors, or extremely energy-intensive, requiring a smelter hot enough to melt metals and burn off impurities. So, much of the gold ends up in landfills—gold bugs can talk up the value of the metal all they like, but we are throwing away about 35 percent of the metal that is produced for medical, electronics, and industrial uses each year. ATMI has developed a water-based solution, safe enough to drink, that dissolves the gold and extracts it from the e-waste. A machine the size of a shipping container can recycle the e-waste from an entire city, with gold electroplated out, 100 percent pure, in the form of a bar of gold every two days. The machine can be easily transported to wherever the e-waste is.

ATMI started out in a very different business. It made specialty gas-storage containers for semiconductor companies. ATMI grew about twice as fast as the semiconductor industry and had better than 50 percent gross margins, but growth in semiconductors has been steadily slowing and is now only about 5 percent annually, averaged across a cycle. So, ATMI took its core competence—a team of PhD combinatorial chemists, plus complex modeling and optimization software—and went looking for problems to solve. Electronics manufacturers and recyclers using ATMI's process are now the lowest-cost producers of gold in the world, and by a long margin.

As a by-product of the gold reclamation process, ATMI's process collects the solder used to attach chips to boards, thereby decreasing the contamination of waste sites from the lead in solder. Moreover, the chips in discarded electronics literally fall off into a strainer basket while traveling through the water bath with the proprietary, nontoxic chemicals. Because the chips were never exposed to high temperature or mechanical strain, they can be cleaned, dried, sorted, and reused in other products—substantially increasing their value beyond the mere metal content. Since introducing the technology in 2011, ATMI has already figured out how to cut the cost of its chemicals by 50 percent and of its capital equipment by 90 percent. The company is just getting started on the huge opportunity it discovered.

ATMI's gold reclamation process is one example of a much broader class of biology-inspired manufacturing and recovery processes. Rather than relying on toxic chemicals, high temperatures, or other artificial catalysts traditionally used to fabricate or recycle materials, these procedures often take place in water solutions, allowing self-assembly based on electrical or chemical gradients. As a result, energy use decreases dramatically. These processes can deliver bright colors, for example, mimicking the optical effect that gives a butterfly wing its iridescent hue without the use of cobalt, which is both toxic and rare. And they can also enhance a property like strength: cellulose (the structural material of plants), chitin (the structural material of insects and fingernails), and calcium (the structural material of snails and crustaceans) can be layered and aligned so they exceed the strength of steel. Because this type of so-called manufacturing doesn't require melting, chemical transformation, or the addition of toxins, the new materials can be reclaimed and used again or simply allowed to biodegrade naturally.

The giant American waste company Waste Management may make a whole business out of turning waste streams into products. Waste Management's core business is collecting trash from homes and businesses and taking the trash to landfills. However, because the total amount of trash is shrinking, the company began looking for additional profit opportunities. Waste Management estimates it could generate $15 billion of revenue annually if it could effectively separate and resell all the material in the roughly 100 million tons of garbage it collects each year—an amount of revenue that would more than double the size of the

Annual resource consumption in America: 86 tons per person

Total materials consumption (annual metric tons per capita)

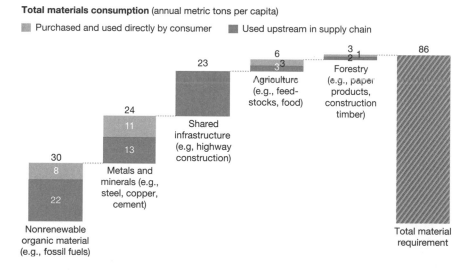

company. Although Waste Management can't comb through everything yet, it already has 131 projects that turn methane gas at landfills into energy and has 17 energy-generating trash incineration plants. In all, in 2011, Waste Management produced electricity that powered 1.17 million homes. Now, the company has set up a pilot plant in Oregon that will take discarded plastics and turn them into oil. The plant is expected to produce 75,000 barrels of crude a year, the equivalent of almost 30 wells of average size in Texas.

Some companies pursue circularity for the explicit purpose of cleaning up the environment, yet make a business out of the work. For instance, Ray Anderson and his company, Interface, recover discarded fishing nets off the Philippines and turn the nylon into carpets.

The rule of thumb in thinking about circularity is: The tighter the loop, the greater the value captured and the stronger the competitive differentiation. Reusing a phone is more valuable than reusing a chip, which is more valuable than melting it or grinding it down to extract gold and silver. Value can be captured both by recovering precious metals and by avoiding using large amounts of energy or water, as well as by avoiding toxic waste products or by-products.

OPTIMIZATION

The new opportunities for optimization range far, far beyond what is happening with cars and represent one of the most important principles for managers. Opportunities are there for just about everyone at every level of a business. The issue is whether to attack a big problem or a small one, but there are inefficiencies everywhere in the use of resources, which are just waiting to be solved.

Some companies are realizing, for instance, that they shouldn't just think about shipping items that are needed very quickly to customers from a factory or a warehouse. It's hard to ship something in less than a day, and it costs millions of dollars a day if, to give an example, a $40 million piece of Applied Materials equipment that is at the center of a semiconductor manufacturing plant sits idle and causes a bottleneck for all production at the $4 billion facility. So, Applied Materials has optimized its parts delivery by keeping track of spare parts no matter where they are. This helps customers find a nearby part to borrow until a new one can be shipped. Similarly, many airlines now pool resources at hubs and provide each other spare parts.

Komatsu goes even further, optimizing use of its equipment by essentially creating a market that lets customers rent to and from each other. Need a $300,000 earth mover for just a few days? Komatsu will help a company find one that would otherwise be sitting idle. Have equipment that is sitting unused? Komatsu will help find someone to rent it.

Kuala Lumpur commissioned a major study of its freight traffic and found ways to coordinate and combine deliveries that improve delivery speed while reducing congestion and pollution by more than 20 percent. UPS reduced fuel consumption and improved safety and speed by rerouting its trucks to avoid left turns. We helped a large utility reduce meter reading costs 30 percent just by restructuring the routes the drivers used to reflect new traffic conditions and customer-use patterns.

The U.S. Air Force has found new ways to have planes fly in convoys, like geese flying in a V. The new patterns, which copy the way geese "vortex surf," save 20 percent on fuel—and the air force uses a lot of fuel; it is the largest single consumer of fuel in the world.

By having each plane fly behind the leader, offset by a precise distance to the side and slightly below, the plane can draft off a vortex generated by the plane ahead that adds lift. The spacing has to be accurate to catch the right part of the vortex, because flying in the downdraft reduces lift. Historical flying patterns were designed based on geometry and pilot visibility, and, during World War II, the position of gun turrets. Implementing the new

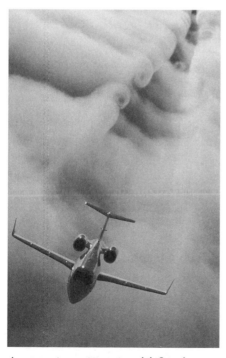

A corporate jet creating vortices while flying low over cloud cover.

configuration was not expensive. It required four lines of code in the autopilot to be changed to maintain the precise separations. Pilots also needed some training not to override the autopilot manually.

As companies consider which opportunities have the most potential, the guiding principle should be: What are expensive assets that are used only a small portion of the time, or energy-intensive equipment that is active without performing a function? This could be construction equipment, shipping containers that are going back empty, or simply planes circling an airport, waiting for congestion to clear. All lend themselves to IT solutions that optimize routing, timing, loading, or sharing.

INCREASE VIRTUALIZATION

Most companies struggle with the two primary dimensions of virtualization—moving activities out of the physical world or simply stopping doing things because they've been automated—because virtualization challenges business models. Sure, a company is happy to interact with clients and customers via e-mail and video conference to make interactions more efficient, and a company is happy to automate the mechanical aspects of interactions. But companies generally don't like to see core activities move into the virtual realm, because revenue always seems to drop more than costs do. Look at newspapers, which get about 16 percent of the revenue from a digital ad that they get from a physical ad that reaches the same audience. Companies certainly don't want people to stop doing things that generate revenue.

Car companies don't want people to drive less, but that's what's happening in developed countries. Miles driven per capita peaked in 2004 in the United States and have declined steadily since then. The reasons aren't entirely clear, but it certainly isn't just the Great Recession. The decline started before the recession and has continued even as the economy has rebounded. Higher gas prices are surely a factor, but probably more important is that many people are doing things virtually that they used to hop in a car to do. Teenagers have shown a declining interest in driving, according to statistics on the age at which Americans get their first license, and the speculation is that the ability to connect via Facebook, Google+, and other social media is one reason. Skype and

A collection of everyday items commonly used by Stefan five to ten years ago that have been replaced by digital apps.

other video-chat software further reduce the need to drive somewhere to see someone. Work is gradually becoming more virtual as people telecommute more often. Virtualization will happen whether the car companies want it to or not, so they need to prepare themselves.

As a demonstration about what other aspects of our lives can go away—or become virtual—Stefan pulled together a list of things he no longer owns or uses, even though they were part of our everyday lives just five or ten years ago, as seen on page 94.

The case of the flashlight illustrates what happens when a company gets caught sleeping. Maglite had pretty much owned the U.S. market for flashlights but missed the shift to LEDs. Fenix of China got there first and won a huge amount of market share. Now, with every smartphone equipped with an LED light, the market is also shrinking considerably— when it comes to flashlights, there is an app for that.

Fast-forward and imagine all the things individuals own that feel as ordinary as an alarm clock did several years ago and that won't be in the market in a few years. The changes will be as small as a business card—and as big as the opportunity that Neal Blue found a few years back.

Blue, the CEO of General Atomics, had a thought: What would happen if military aviation could become virtual? What if he could take the pilot out of the plane?

The answer is: a lot.

Not only would the pilot's weight be taken out of military planes, but so would everything needed to support him—the oxygen system; the instrumentation; everything needed to provide the space for him to operate; safety and escape systems; and even some of the defense mechanisms, given that a less-expensive, pilotless plane wouldn't need to be protected in the same way as a plane with a pilot. Taking out so much weight and eliminating so much space wouldn't just make the plane lighter; the changes would mean that the pilotless plane could stay aloft far longer, carry more fuel or weapons for a given airframe and engine, or have a much smaller radar cross section.

Conventional wisdom was that a drone would take five years and $1 billion to build, but General Atomics spent just $20 million and six months to develop a prototype using a lawnmower engine. When an official from the Pentagon visited, Blue asked if the Department of Defense might be interested in a pilotless plane. Maybe, he was told, once a prototype had been developed. Blue said he just happened to have one flying around outside.

The Pentagon bought a slew of the production technology drones for $3 million to $4 million apiece, a tiny fraction of the cost of the F-35, which represents the next phase of traditional fighter aircraft, flown by pilots. The Pentagon figures it will spend about $1.5 trillion on the F-35 over its lifetime, or about $600 million per plane.

Drones have changed the nature of warfare. The U.S. military uses inexpensive drones to attack targets inside Afghanistan and Pakistan. The use of drones has raised concerns about whether making war is now too easy, including whether military and spy agencies have proper safeguards in place to ensure that they are killing only those who pose a real danger to the United States.

While the customer, the Department of Defense, wasn't necessarily thinking about innovating with pilotless fighters, General Atomics saw the opportunity that improved electronics had created and demonstrated how resource revolutions can make the most of it.

The current generation of drones represents only the first step in where this evolution will go. Drones have mainly exploited cost reduction by removing the pilot, but added the ability to stay aloft for extended periods; a pilot's biological needs would run into limits. So far, drones have not taken advantage of the other major plus that can come from removing the pilot. Historically, airplanes were limited by the strength of materials. Today, many materials can withstand forces of 20 to 25 Gs, where each G is the force the earth's gravitational pull exerts on an object on the ground. But even the most experienced pilots can tolerate only about 9 Gs, and only for a few seconds before blacking out.

A drone could easily perform maneuvers that no manned plane could make. Rockwell Collins has also demonstrated an automated flight control system that allows a computer to continue to fly a plane safely despite its losing up to a third of its wings and half of its control surfaces. The plane's handling requires response at a scale of hundredths of a second—again, something humans cannot do.

Today, with pilots controlling drones remotely from bases in the United States, the air force is reluctant to expand the use of drones because

Principles of resource revolutions

Characteristics of winning solutions
- Superior performance upfront—faster, safer, cleaner, more convenient
- Clear pathway to significantly lower cost
- Ability to deliver at industry scale
- Backwards compatibility
- 50–80% resource productivity improvement; 2-year payback timing
- High-productivity business model

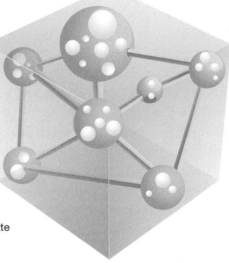

Building blocks
- Interchangeable parts
- Systems integration
- Embedded software; remotely upgradable
- Nanotechnology and biological methods
- Network effects
- Step by step, scale up; customer segment by customer segment
- Computational methods to test/simulate

Organizing principles
- Standard operating system
- Network organization
- Committed champions
- Resource productivity metrics
- High productivity sources and types of talent
- Freelance innovation; crowd sourcing

Sources of productivity
- Substitution: lighter, stronger, cheaper, lower resource risk materials
- Waste reduction: resource productivity is the new lean
- Circularity: designed in closed-loop resources
- Optimization: predictive or real-time analytics to reduce resource requirements or increase asset utilization
- Virtualization: resources as a service

of the vulnerability of communications links to jamming or manipulation. But in a world of Moore's Law, it's not implausible that computers can learn to fly autonomously in contested airspace. In many ways, flying in airspace is a less complicated problem than Google's computers driving a car on a crowded suburban street with pedestrians, people parking, and traffic lights.

While few opportunities will be as high-flying as the one that General Atomics uncovered, a plethora of opportunities exists to either help customers stop doing things in the physical world or to attack new markets and win new customers through savings and convenience. American Airlines pilots are now carrying flight records, navigation maps, and manuals on an iPad, eliminating a 35-pound bag, saving cockpit space, and reducing fuel use by $1.2 million. E-filing tax returns has reduced the costs of processing and record storage while improving the accuracy and speed of refunds.

The opportunities are rife today to drive the next great industrial shift by applying the core principles of the resource revolution. The opportunity in each area is not to use innovation in an incremental way, but rather to reinvent the product and the industry, making things ten times better, delighting the customer in wholly new ways, and creating whole new businesses in the process. Given the technology available in the market today, the results in terms of resource productivity should be staggering.

Interchangeable parts revolutionized manufacturing at the end of the nineteenth century, allowing mass production. Similarly, software has demonstrated accelerating rates of innovation because each new software developer can use and reuse modules of code developed previously. In chapter four, we will show how companies are learning to go even further: packaging industrial technology and software technology and creating scalable innovation in industrial processes that deliver enormous improvements in resource productivity.

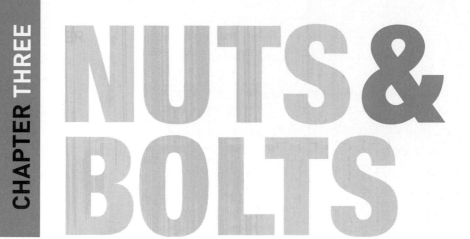

CHAPTER THREE

NUTS& BOLTS

THERE ARE HUGE OPPORTUNITIES TO SUBSTITUTE away from scarce resources. Companies can ask themselves, for example, how to take 80 percent of the weight and cost out of an existing product.

WASTE CAN BE ELIMINATED throughout the system. What will it take to reduce energy use in a company's manufacturing processes by 30 to 40 percent? Where are there opportunities to cut water use by 80 percent or more?

CIRCULARITY CAN BE INCREASED. Where is the next opportunity to mine gold from waste? Where can companies convert equipment sales to services?

VIRTUALIZATION CAN EXPAND SIGNIFICANTLY. What is the next opportunity to take drivers out of machines to increase safety, reliability, and productivity? What else can be done faster remotely and with more expertise?

NETWORK OPTIMIZATION applied to industrial equipment offers significant savings.

CHAPTER FOUR

DIRTT AND SOFTWARE: ASSEMBLY REQUIRED

OF ALL THE INDUSTRIES WHERE THE SEEDS for a resource revolution have yet to be planted, it's hard to imagine one more forlorn than construction.[13] The nail gun and sawzall (a reciprocating saw) may have been the last big innovations. Sure, CAD helps with the design and renderings, but construction in the field happens pretty much as it has for the past century or more. When Tyvek building wrap runs short or too many sawzall blades break, someone makes a run to the hardware store. As the work progresses, so does the pile of rubble that gets shoveled into dumpsters and hauled away. While labor productivity in manufacturing has improved consistently for decades, field construction labor productivity has declined over the last two decades. Between 10 and 15 percent of all material brought to a construction site ends up as waste; 36 percent of all residential and commercial waste in the United States is construction debris. Then, when an occupant's needs change several years down the road (sometimes just several months down the road, in the case of office space), a crew comes in with crowbars, rips everything out, and fills up more dumpsters so that another crew can start from scratch.

---

13   In fact, from an overall speed of building and resource efficiency point of view, we have regressed from 100 years ago when Sears shipped factory-built kit homes all over the western states by rail. The kits included precut lumber, nails, glass, and detailed plans that had been thoroughly tested and could be assembled quickly and cheaply into pretty Victorians or bungalows. Stefan lives in a bungalow built from a Sears kit that was delivered by Southern Pacific and assembled in Palo Alto in 1902 for $500 (about $14,000 in today's dollars) on a plot of land that cost $2. The home came with electric wiring, which was still considered a luxury at the time, plus cast-iron indoor plumbing and a central furnace. These homes were built to the latest standards of comfort and design.

Construction can, in fact, be carried out far more efficiently and, just as we have seen for automobiles, create unexpected possibilities while eliminating waste. The transformation begins with the five principles from chapter three—substitution, eliminating waste, circularity, optimization, and virtualization. The transformation then builds because of the power of the two ideas that we'll explore in this chapter: interchangeable parts and the importance of tying them together with software.

The idea of interchangeable parts comes from the earlier industrial revolutions, when people learned that these allow for much faster production in the factory and for easier and more efficient repairs in the field. As we'll see, the notion of interchangeability can be applied not just to cars and appliances but to entire buildings, factories, work processes, and even infrastructure systems, through the use of modules and standard interfaces that allow both physical objects and processes to be, in essence, snapped together. The result is the same combination of higher performance and quality and reduced waste that earlier industrial revolutions produced. In addition, systems can be deployed faster and have more flexibility to change over time.

Once parts become interchangeable, it is possible to embed software in major industrial applications in ways that have never been done before. The software allows for a faster upgrade cycle, lower cost, and accelerating performance improvement. The whole becomes significantly more than the sum of the parts.

The seeds of revolution for construction have already been planted in the dirt in Calgary, Alberta—or, rather, in DIRTT, a young company there whose name stands for "Doing It Right This Time."

The company has an idiosyncratic history that would be hard to duplicate. Its roots trace to a Danish cabinetmaker with a seventh-grade education, but also to the Curiosity rover currently roaming the surface of Mars and to a toaster owned by a couple in Canada which, as hard as it may be to believe, also inspired the Java programming language. (More about all this a bit further on.)

DIRTT builds interiors, but in a clean, precisely focused factory setting that is hardly recognizable as even a close cousin of the traditional noisy, dusty factory that leads to those piles of debris in homes and offices. When DIRTT has finished the manufacturing, it puts all the pieces into

The bright orange reusable stacking packaging "cookie" allows DIRTT products to be shipped with minimal waste or damage.

a container and ships them to the home or office. A local crew then snaps all the pieces together, using the fasteners that have been attached in the factory. *Et voilà*: You've turned empty space into an office or a hospital or a kids' bedroom.

DIRTT provides more than walls. DIRTT also provides the glass, doors, and shelves, and fixtures that fit into or onto its walls—even bunk beds, medical monitors, and oxygen lines for hospital settings; display screens or control systems; and planters with built-in irrigation for conference rooms. If a company wants it, DIRTT will even throw in a kitchen sink. DIRTT mass produces electrical wiring cut to the exact length needed, color-coding the wiring and attaching connectors that make everything simple to snap together. DIRTT makes cutouts in the factory for anything that needs to fit into the walls. In other words, DIRTT makes the interiors of offices and other rooms, with walls as the organizing principle.

Founded by Mogens Smed, Barrie Loberg, and Geoff Gosling in 2005, DIRTT remains a blip on the radar screen in its market, which totals $100 billion a year just for office construction in the United States alone. Yet, in its seven years of shipping product, DIRTT has won big-name clients, including several large Silicon Valley tech companies; major Wall Street banks; and large hospital chains. DIRTT is using its connections in the oil world in Calgary to expand into the Middle East.

What do these clients see in DIRTT? The first answer is simple: value. Materials and labor in a DIRTT office can cost as much as 50 percent less than the price of traditional construction. (Generally, the more complicated the space, the more DIRTT can save; if a company is just building walls out of drywall, using DIRTT saves little.) Then there's the savings in time. DIRTT can generally have an office outfitted within three to four weeks of when the specs are settled,[14] while traditional construction is unpredictable in terms of timing and is usually measured in months. There's also less noise, dust, and disruption in the construction of a DIRTT project. Most of the labor occurs away from the job site, in one of DIRTT's three factories, in Calgary, Phoenix, or Savannah, Georgia. Final, on-site assembly time totals two or three days. Hospitals have become a big business for DIRTT partly because they can avoid sealing off a whole wing for weeks or months while construction takes place.

Further, custom sizing of DIRTT parts does not cost extra. There is no such thing as a custom size, in fact. Any size is possible. Want a cabinet that is 30 inches wide (a standard office size)? Great. But 28 inches is fine, too. So is 27.5. And the customer wouldn't have to pay more for picking an unusual size. In fact, the company would pay slightly less because it would be using less material. This is the opposite of the traditional ways of the furniture business, where any change in dimension equals a special order that may take two to three times as long and costs extra for manual design and manufacturing.

The initial savings are just the beginning. If something can be snapped together, it can be unsnapped and reused. A customer can decide to have a door open out instead of in, to the right instead of to the left, or slide instead of swing. A customer can reconfigure a wall, perhaps by adding shelves or adding a flat-screen TV to an office to make it a conference room. The customer can make any number of other changes, too—and the installer needs only minutes to implement them, because the adaptability is built into the design. DIRTT says that a company moving into a new space can typically reuse 80 to 85 percent of the pieces from an earlier space. One big customer consolidated five branch offices into twelve floors of one building, essentially just packing up the walls and doors and moving them, along with the printers and file cabinets.

Portable walls even lead to a potential tax break. When classified as furniture for tax purposes, they depreciate faster than a building—in five to seven years, as opposed to thirty to fifty.

---

14 A typical crew of twelve can install about 27,000 square feet of DIRTT-built offices per week to move-in-ready condition.

How has DIRTT been able to deliver such remarkable speed, efficiencies, and savings? DIRTT's methods represent more than an incremental improvement over the prefabricated furnishings customers find at IKEA or Target. The work signals a conceptual breakthrough shared by other innovative companies doing creative thinking about resource use. Smed, Loberg, and Gosling found their own path to resource productivity—in some ways, a path that is highly technical in nature and unique to their industry. Their basic approach, however, is the same one that we see increasingly with other companies, including Boeing, which built its 787 Dreamliner in much the way that DIRTT designs its offices. DIRTT has broken its products and manufacturing processes into the most basic parts and reconfigured how they fit together. The company has unlocked waste, increased flexibility, and eliminated legacy technologies, such as the nail and screw. It has done so by looking at its products holistically.

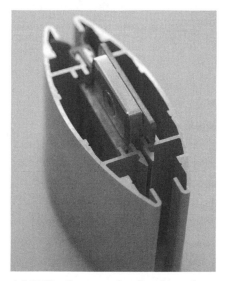

A DIRTT wall connector that allows for seamless installation and removal.

Let's take a closer look at what this means.

To begin with, DIRTT shows the power of starting with first principles. For example, the team didn't think about how to build a better door. They thought about what a door is, from the point of view of the customer's need. It's a physical barrier. It delivers privacy. It opens in a certain direction. It may allow light to pass through while keeping people from seeing inside, or it may be transparent. It blocks noise. Rather than starting with the current product and trying to improve it, the DIRTT team considered separately each of the functional aspects of a door and thought about how to divide the door's physical components to align with those functions, one by one, so that each function could be changed independently of the others. So, the same door frame could mount hinges on the left or right side, swing in or out, or, indeed, not swing at all but be suspended from the top and slide. Same for handles—instead of left-handed and right-handed doors, DIRTT produces one door; the handle can be mounted either way. Want a glass door for light or a solid door for visual privacy, but with airflow? Want a soundproof door? No problem. DIRTT simply reconfigures the panels that go inside the door frame. Want a fancy wood door with custom millwork trim? DIRTT can do that, too, simply by changing the door surface while keeping the same standardized connectors hidden inside.

With walls, the customer can change height, length, thickness, surface material, the position of outlets (or oxygen, water, or Ethernet). The customer can mount a TV, or plants, or a sink, or cabinet, or even a bed to the wall. The beauty of DIRTT's system is that the basic building blocks are the same—the vertical posts, the way the frames of adjacent sections connect, the way panels are attached to the frame.

Everything is parametric, meaning that individual parts are standardized in the way they fit together but that each one can be changed in size, material, or color. Want fabric walls? Change only the surface texture panel. Want a dry-erase board? The surface texture panel also comes in the dry wall surface treatment. Or glass, or wood, or metal. Or even a mounting frame that includes a TV and cable connections . . . or a fish tank.

In the old model, pieces of walls and furniture were connected with nails or screws, nuts and bolts, mortise and tenon joints, staples, or glue.[15] But screws, bolts, and the like are far too crude for DIRTT—by design, they damage the material itself and are thus irreversible. Sure, a contractor could take a wooden desk apart, saw off part of the legs, and reconstruct it at a different height. But the contractor can't make the legs longer again.

---

15 It was a revolution when screw threads were first standardized and each manufacturer could use screws from another manufacturer. We take it for granted today that screws are right-handed except when function requires exceptions—the left pedal on bicycles, the left side of the suspension of cars, New York subway lights (to deter theft by making them impossible to use anywhere else), and Swiss watches (to prevent Chinese knockoffs). But the standardization to make screws interchangeable took more than 150 years. Standard screws became possible in 1800 when Henry Maudslay invented the screw-cutting lathe; and standards took a leap forward when, in 1841, Joseph Whitworth's "British Standard Whitworth" screw was adopted by most railroads. But to finally launch international standards in 1947 required government contracts, a big push by the Pennsylvania Railroad, an international congress in Zurich, and a war in which the United States was supplying Europe. We think of screws as simple, but actually they have at least ten dimensions (gender, handedness, form of thread, angle, lead, pitch, etc.) that have to match for them to be interchangeable.

DIRTT's connectors are nothing like screws or nails. Most of them are extruded aluminum track in complex shapes which, using combinations of straight and curved elements, are designed to ensure close fit and strength but that slide easily in one direction to allow for installation and removal. Assembly and disassembly require simple tools.

Smed learned about furniture from his father, a Danish immigrant to Canada who had just a seventh-grade education but who imparted many lessons to his son—among them, that "a pissed-off customer never pays." Smed started out making traditional furniture but gradually became interested in the modular ideas that DIRTT embodies. He met the key members of his future team, industrial designer and sculptor Geoff Gosling and information systems expert Barrie Loberg, when he was CEO of Evans Consoles, a company that makes consoles that are used in mission-critical control centers such as those at utilities and at NASA. Some of the critical insights powering DIRTT can be traced back to what the team learned at Evans, which built the consoles that control the Curiosity rover on Mars.

Gosling's first degree is in sculpture—he says his painter friends tell him that "sculpture is what you bump into when you're backing up to view real art"—but the consoles at Evans had taught him that he couldn't set his office designs in stone. His designs needed to incorporate the ability to change easily.

Gosling says the design process for command-and-control centers can take five years and is "completely paralyzing." The design of a center to handle 9-1-1 calls in Chicago, for instance, involved some forty-five city departments, all with decision-making power. The design has to be perfect because the stakes are so high. "When you and I make a mistake," Gosling says, "we just backspace and type again. When someone makes a mistake in a C&C room, people die and things blow up."

The design has to stay right, too, for fifteen or more years, even as technology changes, because no one wants to take a control center offline to update it. The design at Evans Consoles became especially complicated during the early 2000s, because flat-panel screens were clearly the future but were not yet the present. No one wanted to design for the clunky old cathode-ray devices, but few customers could afford flat panels in the early days—each screen cost thousands of dollars, and every operator in a control room might need ten. Gosling learned on a Federal Aviation

Administration project that the FAA was going to build cabinets out of plywood and keep a carpenter on the payroll so it could adapt as technology changed.

He began thinking about a toaster his parents had. Over the decades, just about every other kitchen appliance, from the coffeemaker to the microwave, had changed, but the toaster still fit in and kept turning out toasted bread. That toaster helped guide him to his thinking on modularity.

The toaster that inspired Geoff Gosling, cofounder of DIRTT, and his brother, James Gosling, inventor of Java.

(Much later, Gosling went home one night and watched a Discovery Channel piece on his brother, James, who is the father of the Java programming language. Asked what inspired Java, James said that, well, in part it was his parents' toaster. Geoff was stunned. The brothers had never discussed the toaster.)

How did this toaster inspire the object-oriented programming software that became Java? Java is based on the concept of a complex, virtual machine that can power websites and other programs independent of the hardware they run on, whether that is a high-end supercomputer or a mobile phone. James's idea—that one kitchen function could be isolated from other kitchen functions and yet be connected to the rest of the kitchen in a standard way—came to him because he had the same epiphany about the toaster that Geoff had: It had remained the same even as the kitchen around it changed.

The plug for a toaster, while standard today, evolved. Because lighting was the first application for electricity in the second industrial revolution, toasters originally had plugs that literally screwed into the socket for an Edison lightbulb. As more appliances were invented, Harvey Hubbell patented a device in 1904 that allowed a two-prong connector to plug into a light socket. Eventually, people realized they could just put outlets for those two-prong connectors directly into their walls. Because this interface was standardized long before the Goslings' toaster came along, the toaster could rely on it. The toaster also relied on standard sizes and thicknesses of bread slices (at least until bagels became popular). Pop-Tarts were designed to conform to the "bread slice standard."

So, what the toaster embodied was the idea that one kitchen function—warming and browning bread—could be isolated from others—refrigeration, cutting, baking—and still be connected to the total functions in a standard way. Other functions could be upgraded without having to replace the "toasting bread" function, as well.

Object-oriented programming

It is this idea that forms the core of Java, known as "object-oriented programming." Each "object" is a module that communicates what its job is. Other objects don't need to know how that module does its job. For example, an object that can perform integral calculus can do so for any program. Programmers writing code can draw on that object without needing to understand calculus. They simply have to know how to pass on the request—in programming jargon, this is "calling a method"—along with the data parameters that describe the calculus problem to be solved.

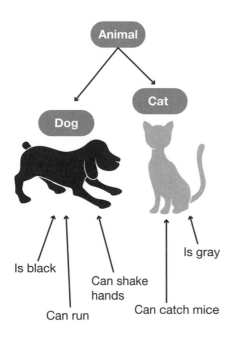

A program using the calculus object could simply say, "Tell me the area under the curve described by these parameters."

This idea has an enormous effect on productivity. First, a programmer writing a new app for the iPhone doesn't need to reinvent any of the functions that already exist, such as displaying on the screen, locating via GPS, or sending a text message. Instead, the programmer can draw on all the other objects that already exist. Second, if, say, someone comes up with an object that performs calculus faster, that new object can replace the old one without requiring any other change on the iPhone app or any other device. The interface is standardized. An app just asks for calculus to be performed and doesn't have to "care" about how the calculation is done. As the software world has shown, there is immense power in these standard interfaces.

In the physical world of tools and construction, a benefit of standard interfaces is that, when one part or module breaks, it can simply be replaced or repaired without affecting anything else. While software modules don't break or wear out, standardization allows Java to run in a "virtual machine" that allows the actual computing hardware to be swapped out with newer, faster, cheaper computers and still run the same software.

Good managers can begin to see how the Gosling toaster[16] could have inspired both modular, interchangeable software objects and modular, interchangeable walls, furniture, and building systems. Each system has standard interfaces. Each object/part can be swapped out or used in new ways. When DIRTT wants to add a new type of cabinet door or a new trim, as the company is now doing to be able to produce high-end residential and kitchen interiors, it simply designs a few new parts or choices. Everything else is already done—the hinges, the connectors, the rest of the cabinet's insides.

There is another connection: DIRTT's design tools and its manufacturing and logistics control system run in Java. So, the Gosling family toaster was a double win for DIRTT. It not only figured in Geoff's insight about modularity but also helped provide a technology, in Java, that lets that insight be implemented.

The connection to Java actually comes through Barrie Loberg, who also worked at Evans Consoles and who had his own epiphany about the need for adaptability and integration. His job was to create software design tools that enabled customers to play around with console plans until they found configurations they liked. After cofounding DIRTT, he

---

16   Given the seminal role of the toaster, we asked Geoff where the toaster is now. He said, "Oh, our sister has it." We wondered whether the sister had any idea just how significant an object she had in her kitchen. It turned out that she did.

applied the same idea to floor plans and prefab construction. In a system he calls ICE, Loberg created the basis for parametric parts and did away with the notion of standard parts. Each part is simply a CAD model that specifies dimensions, materials, weight, and cost. Each aspect of a part can change independently, based on the parameters input by the user or required by the rest of the design. This feature draws on a key capability of Java: that one object can rely on another object and tailor its behavior based on parameters the other object specifies. Does the customer want to insert a door into a wall? ICE will not only add the door, drawn to whatever dimensions the customer specifies, but will automatically reduce the widths of the walls on either side and do anything else needed to incorporate the door into the design.

Incorporating technology that gives video games a realistic, three-dimensional look, ICE also lets customers walk through the design and see it from any perspective, as they're constructing it. Pick a new color or finish, and the image updates instantly. The customer can even view updated versions of the design in real time on an iPhone.

Loberg's system can begin either from scratch or from whatever drawings have been done for the space that's being used. A designer builds out the space virtually, dividing it up into offices, seating areas, cubicles, or whatever is desired. In the background, the software communicates parts lists to vendors' computer systems and continuously generates real-time cost estimates. Thus, a price for the job is always available, and it's possible to tinker, to see how much would be saved by using different materials. Once the design work is done, the specs are automatically generated and communicated electronically to DIRTT's factory. All the necessary parts and materials are ordered, and a commitment on delivery is sent to the customer.

"The picture is the order," Loberg says.

DIRTT's design process can require just hours. Most of the manufacturing process, which involves laminating wood to the metal structural elements that wind up invisible inside the walls or furniture, takes just a few days. Most of the time between design and delivery is spent by suppliers scrambling to keep up with DIRTT.

The software holds all the specs, so that a client who wants to move knows exactly what pieces he already has and is coached on how to reuse as much as possible. "We prefer that the walls live on," Loberg says. "We see recycling as a last resort."

Loberg's work is part of a larger trend to apply information technology to the value chain of making, delivering, and servicing a product—one of the central, decisive elements of any resource revolution and one that we will return to throughout this book. In terms of the five principles we laid out in the last chapter, DIRTT's software enables virtualization of all the design steps and eliminates any need for paper CAD drawings or faxing specifications back and forth. The software, together with the interchangeable design of the components, drastically increases circularity by supporting products' reuse or life extension once they are in customers' hands. DIRTT eliminates a huge amount of waste, because its construction occurs in a controlled factory environment, where the software provides detailed instructions that optimize the layout of pieces on a sheet of steel or a wood laminate board thus minimizing the amount of material that gets thrown away. (The only dumpsters at a DIRTT factory are containers that get shipped back to suppliers to reuse. A recent visit to the quiet factory in Calgary found that the largest amount of waste was trimmings from insulation put into walls. That extra insulation—made mostly from recycled blue jeans—is sent back to the supplier to be processed into new rolls of insulation.) DIRTT also optimizes the construction process to a huge degree. At the site where the office or room is going in, assembly takes far less time than the traditional cutting and pounding. At the DIRTT factories, all the materials that workers need are at their fingertips, not at a hardware store ten minutes away.

DIRTT goes well beyond simply improving the resource productivity of its product. By incorporating the notion of interchangeable parts and standard interfaces and by building on the capabilities of Java, DIRTT begins to change the entire business system, from the initial design all the way through to the eventual reuse of the pieces it manufactures. DIRTT's approach doesn't just create savings; it enables higher performance.

In China, Zhang Yue is using aspects of the DIRTT approach for its boldest application yet and could set a major precedent for China, which has the world's largest urbanizing population and faces immense pressure to construct large numbers of buildings quickly. Zhang, the founder and CEO of Broad Sustainable Building, came to buildings as an engineer, not

China is building the equivalent of 100 New Yorks

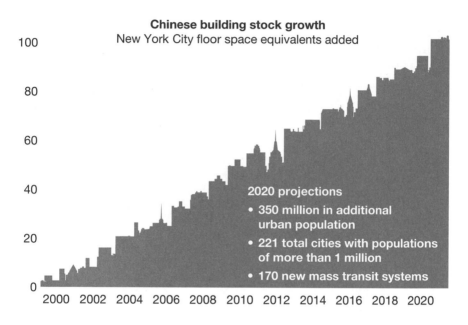

Chinese building stock growth
New York City floor space equivalents added

2020 projections

- 350 million in additional urban population
- 221 total cities with populations of more than 1 million
- 170 new mass transit systems

an architect. He started by making commercial and industrial air-conditioning systems. In 2008, he began experimenting with prefab construction that makes buildings faster and cheaper to design and build, while saving enormous amounts of water and concrete. Now, BSB has a large factory for Lego-like steel and concrete modular blocks. They come with ducts and wiring built in and are hoisted into position on site, where they are connected with standard fasteners. In 2011, BSB built a fifteen-story tower in Zhang's hometown, Changsha, in thirty days.

Zhang, who has amassed a fortune of $860 million, is, as we write this, gearing up for his next big project: Sky City. Also to be built in Changsha, Sky City will be the tallest building in the world, at 838 meters (more than twice the height of the Empire State Building). Sky City will house 30,000 people and have 104 elevators, a hotel, a school, and a massive entertainment and sports complex, plus stores and restaurants. Similar to ___RT, which figured out a way to

Building modular skyscrapers

Modular building techniques employed by the Chinese developer Broad Sustainable Building.

Floor/ceiling modules
The floors of the skyscraper are built in sections at the factory.

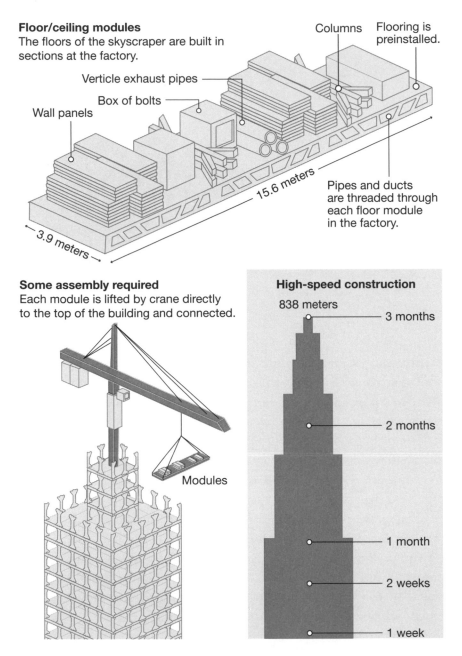

Columns

Flooring is preinstalled.

Verticle exhaust pipes

Box of bolts

Wall panels

15.6 meters

3.9 meters

Pipes and ducts are threaded through each floor module in the factory.

Some assembly required
Each module is lifted by crane directly to the top of the building and connected.

Modules

High-speed construction
838 meters

3 months

2 months

1 month

2 weeks

1 week

mount irrigation systems and plants onto a wall panel, the exterior walls of Sky City will act as farmland and grow plants and food. Zhang intends to earthquake-proof Sky City for a 9.0 earthquake.

Now get this: He intends to assemble the building, on site, in ninety days. He projects the cost to be $1,500 per square meter of space, one tenth the cost of the Burj Dubai, which is currently the tallest building in the world.[17]

INTERCHANGEABLE PARTS: BACK TO THE FUTURE

To see where the DIRTT/Zhang approach can take us—and we're just at the beginning—look for a moment at the history of interchangeable parts. They first appeared in the eleventh century, when Bi Sheng invented movable wooden type in China. In the Middle Ages, the Venetians built their naval power on interchangeable parts. They not only had the largest fleet of their time but could rapidly build, repair, and train crews for ships built of standardized parts, using a standard frame that saved both wood and time in construction. Many people think Henry Ford ran the first production assembly line, but, in 1320, Venice's Arsenale could crank out an entire ship with weapons, sails, and navigation instruments in a day.

Johannes Gutenberg's (1395–1468) movable type printing press, invented c. 1436.

Johannes Gutenberg made just a conceptually straightforward improvement to Bi Sheng's work, yet Gutenberg's metallic movable type slashed the cost of printing, made books accessible to the middle class, and laid the foundation for the modern age. Napoleon conquered most of Europe with artillery whose standard sizes, bores, and cartridges improved accuracy, safety, and reliability, while reducing cost; and then Sir

---

17   By the time this book is printed, we will know whether Zhang delivered on schedule!

Marc Brunel applied the power of standards to the British navy and gave it an edge over Napoleon. Eli Whitney conceived of interchangeable parts for firearms, which Samuel Colt put into practice in the "Colt way" that fundamentally changed the tactics of all wars. The idea spread to clocks, sewing machines (Singer, for example), reapers, and steam engines, until it reached Henry Ford and the assembly line that did so much to enable the second industrial revolution. Rather than be surprised that the idea of standard, interchangeable parts can be applied to buildings, we should be surprised it has taken us so long to discover that fact.

SOFTWARE, SOFTWARE, SOFTWARE

Once a company has broken its products and services down into their core parts and established interfaces that let them interact the way software objects do, the next key step is to focus on how to use software to pull the pieces together in powerful, new ways. Just as DIRTT achieved huge efficiencies in office and hospital construction through proprietary software, companies in virtually every sector can apply information technology and algorithms both to design better products and to add important capabilities inside them.

Currently, the engineering groups involved in thinking about resources at most companies tend to be dominated by civil and mechanical engineers; the IT guys handle desktop computers and phones. The resource revolution requires a major commitment to integrate software engineering capabilities throughout a business and its products, even in traditional heavy industries. This won't just be programming, either. Software engineers will need to design algorithms and use decision theory, while integrating sensors and control systems to optimize capabilities. A battery, for instance, can get considerable improvement from better chemistry but will take the big leap forward when sensors, newly embedded inside, report constantly on key variables such as temperature, so software can constantly tweak the chemical reaction to maximize its output of electricity.

"Big data" will also come to lots of companies that haven't previously had to think about massive computing capabilities. For instance, big data will allow for much more sophisticated analysis of manufacturing processes and raise the quality of production. This has already happened in semiconductors, where KLA-Tencor allows detailed analysis of defects of nanometers of misalignment between successive structures on a chip during the fabrication process. It not only allows bad chips to be marked and later discarded, it even allows subsequent manufacturing steps to correct for slight variations that occur naturally so that nearly all chips come out fully functional. In a technology where a single atom of copper in the wrong place can destroy a $500 microprocessor, real-time data on every manufacturing parameter has turned out to be essential to ensuring output and yield.

Many companies will find they need to borrow software capabilities from other industries, or they will risk being "Amazoned." Way back in the Dark Ages—let's say the mid-1990s—companies were mostly compared with their direct competitors. GM competed with Ford, Exxon with Shell, Deere with Caterpillar. But the Internet provided such an intimate look at every company that customers began to form expectations based on the state of the art in any industry, not just the one in which a potential provider operated. Companies that failed to meet expectations were said to be Amazoned because Amazon made it so easy to buy books, so easy to provide feedback, and so easy to get recommendations on other books to buy that the company raised the standards for everybody. The CEO of a maker of heavy equipment said in the late '90s that he was being criticized for not keeping up with Federal Express. He said that a customer told him, "I pay FedEx $15, and they can tell me to within half an hour when a package will be delivered. I pay you $300,000 for a piece of equipment, and you can't tell me to within a month when I'll get it."

We now live in an iPhone world, and every company needs to live up to the expectations that Steve Jobs created: a world of intuitive interfaces and robust capabilities. Every good manager needs to ensure that all the software on the system is the absolute best.

In general, other industries can be great sources for ideas, especially if the company might share certain technologies. Companies making electric cars will be tempted to stick to the years-long development cycle that is traditional in the automotive world—it's what they know, and they've succeeded with it—but companies like Tesla are using consumer electronics for help with the battery, a key component. Consumer-electronics product cycles last months, not years, so batteries are being continually improved. If car companies can tap into the work in consumer electronics, they will have better batteries, faster. Tesla already does this through a relationship with Panasonic and recently announced a move that could increase the benefits of those ties. Tesla said it will incorporate technology into its cars so that batteries can be swapped out in ninety seconds at a drive-up lane similar to a car wash. While originally developed to speed up battery charging by simply swapping in a fully charged battery for a depleted one, swapping would also allow cars to continue to upgrade batteries on a consumer-electronics cycle. The older, used batteries would find new applications in stationary storage for the grid or in homes, where cost matters more than energy density—space and weight are not as much at a premium when you're not driving the battery around with you.

Just about any component that can be switched to silicon will likewise create opportunities. Silicon components not only typically use much less power than copper coils or mechanical relays and plunge in cost because of Moore's Law, they also can create opportunities to introduce software that will raise performance. While all modern planes have forsaken hydraulic pressure lines and valves for purely electronic "fly by wire" controls, many planes still use heavy electromechanical coils, each about the size of a football and made mostly of copper. Systems flying in prototype planes for the next generation replace these relays entirely with solid-state switches. The change shrinks the space and weight required for switches. It also reduces the power requirements for a plane by some 40 percent. Better yet, the change opens the switches to control via software and, as a result, delivers better performance. The solid-state relays can sense minute fluctuations in voltage and current, detecting warning signs of impending failure or overload. The next generation of control systems will also anticipate power needs based on what the pilot is doing and what the flight plan shows. If full power to climb is about to be needed, the system will ramp down climate controls or other nonessential systems to avoid the big spike in electrical demand normally experienced when a pilot calls for full throttle.

Once a piece of equipment moves control into software, it's relatively easy to establish feedback loops, so that equipment keeps "learning" about what works and what doesn't and can keep optimizing performance. GE has been doing that for years with its jet engines. Sensors inside them monitor key factors that determine performance and can radio ahead for maintenance as a plane is getting ready to land. GE can also then monitor the effects of the maintenance and keep tweaking its system to minimize expense and disruption for its airline customers, while maximizing power and fuel efficiency.

As companies add software capabilities to their core products, they will find that they can—and must—make products as upgradeable as possible. The standard progression in the world of technology is that capabilities

Rise of computing power compared to evolution of animal brains

Author, inventor, and futurist Ray Kurzweil has shown how the exponential growth in CPU performance, as described by Moore's Law, promises to produce computers that are more powerful than humans brains.

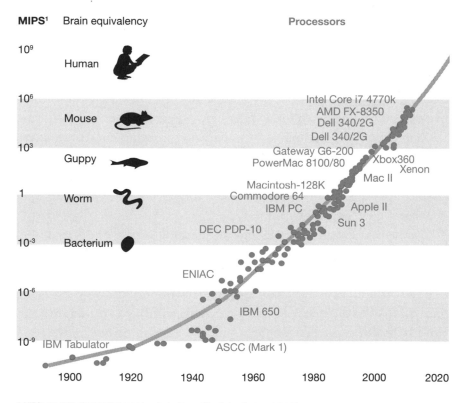

1 MIPSs are units of computing speed equivalent to a million instructions per second.

start out hardwired, because that's the only way to get the necessary acceptable performance. Then, capabilities migrate into software. These days, capabilities are becoming even more abstract: Software can be updated remotely or can even run in the cloud, on centralized servers. NASA shows the progression. The original moon mission software was actually hardwired by hand into physical circuits, because fully functional computers were too large to fit on the spacecraft. Over time, as the electronics improved, conventional software could run on conventional computers in spacecraft. Now, satellites can be upgraded from Earth with new software releases on a regular basis. The progression from hardware to software to remote upgrades is available to far more companies today. Companies that design their equipment and networks to be upgradeable will have a major advantage, because customers don't want to invest in the latest, hardwired technology only to see it become obsolete in twelve to eighteen months.

By setting aside the conventional practice of building offices on site, and instead manufacturing interiors of offices in factories, DIRTT has moved construction away from the traditional three-yards-and-a-cloud-of-sawdust and into the world of resource revolutions. Following in DIRTT's footsteps, companies can break their core product and service offerings into their most basic modules, define the interfaces that let them work together, and search for ways to incorporate the latest software.

Success will only be limited by a company's imagination. For instance, Clean Power Finance incorporates technology from online dating services. An early backer, Gary Kremen, founded Match.com, and Clean Power Finance uses algorithms similar to the dating service's to find the right match of financing with customers.

In the next chapter, we will look at one additional element critical to success: enhancing system integration. By now, the company has identified just about all the parts necessary to succeed, but packaging them the right way is both extremely hard and crucially important. As Mark Twain once said, "The difference between the right word and the almost right word is the difference between lightning and a lightning bug."

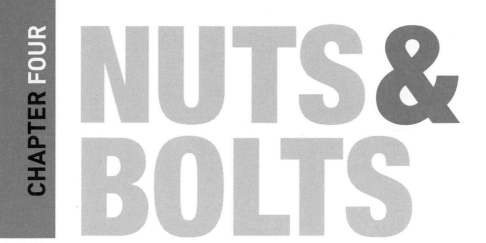

NUTS & BOLTS

In this environment, managers must:

INCREASE STANDARDIZATION AND MODULARIZATION, making inter-changeable parts for the twenty-first century.

FIND NEW WAYS TO DELIVER improved capabilities to customers without relying on the old product architecture.

USE NEW MATERIALS, design techniques, and software analysis.

APPLY SOFTWARE AND ALGORITHMS AND AUTOMATION both "inside" the product and also to the value chain of making, delivering, and servicing—improving product performance and reducing weight and cost.

ALLOW THE PRODUCT TO BE UPGRADED consistently over time, opening up the potential for more software-as-a-service delivery models.

CHAPTER FIVE

SYSTEM INTEGRATION: THE POWER OF MACHINES MEETS THE INTERNET OF THINGS

In one of those predictions that he would surely like to erase from all memory, *New York Times* columnist Paul Krugman wrote in 1998 that "the growth of the Internet will slow drastically." He said people forecasting wild increases were counting too much on "network effects," the notion that each additional phone or computer added to a network increases the value of all the other devices connected in that network and leads to further growth. The flaw in the forecasters' logic, the columnist wrote, is that "most people have nothing to say to each other."

If someone with Krugman's credentials, which include the Nobel Memorial Prize in Economic Sciences in 2008, could underestimate the power of network effects so completely, the rest of us need to take a little time and make sure we see what they are making possible.

Going far beyond the networks of phones, roads, and the like that have been built to this point, the world is now building out the most complicated and powerful network yet: what is being called the Internet of Things. To this point, the Internet has mostly allowed people to communicate with each other and to interact with other devices by, for instance, visiting websites. Increasingly, though, devices are going to talk to each other without the need for any human involvement. Perhaps each person's phone will carry that individual's comfort preferences, and when they walk into a room the device will tell the thermostat and the lighting what setting to use.

The thermostat or even the smoke detector could also recognize when a room is empty and could turn down the heat and shut off the lights (removing tons of frustration from the lives of parents of teenagers). In an office, the thermostats could check on calendars to see that the next day is a holiday, and then they'd keep the heat off. The thermostats could check the weather forecast and see that a day was going to be hot, meaning the building should cool itself considerably overnight, when electricity rates were low. Ericsson, a major developer of communications technologies, estimates that, by the end of the decade, 50 billion devices will be connected to the Internet, and that about 80 percent of those will be talking almost entirely to one another, not to people—in other words, 40 billion devices can be working behind the scenes on our behalf.

The implications for resource revolutions will be profound. In the past, many businesses have operated inefficiently because it's been hard (or simply impossible) for certain machines to talk to each other. On a factory floor, for instance, machines by different manufacturers spoke their own "language," making it more likely that parts of a process would be managed independently rather than as one smooth, integrated system. Likewise, in offices, the furnaces, air conditioners, and other equipment speak only the language of their manufacturers. Because of the Internet of Things, machines will all be able to talk to one another, and there will be billions of sensors and cameras joining the conversation. The possibilities for efficiencies and for new products and services are exceptional.

If all the devices in the Internet of Things are to be any help, though, they have to be integrated properly into products and business models and align better with existing infrastructure, with others' supply chains, and with legal and regulatory frameworks. The devices also have to be designed with interfaces that people understand and can use. Putting new dongles on old systems can actually make performance worse. And we've already complicated each company's operating framework with the challenges we posed in the last chapter. We've said that to break products down into their tiniest modules, based on first principles, managers need to find ways to add as much software as possible—and now we're saying managers have to do all that in the context of this extraordinary new opportunity to gather more information and to improve communication inside the business.

The only way to make this all work is through a huge emphasis on the subject of this chapter: system integration. We'll also look at how to consider new business models, because they will often be necessary to capture the full benefits of the integration.

The discipline of system integration has existed for a long time, but, frankly, most companies aren't very good at it. This is especially true in resource-intensive areas, because the technologies have been in place so long that it hasn't been necessary to integrate new ones. Many utilities, for instance, used to have labs to test how new technologies would be incorporated into the grid but closed them in the 1970s and 1980s, as cost pressure drove industry restructuring.

Besides, the problems are very hard. System integration is more like trying to manage an ecosystem than it is like solving the sort of calculus problem one encounters in engineering school. The complexities of system integration explain why China doesn't yet have a competitive commercial airliner, despite decades of trying. China hasn't mastered the skills that Boeing and Airbus have developed to manage all the tradeoffs among weight, performance, seating configuration, and all the other factors that go into designing the best airplanes.

As Boeing and Airbus have seen, the payoffs for success are enormous—but even if one company solves the problem, the other guy likely won't, simply because the problems are so tough. Bed, Bath & Beyond, for instance, has won a significant advantage through its ability to let a customer visit a store, scan all the items he or she wants to buy when, say, a teenager is going off to college, and have all the items delivered in a box to that student's dorm room halfway across the country. This isn't a simple matter of having the local store box and ship the items or of having the store nearest the college do so—both turn out to be too expensive. Instead, Bed, Bath & Beyond has designed its systems so that every process is performed at maximum efficiency and integrated tightly with all other parts of the process. Competitors, obviously, have been able to see what the company is doing but haven't yet been able to duplicate it.

Done right, system integration can mean that 1 and 1 equal 11. Done wrong, integration can turn 1 and 1 into zero.

Although system integration is hard, there are three things each company can do to greatly increase the odds of success:

- *Recognize the scope of the problem.* Simply realizing that systems are subtle and that lots of variables are interacting simultaneously will give a company a head start.
- *Bring in people with experience.* We'll look more closely in chapter eight at where to find these people (or how to develop them). In some cases, the experience won't exist because the team is dealing with new problems, but each manager will need to find any expertise available.
- *Model whenever possible, then test.* Because systems are so complex, the only way to know for sure whether a process works is to test it. But, these days, a company can do an awful lot of that testing through computer models.

Rocketdyne used to leave residents near Los Angeles spooked, beginning in the 1940s, because the rocket engines it was developing for the military exploded routinely over an area designated for secret testing. Rocketdyne had as many as twenty versions of a new design blow up during testing before getting a design right. Rocket engines are made of brazed copper tubing because, like much more expensive gold, copper is very ductile and flexible and can handle the huge vibrations a rocket engine experiences, without breaking. The challenge is that copper has one of the lowest melting points of any metal, well below the temperature of the exhaust gases jetting out of the engine. So engineers run the liquid hydrogen that fuels the engine through the tubes that form the exhaust nozzle, which brings the fuel up to ignition temperature while keeping the copper below its melting point. Any slight mistake in shape or fuel flow, or any hot spot that develops in the engine, and a section melts—*boom!* Rocketdyne engineers collected the pieces that scattered on the ground to try to figure out what went wrong, adjusted the design, and launched a new version—usually just to have that one blow up, too. By about a decade ago, the company had cut the number of explosions to just two or three during testing. Today, because of advances in computer modeling, the company gets engine designs right the first time—no mysterious explosions necessary.[18]

POWER NETWORKS

To see how system integration will need to occur, we'll look at how the electric grid will be transformed in coming decades. This is an uncommonly hard problem. That's partly because so little has changed over the past century—the joke goes that if Alexander Graham Bell came back to life and saw the phone network and all the mobile devices we use, he'd be stunned, but that if Thomas Edison came back to life and saw the electric grid, he'd say, "Yep, that's about how I left it." The difficulties also come because the changes need to be so profound. The grid needs to go from being essentially a hub-and-spoke system of power plants and their customers to a network as supple and complex as the Internet. While the scope of the system will surely dwarf those most companies are wrestling with, the grid makes for a vivid example of both the changes and the opportunities that each company will face.

Once we explore the system integration issues with the grid, we'll look at the new business models that may be enabled, because resource revolutions will cause so much change that new business models will need to be invented and implemented.

FINDING THE "ON" SWITCH FOR THE ELECTRIC GRID

At the moment, the grid is about where the phone system was in the 1940s. Long-distance phone calls were scheduled two hours or more

---

18 It may be disconcerting to know that the engines for commercial airliners use the same principle. The so-called "hot section" of the engine where the exhaust gases are at their highest temperature and speed just after igniting has a turbine in it that drives both the compressor and fan section at the front of the engine responsible for feeding high-pressure air to provide oxygen for the fuel to burn. The turbine also powers all the electrical, air-conditioning, and control systems in the plane. As in rocket nozzles, the temperature of the engine exhaust gases exceeds the melting point of the metal alloy used to make the turbine blades, and only cooling provided by the fuel running through each blade keeps the whole engine from melting or exploding. Jet engines get tested by letting a frozen turkey get sucked into the front to ensure they stay stable in flight even if the plane accidentally strikes a flock of birds.

ahead of time, and operators had to make the connections manually. A long-distance call could take fifteen minutes to set up.

As crazy as this may seem in our day and age, our utility system tends to schedule power generation and transmission twenty-four hours in advance and in fifteen-minute increments to allow time for manual interventions in power plants.[19]

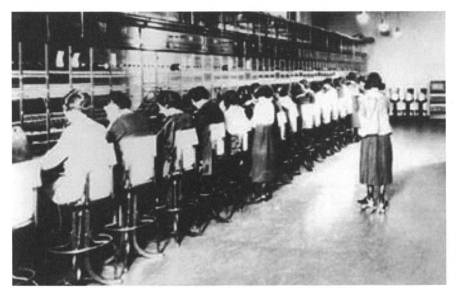

An AT&T switchboard supervisor on roller skates watches over long-distance phone operators in 1920.

But there's hope. In the phone system, after World War II, switches were replaced with automated relays, and the area code system we now take for granted was put in place, removing the need for armies of operators. Then, in the 1980s, Cisco invented the software-defined network (SDN) routers that became core to the network. The routers eliminated the need for dedicated lines for each phone call, driving down costs dramatically and opening up the system to cell phones and Internet communications. The same sort of dramatic improvements will come to the electric grid.

---

19 A few grid operators, like the one in California, are now beginning to experiment with nearly real-time grid controls that can respond within five-minute intervals to additional power demand. But even the best systems are nowhere near the almost instant response we have come to expect from our communications networks.

The modern electric grid traces its roots to the spring of 1885, when Thomas Edison and George Westinghouse competed to define the standard for bringing the magic of electricity to the country. After settling on alternating current, the United States spent most of the next hundred years building out a power grid providing nearly universal service nationally, relying on 5,800 central station power plants. The build-out of the grid has been called the engineering marvel of the twentieth century, but the basic technology of the grid has changed little since the time of Edison and Westinghouse. The average circuit is forty years old, and some are more than a century old. The grid is showing its age.

American inventor George Westinghouse (1864–1914), father of the electric grid.

Today, many utilities still do not know what's occurring on their grid or where. The average utility generally learns about problems with its lines by looking for clusters of customers who are calling in to complain, rather than by receiving information on the problems directly. Issues at substations often have to be addressed by sending maintenance workers into the field to flip a switch, rather than being able to have someone in a remote office make the change—or, better yet, have the grid sense the problem and either fix it automatically or route electricity around it.

Generally, only 20 to 40 percent of the transmission and distribution capacity in the network is in use at a given time, and only about 30 to 40 percent of the capacity of power plants is being used. Many "peaker" power plants sit idle all but a few dozen hours a year, just so they can be fired up to handle demand during the peak of air-conditioning use on the five hottest days in the summer. These plants, by the way, can cost so much to run that utilities can lose money on peak demand despite charging what consumers see as exorbitant rates. Power plants turn only a bit more than half the energy in their fuel into electricity, and more than 10 percent of that electricity is dissipated between the plant and the end user through what are called line losses. Many utilities are still running COBOL code from the 1950s, and some are still rekeying data or transporting tapes to issue paper bills once a month.

Telecom subscribers and data traffic

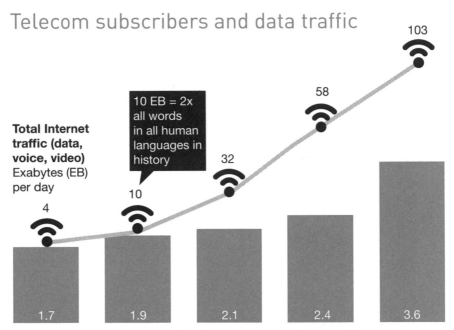

Total Internet traffic (data, voice, video) Exabytes (EB) per day

10 EB = 2x all words in all human languages in history

Total global wired and wireless subscriptions (billions)

Utilities not only have to overcome their massive inefficiencies but have to adapt to the contemporary, rapidly shifting environment. Homeowners are putting solar panels on their roofs, which not only takes customers from the utilities (usually, the most profitable customers) but also requires that utilities figure out how to integrate into the grid the power that the homes sometimes make available. At the moment, in parts of northern Germany, power from solar and wind often becomes available just when the distribution network is maxed out and can't handle any more power, meaning that the renewable sources have to be shut off. Engineers are developing advanced building-control technologies, and architects have designed more efficient buildings that consume electricity during off hours—for instance, cities like Austin use cheap electricity at night to freeze water, then, during the day, circulate air over the ice to cool buildings. New air-conditioning systems can similarly use evaporation to cool buildings instead of the compressors that make current air conditioners so noisy. Such compressionless air-conditioning systems may reduce the use of electricity by 50 percent or more, eliminating much of the afternoon peak that utilities in the United States have typically designed their grids for. Lighting is getting much more efficient, with LED bulbs cutting electricity usage by 85 percent, compared with incandescents. Utilities can continue to drive increasing electrification (including everything from ports to lawn mowers).

Once electric vehicles deploy in large numbers, utilities will have to get used to the power equivalent of a commercial building or small factory unplugging, moving, and plugging back in somewhere else. Utilities are going to have to develop massive capabilities for integrating not only what they are doing but what all the related players are doing, too.

Physicist and inventor of the first transformer Nikola Tesla (1856–1943), with one of his electrical oscillators in 1895.

Plenty of technologies will be able to help with the reinvention. For instance, batteries distributed throughout the grid could reduce costs by allowing stored electricity to be generated in a smooth, steady way, with plants operating at maximum efficiency and with electricity drawn from the batteries as needed—no more need for entire plants to be kept ready all year just for a few hours of work on a few days. Solid-state transformers, which rely on sleek, semiconductor technology and which are currently used in high-speed trains and military airplanes, could provide much higher reliability at

The smart grid

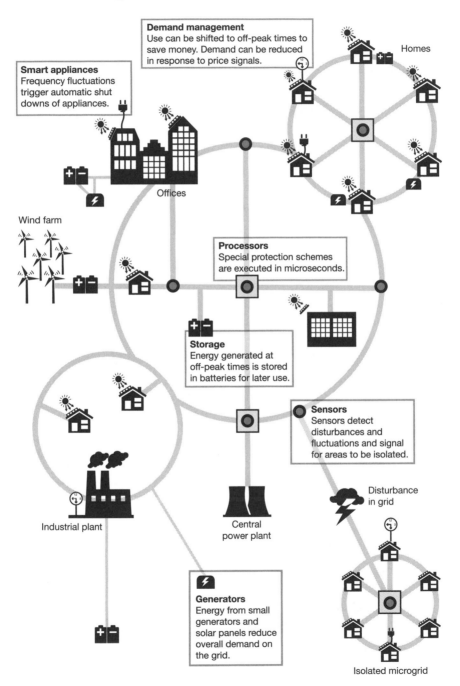

Demand management
Use can be shifted to off-peak times to save money. Demand can be reduced in response to price signals.

Homes

Smart appliances
Frequency fluctuations trigger automatic shut downs of appliances.

Offices

Wind farm

Processors
Special protection schemes are executed in microseconds.

Storage
Energy generated at off-peak times is stored in batteries for later use.

Sensors
Sensors detect disturbances and fluctuations and signal for areas to be isolated.

Disturbance in grid

Industrial plant

Central power plant

Generators
Energy from small generators and solar panels reduce overall demand on the grid.

Isolated microgrid

much lower cost than conventional transformers, which are bulky, copper-based devices; substations will fit in a small vault rather than occupying a full city block.[20] Electric vehicles could act as grid storage, drawing down power when demand is low and plants can produce power most efficiently. Sensors in the network will be able to spot problems in the network and fix them or route around them, much as the Internet does today with data traffic. An array of smart grid meters at homes and offices will enable interactions with users—balancing of the grid won't just happen by generating more power; balancing might also happen by reducing demand for brief stretches. Power will be able to flow in both directions, from where there is more to where it is needed, rather than have a few central plants generate all the power.

But, to get us to a twenty-first-century grid, utilities will need to be superb at system integration. At the moment, the average utility collects about 60 million data points each year—5 million customers and a dozen monthly bills. When smart meters come into widespread use, the average utility may have to handle 5 billion data points every day. The grid will need almost to be redesigned from scratch to get the full benefit of the new types of transformers, the capability to sense problems and solve them automatically, the ability to essentially have little power plants on millions of rooftops as solar prices keep coming down, and so on. Yet, utilities will have to integrate all the potentially beneficial new technologies in an environment where simply installing a sensor on the network can require shutting down for a disruptively long and expensive stretch.

Utilities will need to start by recognizing the extraordinary scope of the challenges and opportunities in front of them. They'll need to ask themselves tough questions at every step. Has the company evaluated all the opportunities to embed software? Is the company involving suppliers actively in evaluating design alternatives? What will it take to create the

---

20 Essentially, utilities will be following the path that computers have already taken. When the first computers were built, beginning toward the end of World War II, they were a rat's nest of wires, used thousands of vacuum tubes, and were the size of a large room. For early military versions, soldiers stood around the room, ready to replace the vacuum tubes as soon as they burned out. Beginning in the 1960s, computers started the transition to solid-state, with transistors etched into silicon. Today, chips routinely contain hundreds of millions of transistors. The switches and transformers that utilities use are the equivalent of WWII-era computer technology, but, thanks to the progress in the computer world since then, have the chance to make several decades of progress in one leap.

tools to evaluate cost, time, and value tradeoffs in design? How well does the new project plug into the global network? And so on.

Regulators will need to be partners on this journey with the utilities. Although regulators aren't known for being on the leading edge of innovation, and although most utilities are more than happy to simply collect a set rate of return on their investments, regulators must confront the scope of the transformation that the grid will go through in the next twenty years and start to map out how to get there from here.

To integrate all the aspects of the grid, utilities will need to invest heavily in software and control systems, or they'll be swamped. Only a very few utilities have a chief technology officer and a software-engineering department. Almost none have the kind of software team that is necessary to deliver the integrated hardware-software control routines that will manage a smart, data-intensive grid.

The good news is that many of the capabilities that utilities will need aren't new, even though they will be very unfamiliar to utilities. While utilities think in terms of millions of interactions with customers a year, not billions a day, cell phone companies know how to manage the volumes that utilities will be facing. Aerospace companies also know how to handle massive amounts of data in a dynamic system. Partnerships are waiting to be made.

Other countries can be good sources for new expertise, too. Renewable generation such as solar or wind power increased from 0.06 percent of total electric power in the United States in 1996 to 5 percent in 2013 without any noticeable impact on grid reliability, but there is uncertainty about how to keep increasing the percentage, given the fragmented U.S. regulatory structure and numerous transmission bottlenecks. American utilities could learn from Germany, where utilities are successfully drawing 36 percent of their power from renewables, on average, and more than 59 percent at peak times. State Grid in China has developed expertise on bringing power from generating centers in remote deserts to the coastal cities without significant losses of power.

Massive computational models will need to be developed for the new version of the grid to ensure that loads can be balanced, that the network can be protected from external attack, and that future changes to the network can be made as software upgrades, without having whole circuits taken down. As we've said, being able to place huge batteries throughout the grid can smooth out the generation of power and make utilities far more efficient—but no one has a basic model for how batteries would change the flow of power on the grid. And that's just the beginning of the long list of issues that aren't yet understood. Companies will need to be willing to experiment endlessly to get the full benefits of switching from a model like the phone network of the 1940s, with its armies of operators, to a model like today's Internet.

Utilities and their suppliers will need to collaborate much more than they do now. Rather than do their own thing so much, every company that contributes to the grid needs to focus on developing standards so that every company, every piece of equipment, and every customer can communicate with every other person or device. Wireless communication wouldn't be a tenth as effective as it is now if telecom companies, makers of wireless routers, developers of phones and tablet computers, and others had all pursued their own approaches to transmitting signals. The magic of Wi-Fi is that standards were established early on so that every person and device can talk to every other person and device. Sometimes, standards simply emerge, as when VHS bested Betamax and became the standard for VCRs. Sometimes, the government sets standards, as happened with the Internet. Oftentimes, though, it's important to have people go through the drudgery of engaging with dozens of other companies and agreeing on standards. It's no fun, but it's important—that approach is what gave us Wi-Fi: An industry-wide group of engineers has worked for years to develop the 802.11 standards.

Electric utilities will also need to coordinate with one another and with other types of utilities in planning, capital upgrades, and scheduling. Much of the instability in the U.S. electric grid comes from two types of problems: trees that bring down lines in storms and bottlenecks in transmission or distribution capacity at jurisdictional boundaries. The first problem is relatively simple to solve: Move the lines underground, as Japan and much of Europe have done. The challenge in the United States is not a technical one but a financial one; putting lines underground is expensive. But collaboration could solve this problem. While living in New York City, Stefan watched his street being dug up by Con Edison, the local electric utility. Then the Department of Transportation repaved the streets, only to have Verizon rip them up again to lay optical fiber and harden its infrastructure after Hurricane Sandy. Moving lines underground wouldn't be expensive if optical fiber, telephone, power, and cable television could all be laid together in a conduit and the street repaved a single time. New York has tried to achieve this coordination by putting a five-year moratorium on underground permits for tearing up streets that were just repaved, but this approach clearly still falls short of syncing up maintenance and improvement plans across utilities.

The same lack of coordination afflicts all the different bodies that produce and distribute electricity. Currently, each utility develops its own capacity plan, and there are more than 3,000 electric utilities in the United

Growth of new data generated by the smart grid

Data generated annually

800 TB

New devices in home enabled by the Smart Meter

Behind the meter

Programmable communicating thermostats come online at scale

600 TB

Advanced distribution automation

Distribution management rollout

Outage management system upgrade

400 TB

Geographic information system deployment

On the grid

Remote terminal unit upgrade

200 TB

Mobile data goes live

START

Substation automation system

Workforce management project

Advanced metering infrastructure deployment

States alone—200 large ones and the rest owned by communities or municipalities. Independent System Operators (ISOs) plan transmission capacity in many markets, but there are dozens of those, as well. In addition, the eastern half of the country, the West, and Texas are not connected; they operate effectively separate grids. Many municipalities run their own power grid, only partly connected to the rest of the state and region.

Balancing the grid becomes much easier and less expensive if coordination happens over a larger area. Differences in wind, sunshine, and temperature can balance out. Simply linking different time zones can help to balance the grid, because daily peaks related to the workday, for instance, come at different times. Our modeling suggests that if you operate a grid that is more than a few hundred miles across and has more than a thousand generation sources, even a mix of renewable energy sources—considered unreliable because the wind doesn't always blow and the sun doesn't always shine—begins to look as reliable as nuclear power plants.

Thousands of American utilities, regulated separately by utilities commissions in each of the fifty states, rarely look at whether coordinating with companies beyond their territory would make upgrades less expensive. The system is designed for shipping commodity electrons and ensuring reliability by systematically oversupplying—the so-called reserve margin where between 2 and 6 percent more power is contracted for than is required by loads in the grid. But the utility business and regulatory models will have to evolve.

SYSTEM INTEGRATION FOR ALL

While it may be that no other industry faces quite the challenges of system integration that confront the grid, the same emphasis will be needed in countless industries. Retailers will need to do a better job of keeping the right sizes, styles, and colors on their shelves to boost sales and eliminate waste. Companies need to improve how they balance fleets of taxis and rental cars, putting the right vehicle in the right place at the right time. Hospitals must become much more efficient at handling patients with different symptoms, different conditions, and different doctors.

Already, Otis has developed a highly integrated approach to make its elevators operate as efficiently as possible. Each elevator talks to the central

Otis Elevator Company founder Elisha Graves Otis (1811–1861) demonstrates his safety mechanism at the Crystal Palace in New York City in 1853.

service center, not only reporting error messages but also reporting usage hours, cable wear, and waiting times between when buttons are pushed and when elevators arrive, so that the system can use these inputs to improve service. Otis software can reprogram the default position for empty elevators so that they go to the lunch floor of a building between noon and, say, 2 p.m., rather than wait on the ground floor as they do first thing in the morning. The information also flows the other way: Service personnel at the control center can address many elevator issues remotely, can shut off a floor for construction, and can even quickly rescue people who are trapped in an elevator because of an outage, without ever coming to the building.[21]

GE demonstrates the crucial benefits from system integration that are available at many companies. It decided to manufacture some energy-efficient water heaters in Louisville, Kentucky, bringing production back from China in 2012. That was partly to reduce shipping costs, partly to take advantage of the low electricity costs that the shale oil and gas revolution has provided, and partly to cut the time it takes to turn an order into a water heater in the back of a contractor's truck in the United States. It used to take four weeks to ship a water heater from China to the United States, then another week to clear customs; today, the time from factory to warehouse is thirty minutes. When manufacturing took place in China, GE design engineers simply produced the specs and let the outsourcer worry about how to make it.

---

21 Otis has been working on system integration for a long time. In the Loma Prieta earthquake that hit San Francisco in 1989, the control center knew instantly that an earthquake had hit, because every elevator in the city simultaneously demanded maintenance.

Once manufacturing came back in-house, GE's designers, engineers, manufacturing experts, line workers, and sales and marketing staff all got together. They realized that the existing design required a tangle of copper tubing that meant lots of difficult welds and that created reliability and maintenance challenges for field service. GE completely revised the design. In the process, GE reduced materials costs by 25 percent and cut manufacturing time from ten hours in China to two hours in the United States. Even though wages here are so much higher than in China, the water heater made in the United States retails for almost 20 percent less than the one from China. Quality is up, too, because those difficult welds were designed out, so the number of repairs covered by warranty have dropped. Based on the early successes that have come from an integrated approach to design and manufacturing, GE is spending $800 million to expand its appliance manufacturing in Louisville.

In 2008, ArcelorMittal "twinned" an underperforming steel plant in the United States with a state-of-the-art facility in Ghent, Belgium, and made remarkable strides by bringing the plant in Burns Harbor, Indiana, up to the Belgian plant's standards for system integration. The plant in Indiana did away with its old system of phone calls, paper, and brainpower and installed sensors and computerized control systems. The system tells workers when to pour iron into ladles, when to mix in alloys, and when to cast steel into slabs. Workers were able to reduce the amount of steel they trimmed off the sides of coils by the equivalent of 17,000 cars a year. The mill has increased output by 20 percent because smoother processes mean fewer backups; backups cause steel to cool, and then the steel must be reheated—and, in steel, temperature is money.

The union rep at Burns Harbor says: "Steel working used to be 80 percent back and 20 percent brain. Now it's the other way around." A *Wall Street Journal* reporter asked the plant manager if he'd one day be able to run the plant by himself with just an iPad. The reply: "That's an open question."

BUSINESS MODELS FOR THE FUTURE

As companies work through complex integration issues, they will also have to be open to experimentation with their underlying business models. For instance, as more solar power is generated from the rooftops of homes and offices, utilities will need to be both big buyers and big sellers of power. The enormous costs of maintaining the grid will have to be distributed over significantly fewer kilowatt hours of use. Utilities will need to charge for backup capacity rather than kilowatts

Business models will, in general, require careful attention during the resource revolution. The core of the problem is one very similar to the innovator's dilemma described by Harvard professor Clayton Christensen. A company at the top of its game has accumulated a number of rules of thumb—implicit assumptions and beliefs about what has been central to its success. New technologies and business models belie or change some of those assumptions, but they only seem sensible if the management team can become aware of those implicit assumptions and mind-sets and suspend them for a moment to contemplate the change. It's very hard to do that with the inherited wisdom, experience, and lore of a company. This is why the failures of incumbents to capture the benefits of disruptive innovations are a result not of bad managers, but of good managers practicing what they have done best. Incremental innovations can quickly be scaled and incorporated. Disruptive innovations require changes in customer sets, business models, or performance metrics that are no longer consistent with what led to success in the past.

The issues in the resource revolution will be even more complex than those Christensen has described. His examples concern changes within one industry—for instance, the electric arc furnace and mini mills displacing the classic Linz-Donawitz steelmaking process. In the resource revolution, the landscape is much broader. Consumer electronics can disrupt the automotive market, for instance, by sparking innovations in batteries that could make electric vehicles a huge market. Cars might then disrupt utilities by becoming distributed storage throughout the grid—homes could run off cars directly or use batteries removed from cars, and download electricity at cheap rates overnight.

Silver Spring Networks, the leading provider of the sensors and software that make a smart grid possible, shows the kind of new business model that service providers will be able to deploy on top of the transformed electric grid. Service opportunities will be everywhere. The founders of Silver Spring Networks actually got their idea from supermarkets. While working on a supermarket project at Procter & Gamble, Eric Dresselhuys realized something fundamental about the bar code scanners at checkout lines. An intensive study showed that the scanners did not increase the accuracy or efficiency of the checkout process but were most helpful in the supply chain. The bar-code scanner readings enabled retailers to more accurately gauge customer demand and forecast and react to changes.

Dresselhuys applied this same logic to the grid. Silver Spring meters do not provide more accurate readings of individual electricity usage, but rather of the entire grid system. These meters allow utility companies to quickly know and respond when lines go out and help utilities anticipate and respond to changing loads on the grid. The ability to replace meter readers with automated systems pays for the installation of the new equipment, but the major impact is increasing grid reliability while decreasing the operating costs and capital requirements for the grid. During Hurricane Sandy, utilities with smart meters in place had fewer customer outages, and the outages were much shorter than those for utilities still using the traditional hunt-and-peck method for getting networks back on line.

Another start-up, AutoGrid, works with Silver Spring Networks to provide another layer to the new business model. AutoGrid uses the latest in data analytics and information technology to analyze smart-meter readouts, providing utility companies with comprehensive metrics on electricity use, allowing them to better prepare for changes on their grid.

C3 Energy takes the insights one step further. It was launched by Tom Siebel, who founded Siebel Systems in the mid-1990s and pioneered tools for sales force automation, before selling the company to Oracle in 2005 for $5.8 billion. C3 helps utilities use the massive amounts of information they are collecting to improve customer satisfaction, lower costs, and improve network performance. C3 has developed analytical tools that take real-time data from the utility network and produce a series of dashboards that prompt decisions by utility managers. For example, customer account managers now can look at the energy-use patterns of customers and provide very specific feedback to improve customer performance— the utility can call a big-box retailer and tell it that an air conditioner is still on even though a store is closed, or that fluctuations in the store's electricity usage mean a compressor on the AC is about to fail. C3's tools also enable operating managers to reduce the losses of electricity that come from the uneven increases and decreases in flows across the network—and cutting losses across the country from today's roughly 10 percent line to between 3 and 5 percent would be the equivalent of eliminating the need for dozens of power plants.

Opower, which we described in chapter two and which is building a successful business by using big data to encourage consumers to reduce their electricity consumption, also shows the power of new business models.

In the next chapter, on how to get innovations to scale, we'll examine the learning curves that shaped the lightbulb and LED markets. And in chapter seven, we'll look at one final, extremely effective example of a new business model: the innovations in financing for solar systems that have made them attractive to a mass market.

We will also see one additional element critical to success: timing. This can cut both ways. Companies can fail when consumers or governments aren't ready for a particular resource innovation. But large companies can also be upended by upstarts when they misjudge how quickly technology can evolve or how substitute technologies or business models can leapfrog to the state of the art.

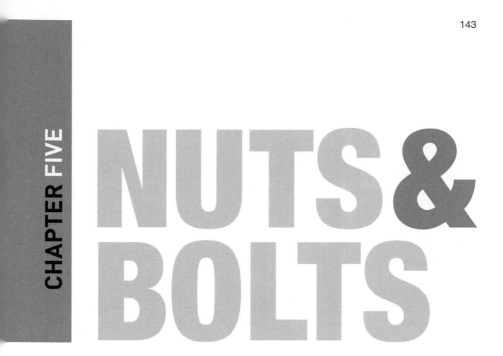

CHAPTER FIVE

NUTS & BOLTS

To get the most out of resource innovation, companies must focus relentlessly on system integration. That means:

INTEGRATING INDUSTRIAL EQUIPMENT into digital networks boosts throughput, yield, and efficiency.

STANDARDS FOR INTEGRATION ARE ESSENTIAL for ensuring network stability and increasing economic returns.

OPTIMIZING NETWORK PERFORMANCE. By understanding how the pieces in a network work together, efficiencies can be maximized.

MODELING OVERALL SYSTEM PERFORMANCE as much as possible, and coordinating with other participants in the system.

TESTING, TESTING, AND TESTING—nothing gets in the network unless it makes the other pieces better.

LOOKING AT NEW BUSINESS MODELS, integrating software and services with traditional equipment businesses.

CHAPTER SIX

TIMING IS EVERYTHING

Percy Spencer, an engineer at Raytheon Corporation, accidentally melted a chocolate bar in his pocket in 1945 as he stood near microwave radar transmitters that the Allies had used to track enemy aircraft during World War II. Companies were investigating commercial uses of military technology, and Spencer tested how other items would react to microwaves. He tried some corn kernels and created the world's first microwave popcorn. He also heated an egg, which dangerously exploded in a scientist's face. At that point, Spencer and his colleagues created a metal box to trap the high-density magnetic field created by a microwave, focusing energy on the liquid molecules in the food and limiting the collateral damage from the heat that built up. The Radarange was born.

But, at almost six feet tall and weighing 750 pounds, it cost $5,000 in 1947. It did not sell well. Five years later, Raytheon licensed the technology to Tappan Stove Company, which marketed the device for roughly $1,295. That was still too expensive. Fast forward to 1967, when Raytheon bought Amana and marketed a countertop model for $495. That price opened the kitchen market for the first time, but a mass market didn't become possible until 1970, when a low-cost magnetron developed in Japan allowed prices of microwaves to fall to $300 and federal radiation safety rules reduced the public's sense of the risk of having a microwave in the house. Some 40,000 units sold in 1970, and sales soared to a million units a year by 1975. By 1986, when microprocessors had improved the control panel, more than 25 percent of American homes had a microwave—but it took four decades to go from those first kernels of microwave popcorn to a time when it could be popped in kitchens across the country.

Although many who write about innovation focus on the danger of being late to market, the Raytheon story shows that being too early can be painful, too.

Getting the timing right is extremely important in resource revolutions, even more so than normal. Markets can change suddenly if a surprise shortage occurs in some resource and prices skyrocket or if some innovation, such as shale oil and gas, solves a huge problem. Even when there isn't any particular surprise, the takeup of a new product can be so slow as to be almost unnoticeable, then surge once a threshold is passed in price or performance—almost no one bought a Radarange at $5,000, but, at $200, microwave ovens became a must for just about every household in the United States.

Enter the market too soon, and it won't know what to do with the innovation. Too late, and others will have locked up the market. The classic large company response of "buying the way in later" won't work when transitions are fast. The new entrant's valuation and multiples may make them too expensive to acquire.

To get the market timing right is both an art and a science. In this chapter, we'll focus on the science, the elements that a manager can, to a large extent, control. That science consists of three parts. First, when thinking about timing, it's crucial to be thinking about products that mark a breakthrough, not just incremental progress. The market will barely pay attention to incremental changes. Second, it's important to understand that change in demand will almost certainly come in a burst once a threshold is crossed. Third, it's crucial to start investing well before that threshold is likely to be hit, both to be prepared and to provide a margin for error in case the market shifts sooner than expected.

FINDING THE BREAKTHROUGH

In thinking about timing entry into a new market, price spikes or potential price spikes can indicate an area where innovation is sorely needed. The normal analysis needs to show that the market is sufficiently large and that a company or a product can gain sustainable competitive advantage over the existing product. But when technologies are changing rapidly, a new product can't just beat the current state of the art—it has to be 50 to 80 percent better.

That improvement could just be in terms of price, as occurred with shale gas, when it took the price from $12 per thousand cubic feet down to less than $3. But that sharp improvement could also be based on some combination of price and performance—slashing total cost of ownership over the life of the product, helping the purchaser generate revenue, and so on. The iPod actually cost more than the Walkman it was replacing, but it was more portable, more reliable, and more flexible and had dramatically more content easily available for play.

Asking for a 50 to 80 percent improvement may seem to be too ambitious. That's far more than is necessary in traditional endeavors. Geico has built a huge business on the prospect that customers willing to spend fifteen minutes answering questions might save 15 percent on car insurance. Part of that goal of 50 to 80 percent is margin of error, because shooting for rapid price declines increases uncertainty; and part stems from the fact that competitors will get 3 percent to 5 percent improvement in their products every year, or sometimes 10 percent to 15 percent improvement every generation, each of which might last a few years (which is mathematically the same). Most disruptive technologies take a couple of years to adopt, so it takes a step change of at least 50 percent to really make a new technology superior to refined versions of the old. Just getting 10 percent better than the current best practice is not enough. Also, from the customers' point of view, adopting a new technology involves risk, and customers require that the payoff be big enough.

In fact, sometimes 50 to 80 percent isn't a big enough improvement. In an industry that can draw on semiconductor technology, for instance, companies sometimes brag about being able to deliver a threefold improvement in four and a half years—but Moore's Law does at least that with just about all semiconductor technology.

Even without semiconductors, resource-based industries can exhibit similarly extraordinary improvements in the early stages. The more general version of Moore's Law is called a learning curve—it measures the amount of cost reduction or performance improvement achieved over time as a function of the cumulative installed base. For managers to predict breakthroughs and judge their timing, it is essential to understand which technologies have steep learning curves (i.e., are improving quickly) and when that learning curve suggests that a given technology will undercut an existing one to open up an improvement gap of 50 to 80 percent. For example, electricity cost some $5 per kilowatt hour in the late 1800s, while most people pay roughly 2 percent of that amount today; most of the progress came between 1890 and 1920.

The result is that it isn't enough to just be better than the competition; a new product has to be way better than the rivals'.

Numerous subtleties affect timing in a resource revolution. For one, rapidly falling prices can actually slow adoption. As consumers and companies debate whether to buy now or later, a perfectly rational response to plunging prices is to wait. Why buy today when the product will be much cheaper in six months? This issue has hurt solar, among other technologies. Solar systems have a useful life measured in decades, and customers don't want to commit to systems now, given that prices are dropping so fast that systems will be much better in six months or a year. (As we'll see in chapter seven, there are ways to get customers to commit now, but they require new business models.)

In addition, when consumers consider adopting a new technology, they won't necessarily do so even if it's clearly better. They want to see multiple options, to increase their comfort, and be sure they can find the version of a product that is just right for them. While many people have expressed disappointment in the early sales of electric vehicles (Tesla aside) and have cast aspersions on the technology, the real issue is that consumers simply aren't ready, given the limited number of brands and models available and given the uncertainty about commitment by manufacturers. When the Prius was the only hybrid option on the market, the demand was constrained, but, with some sixty-five electric and hybrid models on the market for fall 2013, the opportunity for consumers to find the car they want with electric or hybrid drive has expanded dramatically. Once more brands—including the German car makers, with their great engineering, and the Korean companies, with their paradigm of high quality and affordability—reach the market, demand for EVs and hybrids should expand. As a result, even though a linear extrapolation would have electric cars account for less than 10 percent of sales by 2020, it is equally likely that 50 to 60 percent of the new cars sold will be electric or hybrid.

Speed of market penetration for new innovations

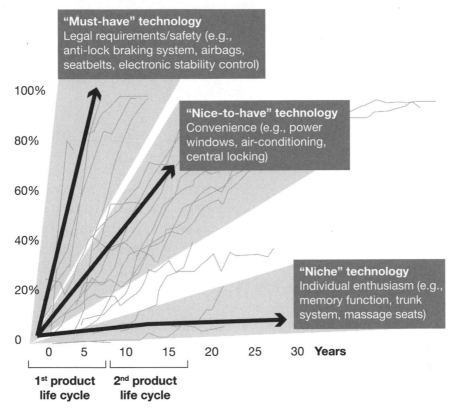

Auto technology adoption curves
Market penetration (percent)

Consumers aren't always rational, either, when considering a new technology. Even if there is a great payback on an investment, they may be put off by higher up-front costs. Up-front cost has been an issue with electric cars, with LED lighting, and with many other new technologies. Generally, if a payback can't be provided in less than two years, consumers and many companies won't be interested.

Looking at decades of data on the car industry shows that, if something is required by regulation, it still takes a decade to be fully adopted; if something is 50 percent better than what it replaces, it takes fifteen years to achieve 80 percent adoption by consumers.

Beyond understanding the customer's desires and behavior, it's important to look across the board—at the supply chain, at the retail channel, and at any government regulations. Energy efficiency products show what can happen when a technology is mature but the supply chain and regulations don't line up. Many such products reached cost effectiveness long ago. They generally pay for themselves within two to seven years. But supply chain issues hold back demand—many aren't in stock at, for example, Home Depot, and contractors often aren't familiar with the products.

CROSSING THE THRESHOLD

Sometimes, it's hard to think about a threshold because the technology isn't there yet. The problem to be solved is still in the basic-science stage; it hasn't reached the engineering world. In such situations, it's crucial to not zero in on a single solution, because it's too hard to identify which one will produce results. Instead, the right approach is to keep applying pressure at numerous points, until something clicks.

With agriculture, the market is ready for innovation—and then some. The Green Revolution produced major gains, with the fertilizer revolution at the beginning of the twentieth century and then, starting in the 1960s, better seed technologies and improvements in irrigation. But those gains have now run their course, and far more is needed to feed the billions who will enter the middle class by 2030 and who will want not only more food, but better food. The prospect of widespread water scarcity compounds the pressure on agriculture to produce productivity breakthroughs.

As a result, Beyond Meat and other start-ups are attempting to essentially reinvent beef and chicken. They have come up with ways to grow crops that provide the same protein but in a way that is several times more efficient in terms of land, water, and production. It takes 2,000 gallons of water and fifteen pounds of feed to produce a pound of beef. Getting the texture and smell to match the real thing is tricky, but Bill Gates, among others, has written that he was fooled in a taste test between Beyond Meat's chicken substitute and real chicken. His seems to be a

Protein prices

Commodity wholesale price per kg of protein
USD/kg

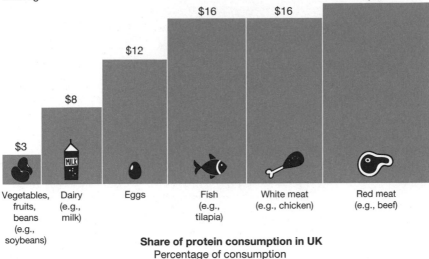

Vegetables, fruits, beans (e.g., soybeans)	Dairy (e.g., milk)	Eggs	Fish (e.g., tilapia)	White meat (e.g., chicken)	Red meat (e.g., beef)
$3	$8	$12	$16	$16	$18

Share of protein consumption in UK
Percentage of consumption

minority opinion at this point, but the substitutes could certainly start finding their way into highly processed forms, such as chicken nuggets. Pronutria, a start-up in Cambridge, Massachusetts, hopes to dispense with food itself, in many cases, and deliver nutrients into the body in pure form. The company is working on what might be called medical food: purified forms of amino acids that have medical benefits, including preventing cardiovascular disease.

Even when technology has passed out of the basic-science stage and into the world of engineering, it's still easy to be wrong about how quickly adoption will occur. When the federal government first starting pushing the idea of solar power, in the 1970s under President Carter, electricity from solar cost twenty-two times as much as power from the grid. Businesses jumped into the market, but there was no way, even with subsidies, that solar made sense as a significant source of power. Carter had solar panels put on the roof of the White House, but that was an empty gesture. Almost no customers followed, and Ronald Reagan had the solar panels removed.

Pace of new technology adoption

Percent of population to adopt in U.S.

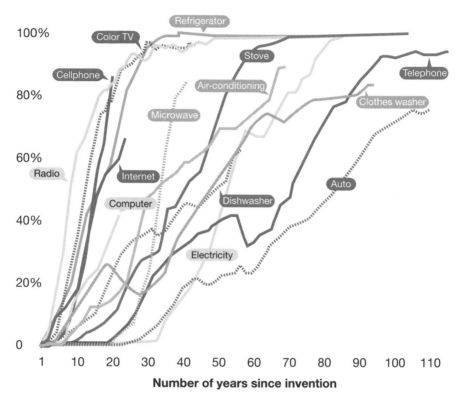

INVESTING EARLY

Because of the uncertainty, a rule of thumb is to start investing two product cycles before a product will likely hit the mass-market threshold by providing that 50 to 80 percent improvement, achieving customer readiness, etc. Product cycles vary: Phones are on about a six-month product cycle, while cars are still on a seven-year cycle. But investing at least two product cycles in advance provides some room for error in timing the market, builds important product manufacturing experience, and begins to develop brand recognition. Investing at that point also provides time to work out the kinks that invariably appear with a radically new product.

The history of lighting, leading up to the LED, shows both how long some time frames can be for new technologies and yet, how their progress must be continually mapped out and tracked.

FROM SWAN AND EDISON TO THE LED

Joseph Swan patented the electric lightbulb in the United Kingdom in 1869, and Thomas Edison commercialized the new technology in the United States in 1879. The electric lightbulb represented a revolution in productivity, extending the work day and enabling study at night, increasing urban safety dramatically through street lighting, and extending downtown business hours. The lightbulb prolonged human eyesight by years by providing enough light to read by at night and extended lives by taking the soot of gas and kerosene light sources out of the air in the standard home.

The economics of the lightbulb were dramatic. In ancient times, it took 160 days of work to buy an hour of light from an oil lamp—artificial light was the province of kings. By 1800, the development of paraffin candles meant that an hour of light at night cost two days of labor at standard wages—light was the province of the rich. In the latter half of the 1800s, coal, gas, and kerosene made lighting a middle-class privilege—two hours of daylight work could buy one hour of light at night. Then the incandescent lightbulb made the technology ubiquitous: By 1950, eight seconds of work could buy an hour of light at night, and today it costs only half a second of work to buy an hour of

Thomas Edison (1847–1931) in 1915 with his Edison Effect bulb, the precursor of modern electronics.

light. Some 300,000 lamps were sold in 1885; roughly 1.5 billion bulbs were sold in 2010.

But the incandescent lightbulb is, in fact, a very inefficient technology. Roughly 95 percent of the electricity that goes into a bulb is emitted as heat, not light. With a traditional dimmer, the bulb still consumes the same amount of electricity; it's just that more energy is emitted as heat and less as light. So much heat is emitted by lightbulbs that a commercial building devotes some 5 percent of its energy usage to getting rid of the heat that the building produces simply through lighting.

In addition to the heat problem, lightbulbs don't last very long. With just moderate use, an incandescent bulb may last only two years. In some settings, such as factories and big stores, that short life can be a real problem, because changing a bulb can be disruptive and expensive. Changing a single bulb in a Walmart sign on a store's façade may require a crew and a cherry picker and cost hundreds of dollars. Changing a single streetlight similarly costs hundreds of dollars—and many cities are strapped for cash.

Looking at concerns about potential spikes in electricity prices, the industry could have seen for decades that better lighting represented a juicy opportunity for innovation. The market is huge, too—in addition to those billions of bulbs purchased each year, lighting consumes 12 percent of the electricity used in the United States, at a cost of tens of billions of dollars a year.

The problem has been that the technology wasn't ready. Managers made some progress with compact fluorescent bulbs, but, among their other shortcomings, compact fluorescents require toxic chemicals such as mercury and pose a disposal problem. Many consumers strongly dislike their slow response turning on, their double-helix shape, and their relatively blue light.

The answer, as has been clear for some years now, is the light-emitting diode, or LED. LEDs require only 10 percent as much electricity as incandescents to produce the same amount of light. LEDs generate almost no heat. LEDs can deliver much better color quality than both incandescents and compact fluorescents. They can integrate motion- and light-sensing features to ensure the lighting is just right for the working environment. They can last twenty to thirty years—in fact, they don't burn out; they just eventually dim. By 2030, LEDs could contribute to greater energy efficiency in buildings that could save 21 quadrillion BTUs annually. Those

Making light affordable

Total lighting output by source[1] (teralumen-hours per year)

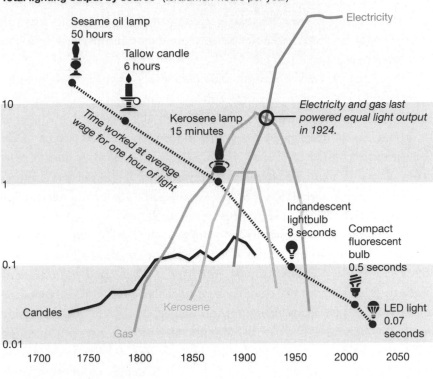

Sesame oil lamp
50 hours

Tallow candle
6 hours

Electricity

Kerosene lamp
15 minutes

Electricity and gas last
powered equal light output
in 1924.

Time worked at average wage for one hour of light

Incandescent
lightbulb
8 seconds

Compact
fluorescent
bulb
0.5 seconds

Candles

Kerosene

Gas

LED light
0.07
seconds

1 Based on United Kingdom data.

savings would be valued at about $100 billion per year based on today's commodity prices. But LED technology has taken more than a century to come into its own.

The LED traces its roots all the way back to Edison's lifetime, in 1907, when a scientist working on radio technology at Marconi Laboratories in the United Kingdom ran an electric current through a variety of substances and found that some semiconductors gave off light. By the 1920s, an LED had been produced; but semiconductors are complicated materials, and there wasn't a clear commercial application. Further breakthroughs didn't come until the electronics industry deepened its understanding of semiconductors in the 1950s and 1960s as it laid the groundwork for computing devices. When an engineer with General Electric produced an LED that emitted red light in 1962, LEDs began to show up in commercial settings, such as indicators on control panels. Early calculators used the LEDs because of their brightness and light weight. But utility was still limited, both because the light was only one color and because it was of very low intensity.

The industry faced two major challenges: make the LEDs brighter and learn how to make green and blue LEDs to complete the red-green-blue color spectrum that allows for every color in the palette. Light output improved as producers learned how to dope semiconductors. Green LEDs were invented in the 1980s, a breakthrough—thanks to evolution on a green planet, the human eye is several times more sensitive to green light than red. Finally, in the 1990s, Shuji Nakamura of Nichia did what many thought was impossible: He invented a blue LED.

This meant it was going to be possible to blend different colors and produce the entire visible spectrum. The advent of the blue LED also meant that LEDs could now produce the sort of white light that incandescents produce. It has been known since the days of Sir Isaac Newton that blending colors will produce white light; Newton managed to do so using just blue and yellow light. The Nichia LED also operated at high intensity, meaning LEDs were going to move out of control panels and into standard light fixtures. Haitz's Law, named for Roland Haitz of Agilent Technologies, holds that LEDs' cost per lumen of output will fall tenfold every decade—the lighting version of a learning curve.

LEDs are highly complex devices. In tiny packages, they must combine emitters of multiple colors, lenses, heat sinks, and a sort of buffer to protect the delicate electronics from any surges in voltage. So, early versions of LEDs were hard to produce and, thus, expensive. But once a blue LED was invented, LEDs stopped being a science problem and became an engineering problem, the kind that, while still difficult, is solved routinely by companies. LEDs were destined to have a major commercial impact.

This was the time when companies, seeing the prospect of far more than a 50 to 80 percent improvement, should have started looking for the threshold that had to be crossed to turn LEDs into a mass market and should have started investing—at least two product cycles ahead of time.

Not everyone noticed. GE, for instance, kept investing in its traditional incandescent business and was late to the transition. Founded by Edison, GE had built a lighting and appliance business that produced more than $12 billion of annual revenue and generated more than $1 billion of operating profit in the first decade of the new millennium, so the company was in no hurry to move to a new technology. Looking to its competitors, as opposed to the possibility of a surge in electricity prices, GE also saw no great reason to hurry; the market, with technology that had been mature for more than a hundred years, had narrowed to a handful of major companies, and they were all generally content with the status quo. GE researchers also thought it would take LED technology many years to migrate from niche technology to general lighting.

When Cree successfully launched an LED lighting business, GE considered selling its lighting business, but the Great Recession of 2008 derailed the plan. When the economy had recovered enough that a buyer might have emerged, the technology had moved on from incandescents. GE's lighting business has declined steadily, and its lighting and appliance business as a whole has shrunk by about a third from the mid-2000s. So, even though LEDs today account for only about 2 percent of the market, GE has found no takers for the incandescent business.

The United States and many state governments have also been behind the curve. California invested hundreds of millions of dollars annually to promote the use of compact fluorescents in recent years, even though it's been clear that LEDs would be a much better solution. The federal government takes more than a year to approve new LED technology, whose product cycle is only six months; in other words, by the time new technology reaches the market in the United States, it is already obsolete in other parts of the world.

Utility regulators will also find themselves facing problems because they aren't factoring in how LEDs will decrease energy use. In the United States, LEDs could account for 80 percent of lighting by 2020. Switching to LEDs could mean a 1.5 percent decline per year in electricity consumption, eliminating the need for 30 power plants annually and cutting annual spending on electricity by $25 billion by the end of the decade. Yet regulatory models for electricity consumption assume a steady increase in demand. When customers can increase their use of lighting services without increasing their demand for electricity, the traditional utility model could face difficult times.

Once change comes to a resource revolution market, it can come fast.

Meanwhile, small companies such as Cree seized the opportunity that the incumbents left sitting on the table. Founded as Cree Research in 1987, the company initially was a technology player and sold silicon wafers to other technology companies for use in their LEDs. Six years later, the company had just thirty employees. But Cree recognized the importance of Nichia's blue LED and soon followed with its own blue capabilities. Cree developed its own lightbulbs because supply chains were not ready to make lightbulbs from the Cree base materials and because the lighting solutions on offer tended to be poorly designed for real operating environments. Partly because of the expense of LEDs, the market wasn't ready for wholesale replacement of incandescent bulbs. But Cree went ahead and invested in the technology anyway, to be ready when the market hit the steep slope of the adoption curve.

Cree chose its early customers carefully. It focused on overhead lighting, where the fact that LEDs emit light in a straight line like a laser, rather than glowing like an incandescent bulb, wasn't a problem. Cree worked with industrial customers, for whom the savings on replacement costs outweighed the high costs of the bulbs. Based in North Carolina, Cree also drew lean manufacturing and system integration expertise from the textile mills that dot the landscape around Durham. Lean manufacturing expertise has made Cree so efficient, even with such high-tech devices, that it has consistently been able to sell bulbs for less than its competitors. The company's annual sales now top $1.4 billion, and prospects are so rosy that the market has awarded Cree a $7.5 billion valuation.

LEDs still have a ways to go because of consumer adoption issues. Today LEDs cost about $8 to $12 apiece at Home Depot, versus perhaps sixty cents for an incandescent, and consumers have first-cost sticker shock. But prices are falling so fast that LEDs will soon hit $4 to $6 apiece, and consumers, at that point, should make the switch in a flurry. Because LEDs use 90 percent less electricity than incandescents, they will pay for themselves in a year or less. And, because the costs are driven by Moore's and Haitz's laws, the LEDs should cost less than a dollar by 2025, at which point every home will want dozens.

The other benefits, while not highly valued by consumers, will help make the argument that LEDs are a no-brainer for businesses—the tenfold increase in the lifetime of a bulb, the lack of heat, and so on. Many offices have already switched to LEDs to save on air-conditioning,[22] and cities, factories, hotels, and large stores have also made the change because of the maintenance savings. Moreover, LEDs are expanding rapidly in many consumer applications—great LED TVs, handheld devices, computer screens, LED headlights and brake lights in cars, and LED billboards. All are combining to drive down LED prices and improve LED performance at a rapid clip.

Once the switch to LEDs occurs, it will fundamentally shift the market dynamics for manufacturers as the long life of the bulbs slashes the number of new bulbs needed each year—when a homeowner replaces a two-year bulb with a twenty-year bulb, the turnover rate falls by 90 percent. When Vice President Joe Biden and then Energy Secretary Steven Chu visited Cree headquarters in 2010 to announce that Cree had won a grant for advanced clean-technology manufacturing as part of the American Recovery and Reinvestment Act, Chu made his staff nervous because he insisted on writing up his own remarks, but he won the crowd with a lightbulb joke. "How many people does it take to screw in an LED?" Chu asked. "Zero. Grandma screwed it in twenty years ago, and it's still working."

As will be the case with numerous other technologies that spread in the resource revolution, the switch to LEDs will actually just be the beginning of the opportunity for managers. The economics will drive the changeover, but LEDs aren't just cheaper incandescents; they come with a whole new set of capabilities.

Because LEDs are based on semiconductors, they can be easily controlled by software. They can be dimmed automatically, based on sensors that monitor the amount of light that is needed to augment what is coming through windows. LED lighting with appropriate sensors can improve building safety by detecting fires, whether people are in the building, etc. They can adjust color for time or mood. Indeed, software-driven LED

---

22 LEDs' lower heat output does have one disadvantage—LED lightbulbs in traffic signals do not burn off snow as rapidly as their incandescent counterparts, requiring new traffic signal designs in cold climates to avoid snow buildup.

packages can integrate with the grid, allowing for small reductions in demand to balance load as the system requires. That change will reduce capital requirements for the grid and improve its resilience.

Organic versions of LEDs will allow for flexible forms of lighting. The color spectrum from LEDs is much wider than from incandescent or fluorescent bulbs, offering even more opportunities for creative thinkers. Each LED bulb can easily be given its own IP (Internet protocol) address and can be controlled individually. Already, companies are marketing apps that can change the colors that LED bulbs emit and, perhaps, create a light show in the family room.

So, while there are still some market acceptance issues for LEDs to work through, it should have been clear to all concerned for quite some time that the future for lighting is, well, bright—as well as dynamic and multicolored.

Thus, there will be plenty of opportunities to sell services that build on the success of LEDs, and companies should be thinking now about how to develop them so that they don't miss out, as GE did. There will be opportunities to sell software that manages the lights to increase productivity in an office, security systems that use data from sensors in the bulbs, software that provides variable light displays, and more. The overall lighting market could go from rapidly shrinking to rapidly expanding in the course of less than a decade.

The key will be to explore and develop the new attributes from LEDs and not just assume they will be a straightforward substitute. It's these new attributes that can make a market extraordinary and define a market leadership position for the next century. To take advantage, managers need to be forecasting when the mass market threshold will be reached for whatever product or service related to LEDs they intend to offer. They need to be constantly updating those forecasts, using the latest performance information to keep them relevant in what will be a fast-changing market. Then, managers must integrate the new technology into the product line two cycles before the threshold is expected to be reached.

Likewise, industries that will be affected by the spread of LEDs also need to be preparing now and getting ready to invest two product cycles before LEDs reach whatever thresholds will matter to them. Utilities, in particular, need to be preparing for a sharp fall in the need for electricity for lighting. Builders should be getting ready both for the new capabilities that LEDs will allow and for a reduction in the need for air-conditioning that gets rid of the heat from lights. Regulators should be preparing, too, because once LEDs hit whatever the magic price turns out to be, consumers are going to change their behavior almost overnight.

In the next chapter, we'll explain how to prepare the market and how to bring production to scale, to take full advantage of that magic spot on the adoption curve where demand starts heading almost straight up.

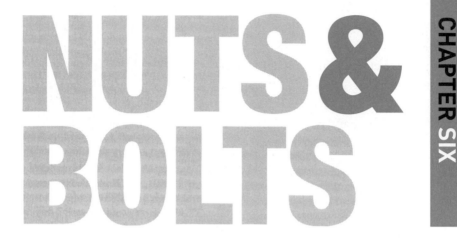

SUCCESS IN A RAPIDLY CHANGING MARKET requires getting the timing right.

UNDERSTANDING LEARNING CURVES is essential in order to predict the disruptive potential of new technologies. By quantifying learning curves, managers can identify the threshold where a product goes from being an incremental luxury good to something every customer wants.

THIS USUALLY REQUIRES A 50 TO 80 PERCENT IMPROVEMENT in cost and performance in comparison with incumbent technologies—just getting a little ahead is not enough to drive substitution.

MANAGERS SHOULD SCALE THEIR PRODUCT when economics allow something like a two-year payback period—if the period is longer, the market will spend time on other products.

INVESTMENT SHOULD BEGIN TWO PRODUCT CYCLES before the mass-market threshold is expected to be reached.

THE MAJOR SUCCESS OCCURS when the new attributes for the product become apparent, moving beyond just substitution.

CHAPTER **SEVEN**

MAKING IT MATTER: SCALING AND COMMERCIALIZATION

SOLAR POWER GOES BACK AT LEAST to the ancient Egyptians, who used pools of water to capture solar heat during the day and then ran the water through pipes to heat their homes at night. The Romans used mica-and-glass windows to capture solar heat in their homes and in greenhouses—the warmth of the sun mattered so much that the sixth-century Justinian Code specified that every individual had "sun rights." But when the Dark Ages set in, most technological innovation ceased. The understanding of solar power barely progressed until the nineteenth century, when Heinrich Hertz discovered that electrodes produced a stronger spark in the presence of ultraviolet light, a phenomenon that is now known as the photoelectric effect and that would eventually become the technological basis for today's solar panels.[23]

Scientists still had little idea about the cause of the photoelectric effect until the beginning of the twentieth century, when Albert Einstein published a paper on it. Einstein, a twenty-six-year-old freshly minted PhD, had been unable to find a faculty position but still decided to tackle what he considered to be some interesting problems, while working as a patent clerk. In 1905, during perhaps the most impressive stretch of hard

---

23 Technically, Alexandre-Edmond Becquerel discovered the closely related photovoltaic effect even earlier, in 1839, while working with solutions of silver chloride. But, because he was using a liquid, his work did not lead to useful devices. Charles Fritts built the first solid-state solar cell in 1883 by coating selenium with extremely thin layers of gold, but it converted less than 1% of sunlight to electricity and was not a practical device.

thinking in the history of hard thinking, Einstein published five papers, the most important of which was on the photoelectric effect and the nature of photons, the particles that make up light.[24] Prominent scientists, including Niels Bohr and Max Planck, disputed Einstein's description of the behavior of photons for years, but experimental evidence kept supporting Einstein, and his theory became widely accepted by 1920.

At that point, the scientific basis for solar energy had been established, but little progress occurred for more than three decades. Solar technology remained a lab technology, not ripe for commercial use, until the photoelectric and photovoltaic effect crossed several times with another technology that has dramatically shaped the last fifty years: yes—semiconductors and the transistors and integrated circuits built on them.

Semiconductors get their name because current can flow through them at certain temperatures and voltages, but not others. William Shockley, John Bardeen, and Walter Brattain used the sometimes-conductive nature of germanium to build the first transistor at Bell Labs in December 1947. Russell Ohl had already used the same property, in silicon, to let sunlight generate voltage when hooked up to a circuit or electrical device. He patented a silicon solar cell in 1946. Bell Lab scientists further developed Ohl's basic solar cell, and, by 1954, reached 6 percent efficiency—meaning that 6 percent of the energy in the sunlight was being converted into electricity. By 1960, efficiency reached 14 percent at Bell Labs, fully thirty times the efficiency of two decades earlier. Cells were still extremely expensive, but they could finally provide useful amounts of electricity—more than a hundred volts and several amperes of current. (A car headlight draws about five amperes.) Solar power was finally ready to emerge from the lab.

After the Soviets launched Sputnik in 1957, the United States went into technological overdrive, feeling that it needed to launch a satellite of its own as soon as possible. One prescient scientist, Hans Ziegler, argued

---

24 That, at least, was the judgment of the Nobel committee, which awarded Einstein the prize in physics in 1921 for that work. Among the papers deemed not as consequential was the one Einstein wrote on special relativity, which included the formulation $E=mc^2$, which became the basis for the development of nuclear energy. While writing his Nobel Prize–winning paper on the photoelectric effect, Einstein was passed over for promotion at the patent office because he had "not fully mastered" technology related to electrical signaling. Go figure.

Learning curve for solar innovation

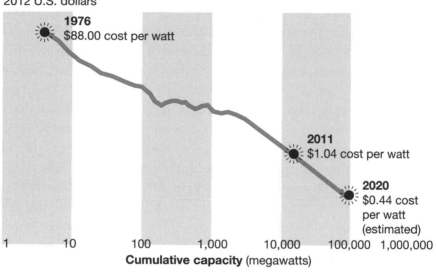

Solar cell module cost per watt
2012 U.S. dollars

1976
$88.00 cost per watt

2011
$1.04 cost per watt

2020
$0.44 cost
per watt
(estimated)

1   10   100   1,000   10,000   100,000   1,000,000
Cumulative capacity (megawatts)

that the United States should use solar power and got a solar cell designed into the Vanguard 1 satellite in 1958. The panel produced less than a watt of electricity, but that was enough, and the solar panel worked indefinitely, while the conventional batteries in the satellite died after a few months. By 1959, solar power had become standard for all new satellites because it provided the greatest lifetime power output per weight, and lifting even one pound of satellite into space cost more than $20,000. (Only recently has the cost dropped below $5,000 a pound.)

Solar had won its first geographic market: outer space. It wasn't much of a market, of course—plenty of territory but not an awful lot of customers.

IT ONLY MATTERS AT MASSIVE SCALE

As solar shows, resource productivity doesn't become relevant until it reaches massive scale. The world consumes roughly 1.3 trillion gallons of oil every year, along with 110 trillion cubic feet of gas, 17.6 trillion pounds of coal, and 2.4 trillion gallons of water. Resource challenges are denominated in billions and trillions. Any solutions must be able to scale.

But scaling new technologies is notoriously difficult. It's hard to move from the lab bench to the pilot to full-scale manufacturing. The rule of thumb is that every tenfold increase in the scale of manufacturing increases complexity by a factor of a hundred. Customers and businesses can be hard to budge—current technologies work just fine; any new technology may be more costly and less reliable; and, in general, consumers don't want to think about the resources they consume. Fitting disruptive new technologies into existing networks can be tricky—and trying to build new infrastructure to support an innovation can be even trickier. Even if everything else goes right, financing may still pose a major challenge. The amount of money required for resource productivity can be staggering. Having solar power replace a hundred 500-megawatt power plants (roughly one-sixth the total of those currently using coal in the United States) would cost $100 billion to $150 billion, even at today's low solar costs, and that figure doesn't take into account the expense of storing solar power for nighttime use.

To get innovation to scale, companies have to think explicitly about the problem. That may sound obvious, but many people miss this part. They focus so much on figuring out technology that they don't pay enough attention to whether it can operate at scale. Lots of things work on the lab bench but not in the factory or in the market. Even if something is truly cool, it doesn't count unless it can be done at the scale of billions and trillions.

Once they identify the issue, companies have to do three things to succeed:

- *Make it easy for customers to switch.* The personal energy required has to be low, and the benefit has to be obvious. There should also be an upside surprise—customers won't switch en masse if they're just being offered a variant on what has always been available.
- *Focus on the whole ecosystem.* This includes a hard look at manufacturing, which can be a thorny problem. It's not enough just to focus on a product; it's crucial to understand whether the supply chain can

provide the necessary commodities, parts, or services. It's necessary to figure out ahead of time how to sell and service a product.

- *Provide a committed champion,* the kind of leader who will stick with problems and carry an innovation all the way to market.

SEEING THE LIGHT

In the case of solar, even though the technology worked at useful scale by the 1950s, and even though a real market existed, solar stayed a space-only technology, more or less, for close to forty years. Solar was expensive, and the allure of "going green" wasn't strong enough to get people to spend so much.

The goal became "getting to planet Earth." NASA loved the technology, but NASA had highly idiosyncratic needs and large budgets, where cost per pound mattered more than cost per watt. There weren't any other NASAs out there. Almost no one else cared.

The second market for solar turned out to be buoys that measured and surveyed waters, plus offshore platforms owned by oil companies, which bought up most of the solar companies in the mid-1970s. But solar had a hard time spreading beyond these remote applications, and oil companies simply shut down many of their solar operations altogether when oil prices dropped after the Arab oil embargo ended and concerns about having alternate supplies of energy waned. So, solar had made it to planet Earth but was still stuck offshore.

This was when committed champions made their mark. Martin Green, a professor in Australia, had a breakthrough in the efficiency of the conversion of sunlight to electricity. T. J. Rodgers, the CEO of Cypress Semiconductor, and Dick Swanson, a professor at Stanford, founded SunPower in 1985 and stuck with the maker of solar cells through thick and thin. Rodgers financed the company out of his own pocket for a time.

As is often the case with resource productivity, breakthroughs on cost required that the problem be attacked from every side. Researchers experimented with every conceivable form of semiconductor. Engineers at Boeing and other firms used lenses to collect more sunlight and concentrate it on the solar cells or to split sunlight into different wavelengths and direct each color to the part of the cell that would most efficiently produce voltage. Engineers tried different shapes, such as cylinders, for the solar collection surface and experimented with nanomaterials with large surface areas to catch more sunlight. Motors and sensors were used to continually reposition solar panels and track the sun. Anything—and everything—to either produce more electricity or drive costs down.

Many countries got involved, too. German and Japanese companies invested throughout the 1990s, and the German Renewable Energy Act of 2000 kicked the solar market there into high gear by providing incentives for deployment of solar. These incentives did not pick a winning technology, but they offered a stable market with a twenty-year commitment that allowed private companies and capital to invest in technology that would take a few years to mature. The incentives were designed to decline gradually over twenty years, by which time solar should be below grid parity and be commercially attractive without subsidies.

Eventually, enough ideas succeeded that the cost of solar power has fallen from more than $3.30 a kilowatt hour in 1970 to less than $0.15 in 2013 and is headed to $0.06 in the next few years. (Power from the grid currently costs about $0.10 a kilowatt hour.) In many countries, solar is already one of the cheapest forms of power to build *without* subsidies. It's more cost effective than new nuclear, new coal plants, new oil plants, and new gas plants outside the United States (where shale gas has reduced power prices).[25]

But getting solar to dry land still required some serious focus on the whole ecosystem. It wasn't enough just to get the cost of the panels down. For instance, the universe of installers had to be developed. Utilities had to do some work so they could balance their systems despite the

---

25 What changed? Originally, solar cells were made on 4-inch round semiconductor wafers. Because those are 99.9999% pure—which the product needs because a single atom of contaminant can destroy the microprocessors—they were very expensive. But solar cells are much simpler devices than computer chips and are much more tolerant of manufacturing defects. So, solar cell makers switched to lower-purity silicon and also produced them on square wafers, which are easier to fit together into rectangular modules. Over a number of years, solar cell makers introduced several other innovations, including reducing cell thickness by more than 40% and roughening cell surfaces so that the ridges and valleys trap light instead of reflecting it like a mirror. (This is why most solar cells are dark blue or black rather than shiny like a silicon chip.) Manufacturers connected the wiring to string panels in the factory, rather than doing so in the field. These innovations have come together to give solar the fastest learning curve outside of Moore's Law—a 20% cost reduction with every doubling of the number of installed solar panels. There is still room for breakthroughs, and many companies are pursuing promising ideas.

Retail grid parity is here

- ● Residential power demand (2012); TWh/year
  O = 50 TWh/year
- Countries/states where best-in-class solar is currently economically competitive for some utility customer segments (i.e., small homes, large homes, commercial)
- Forecasted cost of residential solar PV system in 2020

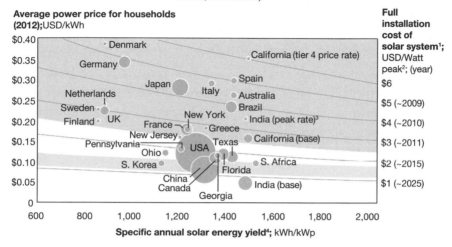

Average power price for households (2012);USD/kWh

Full installation cost of solar system[1]; USD/Watt peak[2]; (year)

$0.40 — Denmark — California (tier 4 price rate) — $6
$0.35 — Germany — $5 (~2009)
$0.30 — Japan — Spain — $4 (~2010)
$0.25 — Netherlands — Italy — Australia — $3 (~2011)
  Sweden — Brazil
$0.20 — Finland — UK — France — New York — India (peak rate)[3] — $2 (~2015)
  New Jersey — Greece
$0.15 — Pennsylvania — USA — Texas — California (base) — $1 (~2025)
  Ohio
$0.10 — S. Korea — Florida — S. Africa
  China
$0.05 — Canada — India (base)
  Georgia
0
600   800   1,000   1,200   1,400   1,600   1,800   2,000

Specific annual solar energy yield[4]; kWh/kWp

1 Cost to generate power with solar cells corresponding to solar intensity, using the following assumptions: 5% cost of finance, 25-year lifetime, 0.3% annual degradation, fixed O&M 1% of full installation cost; includes module, balance of system, and soft costs with margins. Soft costs also include customer acquisition costs and permit fees.

2 Watt peak measures solar output at noon sun intensity.

3 Only 2008 data available. Peak rate refers to rate without artificial cap imposed to close the peak power deficit filled by diesel generated power.

4 Amount generated by a south-facing 1 kWp module in 1 year (a function of solar intensity).

infusion of solar power. Utilities also had to change policy to enable "net metering," ensuring that customers would get credit for the electricity they contributed to the grid and only be billed for the net amount of electricity they used.

But the biggest change was in the mind-set and business model of how to deploy solar power—the siting, the ownership, and the financing. While some of today's utility-sized projects, such as those in the Mojave Desert, are certainly intriguing and will produce large amounts of power for the traditional grid, from a utility's point of view solar does not look as attractive as fossil fuel, nuclear, or hydropower. A fossil-fuel-based central station power plant isn't exactly a world beater—the percentage of energy in the fuel that is actually turned into electricity has remained relatively static for fifty years—but legacy technologies have been the basis of large capital projects that engineers know how to build and run. They allow a utility to assemble detailed documents and recover the cost of the large project. That's the one kind of marketing that utilities understand well: marketing to regulators at utility commissions. Solar is seen as risky and unreliable.

With utilities only signing up for solar when the regulator required it as part of a renewable mandate, some innovative companies began looking to sell directly to consumers, but there were problems there, too. Look at a typical homeowner. He wants the lights to go on and the air-conditioning to work during summer. He would like to save money if possible. But he may not care about green energy. He likely won't pay much to get it, rather than use conventional sources.

In some cases, using solar made economic sense for homeowners, especially with subsidies, but solar companies were asking consumers to make a decision that was simply too complex. Consumers were being asked to compare apples and kumquats. On the one hand were solar systems, where almost all the cost comes up front but where electricity is essentially free once the panels are installed. On the other hand was traditional power, which consumers purchase by the kilowatt hour for about eight to forty cents apiece, depending on the local rates. Consumers also faced the choice between a complex solar installation project on their roof and simply placing a phone call and flipping a switch for conventional energy.

The result of the comparison was predictable: The status quo won. "Customers are used to buying power, not a power plant," says Edward Fenster, one of the two CEOs at SunRun, a solar company based in San Francisco.

Because solar customers were being asked to pay up front—perhaps tens of thousands of dollars—no matter the economic argument, they just about always felt they had a better use for their hard-earned dollars. For good measure, consumers were being asked to make these comparisons on a subject that holds almost no interest for them.

As if those obstacles aren't high enough, there's even one more problem with selling to consumers, one that isn't as apparent: We call it the innovator's headwind. It stems from the fact that costs will continue to decline rapidly for solar. Even if solar is a good deal today, it will be a better deal in a year, so why not wait? This same problem shows up in consumer electronics, as we noted earlier, but the lifetime of those products is short enough that people tend to hesitate less. We all trade our phones in every two years and our TVs every seven years, but a solar system will last twenty-five years or more. Once someone buys one, that family really doesn't want to find out two years later that they could get 40 percent better performance for the same price.

To get over these hurdles, a few innovative solar companies finally turned the problem on its side. Rather than stubbornly trying to sell customers on the environmental benefits of clean energy or on long-term financial savings, they have reinvented their business models.

Companies like SunEdison, and a few years later SunRun and SolarCity, have found great success by taking a lesson from the automotive industry as well as one from their direct competitors, the electric utilities: These companies have gone from being makers of products to being providers of services. The breakthrough was to relieve the individual homeowner of the burden of ownership of expensive machinery. Just because our homeowner has a solar unit on the roof of his property doesn't mean he needs to own it. Instead, he's buying a service, sort of like leasing a car, except he's paying for electricity.

For consumers in markets with high retail electricity prices, like California, the incentive to switch is significant, and the profit for the solar companies is attractive. SunRun can put solar panels on a roof for the equivalent of $0.15 a kilowatt hour and charge the customer $0.25 a kilowatt hour. SunRun earns a 20 percent return on the capital it invests. Yet the customer saves $0.10 a kilowatt hour off the rate the utility would have charged him. That can add up to hundreds or even thousands of dollars a year—and he hasn't had to do anything other than switch where he sends his electronic payment each month.

SolarCity, SunEdison, and SunRun provide very little of the financing directly. Goldman, Wells Fargo, Bank of America, Google (through its investing arm), pension funds, and even Warren Buffett (through his insurance companies) are providing the capital. Because solar has turned out to be substantially less risky than initially estimated, the cost of this financing has dropped. Often, manufacturers guarantee the technology for 20 to 25 years; installations are becoming more standardized, and default rates on solar energy payments have proven to be modest, making solar an attractive return investment, especially while interest rates hover near historic lows.

The solar companies have had to figure out how to target the right home-owners, and it hasn't been cheap. The cost of attracting a customer can run to $5,000, which is often more than the cost of the panels that are installed. The companies currently focus on people who want to show off their house; who have AAA credit ratings and are used to financing mortgages, cars, and other luxury purchases; who often have elementary-school-age children; and who want to make a statement about their values. But the pitch isn't "put on a sweater and save the planet"; the pitch is "we guarantee a low rate, make the experience convenient, and improve resale value." Psychology and tactics make all the difference, as OPower (profiled in chapter two) learned with its "be better than your neighbor" approach.

Until solar companies developed the ability to narrowly target customers who were willing to buy, solar was going nowhere fast. Now, some solar companies have come up with strategies that break with tradition—the kinds of strategies that produce resource revolutions. A resource revolution doesn't just require great technology. It requires reaching the correct customer in the correct way.

Solar installations directly on top of buildings are now taking off in many parts of the country and will continue to do so, even without subsidies.

MAKING IT EASY FOR THE CUSTOMER

The problem that solar faced is so familiar among companies that make breakthroughs in technology that there is a name for it in Silicon Valley: "crossing the chasm." The term, coined by author and consultant Geoff Moore, has been a touchstone for a generation of Silicon Valley start-ups. He refers to the gap between early adopters and the mass market as a chasm and says crossing it is the key challenge.

Innovators can be deceived into thinking they've found their market quickly—there are enough hard-core believers in a green technology like solar that the initial uptake for a new product can be swift. But in our experience that segment is at most 10 to 15 percent of the population, so achieving mainstream acceptance means appealing to people who couldn't care less that the power they use is green. Concerted efforts are required to get costs down enough to appeal to a broad audience and to select which initial markets to develop as a way of creating a foothold on the far side of the chasm.

Resource technologies, it turns out, are especially susceptible to this struggle. Rene White and Steve Kimball of Moore's Chasm Group, who have worked extensively with traditional tech companies in Silicon Valley and, more recently, with resource tech companies, said that companies focused on resource productivity face two daunting problems when bringing innovations to market.

For one, product cycles are longer than for other businesses built on innovation, which means adoption cycles are longer, too. High-tech leaders are accustomed to rapid turnover of products—think about how often a new iPhone comes out. This allows for new products to enter the market quickly. If customers buy a new phone every year, then there are more opportunities to sell them a new phone and break into the market. Conversely, look at the challenge facing solar. Until recently, power generation was only done by utilities, and power plants last for decades. Electricity demand is growing slowly, so there is little need for additional plants. Because existing technologies have worked well for a hundred years, those in the energy and industrial sectors are not accustomed to thinking about innovation—many utilities have shut down their R&D departments.

The same logic applies across the industrial sector. As White and Kimball describe the situation, the people who should purchase resource technologies are the least likely to think innovatively enough to buy them.

The second problem is that the energy and industrial companies that tend to develop resource technologies do not have experience in connecting with the psychology of their consumers to create appealing products. In other words, not only are the purchasers of resource-related technology less likely to think innovatively, the companies creating and marketing these technologies are not used to factoring consumer preferences into their efforts.

The problem often occurs in the very conception of what the product does, how it should look, and what audience it is being created for, and extends equally to marketing. In the case of solar and other alternative energies, providers often go to market via utilities, which are notoriously poor at marketing. Many still talk about how many "meters" or "rate payers" they have rather than speaking of users or consumers. Because technologies change so little in the energy industry, till now there has been no need to understand customers' desires.

White and Kimball say that "enterprise buyers [B2B] are often just as emotional in their purchases as are [individual] consumers." In other words, big-scale energy and industrial purchasers want that same cool-product appeal in their purchases as do the rest of us when we buy the latest mobile phone. But when is the last time anyone marketed a sexy solar panel?

So getting to market with an innovation, already difficult in traditional technology, is that much more difficult for resource technology.

As solar shows, there is also a need to remove what economists call capital intensity from the equation (e.g., finance the up-front cost through a bank). Resource revolution technologies often are more capital-intensive than traditional products. If not explicitly addressed, this capital intensity can impede adoption. As we saw in chapter six, LEDs are already cheaper over their 25,000-hour lives than incandescents, both because LEDs last so long and because they consume some 90 percent less electricity—but who wants to pay $25 for a lightbulb? Consumers have shown that they'll only consider investments with a one- to two-year payback, and businesses, even though they should be more rational, take the same view or just a slightly longer view of resource-productivity investments. While we have seen companies make investments with a four-year payback, very few will make clean-tech or disruptive technology investments that generate returns in seven years or more, even though many of them do so routinely in their core business when launching major product investments or building manufacturing plants.

As the solar industry learned, it's also crucial to conform to consumers' deeply ingrained expectations, even while subtly altering the entire landscape. Backward-compatibility does not end when, on the most basic level, each company makes sure that the new plug fits into the old socket. Backward-compatibility includes psychological and habitual dimensions, especially convenience. Customers shouldn't have to change anything about their behavior to use the new product or service, even if the underlying technology has changed radically. Ideally, the new offering is even more convenient than the old. That's what many solar companies missed early on but what others finally got right when they provided consumers with no-muss, no-fuss installations and let them buy power rather than power plants.

CalStar, a Wisconsin-based building-products manufacturer, has managed compatibility extremely well. Its product is radically more efficient while remaining radically similar to what it will replace: cement. Joel Rood, the CEO of CalStar, told us, "Rather than the traditional method of firing clay at very high temperatures, which produces enormous amounts of greenhouse gases, CalStar has developed a process that involves no firing at all. It takes fly ash, a coal by-product, and uses a chemical and hydrating process, augmented by curing, to produce a material very much like traditional cement."

Because "very much like" isn't good enough, CalStar has focused on parts of the building materials market where its product behaves exactly like traditional materials and where regulators don't need to certify the new technology for use (a slow and arduous process). For instance, the company has used its technology to make bricks and pavers that are indistinguishable from traditional products. CalStar gets a bit of attention because its process is so much greener than the traditional one, but what really matters is that CalStar will eventually be able to underprice the competition. After all, its main raw material is a waste stream from another industry, and it doesn't have to have a kiln constantly heated to 1,450°C. The company says it is close to optimizing the design of its plants and will be able to roll them out nationally, while breaking even on cash flow within the next couple of years.

· Even better than just fitting into the existing way of doing things, there are many times when it's possible to have a new product deliver an upside surprise, the sort of thing that consumer products companies have long referred to as "customer delight." As we've seen, Tesla didn't just build an electric car designed to duplicate existing ones. Tesla built a beautiful, high-performance car that appealed to enthusiasts and won the *Motor Trend* Car of the Year award. A Tesla isn't mainly an electric car; it's a sexy car that happens to be electric. (Fisker Automotive, meanwhile, took the straightforward approach and failed.) Likewise, LEDs don't just save money because they use less electricity than incandescents. LEDs also need replacement far less frequently and can be easily managed individually and remotely.

FITTING INTO THE ECOSYSTEM

Many managers become so fixated on the challenges of establishing a product's viability in the market that they fail to consider how to manufacture it at scale once the product takes off. Getting production and installation to scale is just as necessary and important. The key is moving forward in a gated process, step by step, and to import as much expertise as possible from other industries that have already solved the manufacturing and supply-chain problems.

Lots of innovations look great on the lab bench, where conditions can be controlled perfectly and bad batches can be tossed without a second thought. But those innovations are vastly harder to pull off at the pilot stage and are an order of magnitude harder in a manufacturing setting, where changes to equipment or settings are more expensive and have to be simple enough to be made by operators rather than by R&D engineers, who have a deep understanding of the science and technology. A certain number of hours needs to be logged at each level of the manufacturing process before an innovation can move from the lab bench to the pilot or from the pilot to full-scale manufacturing. It's tempting to rush, but moving too fast will cause more problems than gain. It's much easier to sort out problems at early stages of the move to manufacturing.

Biofuels demonstrate the complexity that comes with scale. They were going to be the answer to energy security, providing cheap gasoline and diesel that would displace $120/barrel oil. However, the constraints soon became clear. Cellulosic ethanol plants were much more expensive to build and harder to control than the lab test had indicated—that tenfold complexity in scale-up bit with a vengeance. The better answer, it turned out, was to translate biomass into chemicals—much smaller volume but high value. Companies like Solazyme, Amyris, and LS9 Inc. found that they could be profitable at a much smaller scale by focusing on chemicals such as those that are used in dietary supplements and skin care.

The same challenges have held back attempts at further innovation in solar. It's relatively easy to identify materials other than silicon that could be more efficient, to design photovoltaic structures that use less material and are thus less expensive, or to design a process that prints solar cells in a steady stream rather than producing them one at a time in a vacuum chamber. The challenge is in making these innovations scale up and produce reliable, high-efficiency cells day after day. Solar companies backed by recent venture capital have focused on new cell structures and materials they could patent. They left thoughts about how to scale plants and equipment for later—and they are paying the price.

The best predictor of success is not actually the performance of the best cell, which tends to be the focus in the lab but says little about what performance can be reliably generated at scale. The best indicator is the variability of output—that is, the ratio between good and bad cells and the difference in power output between the best and the worst.

It took even FirstSolar, arguably the most successful new solar technology start-up in recent years, more than five years to go from a working cell to a functioning production plant. The only shortcuts that we have seen work involved calling in experienced help. For instance, Stion, a leading thin-film solar panel manufacturer, has created high-efficiency and low-cost thin-film solar modules by utilizing low-cost industrial tools from established industries and supply chains. Stion worked early on with TSMC (Taiwan Semiconductor Manufacturing Company), which is the largest integrated-circuit foundry in the world and which has deep understanding of semiconductor devices, deposition technologies, and industrial engineering for new plants. Stion and TSMC engineers worked side by side to scale up and industrialize the Stion cell technology. This keeps costs down, in an industry where competition on cost is brutal.

One resource technology company has taken a novel approach to scaling efficiently and rapidly, using early field trials. LanzaTech produces fuel and valuable chemicals from waste gases it collects from heavy industries, including steel manufacturing, oil refining, and chemical production. Rather than conducting all initial tests in a lab, with synthetic substances, as most companies would, LanzaTech has tested its product in the field from the beginning, using gas from real plants. As a result, the company has a robust process that can handle wide variances in the amount of hydrogen in the waste gases it processes.

To increase the likelihood of success, LanzaTech used an organic compound already known to effectively turn waste gas into materials that could then be processed into fuel or chemicals. Although this may sound like science fiction, Prabhakar Nair, vice president of business development at LanzaTech, says the compound is "bacteria found in the intestines of rabbits." Having limited the complexity of its process and conducted many trials in a real-world environment, LanzaTech has demonstrated its technology in projects in China and is ready for commercial launch.

To win the race for scaling, companies must begin with rapid prototyping. The leading resource revolution companies have a disciplined scaling process, times-ten at a time: lab scale to pilot scale, pilot scale to commercial scale, commercial scale to world scale. The key is to measure and monitor the performance of each element of a process at each stage and to move through the gate to the next stage only when performance is seamless. Doing this times-ten at a time provides a solid analytical foundation for identifying and addressing problems early, when they are cheap to fix, rather than encountering difficulties later in the process.

Companies also must design for manufacturability. Simple designs that are easy to repeat are much more sustainable—cheaper to manufacture, easier to maintain, simpler to recycle at the end of life. Sometimes this requires a higher-cost piece, like the aircraft-grade aluminum base board on the Apple Macintosh, but the benefits from simplicity far outweigh the piece-part cost advantages of a more complex product.

In addition, supply chain management must be integrated. The ability to get the materials required to make and deliver a product without interruption in a highly distributed market represents one of the biggest challenges for most companies today. When the Fukushima nuclear incident occurred, technology companies discovered that they were highly dependent on a particular resin that was manufactured only in Fukushima prefecture. The ability to build supply chains with the resilience to respond to major disruptions can differentiate companies quickly.

As we'll see much more in chapter eight, companies should also focus on developing an operating process. Standard, repeatable operating processes are the backbone for scaling companies. The Lean and Six Sigma tools developed by Toyota, Motorola, GE, and others provide a useful starting point for eliminating waste and variability in production. The best companies, however, are integrating these capabilities into a package that everyone can execute—both employees and contractors know the standard operating procedures at Alcoa, Honeywell, Boeing, and GE. Companies that know how to develop integrated operating systems across their whole ecosystem, and not just their employees, can change faster than those that don't.

Finally, companies must focus on the adaptation and integration of technology. In today's environment, no single company will be able to invent all the key elements in its production system. The key, instead, is being able to identify great elements that others have already developed and adapting their technologies. Companies also have to manage each new standard release package in a disciplined way that can be repeated across the organization.

As each company builds these skills and heads to scale, watch out for the unintended consequences that often arise. As ethanol made from corn reached scale in the United States, accounting for nearly 10 percent of the gasoline pool, ethanol consumed more than 40 percent of the U.S. corn crop. Corn prices soared, corn exports fell, and the net environmental benefits turned out to be marginal. Instead of energy security, we developed food insecurity. Instead of sound energy policy, we had farm subsidies.

Reaching scale can also place extraordinary pressure on infrastructure. The Airbus A380, when it arrived in 2005, actually broke runways because its landing guidance system was too precise and hit the same point in the runway each time. (A little randomness introduced into the software helped a great deal.) The development of shale oil in the United States has been slowed by the lack of pipelines needed to bring the light crude to market. The U.S. pipeline network developed south to north, bringing Texas, Oklahoma, and Louisiana crude to the Northeast. Now, the country needs a west-to-east system, bringing oil from North Dakota, Ohio, and Pennsylvania to the Northeast. Today, Hess uses trains to take crude from its wells in North Dakota to a barge in upstate New York, which then goes downriver to refineries in New Jersey. The complexity of this temporary supply chain adds $10 to $15 a barrel to the cost of the crude.

Shale oil likewise faced an unexpected hurdle when drillers realized that the production of guar, a natural gum, was far smaller than they required. The little guar bean, cultivated mostly in semiarid land in Pakistan and India, produces a natural, water-soluble polymer that forms a gel used in hydraulic fracturing operations to enable better oil flow. Guar prices shot through the roof, cutting margins for some suppliers significantly.

Likewise, severe competition has arisen for the rare earth metals used in magnets critical to electric-drive technologies. The U.S. treats rare earth metals as a national security issue, causing friction with China, the primary producer of rare earths, which has decided to limit exports.

But not all supply chain constraints are upstream. Sometimes, the deployment or service infrastructure present obstacles. For instance, one of the major barriers facing electric vehicles is not a shortage of lithium mining but a shortage of battery-charging and -swapping stations. Customers face "range anxiety" about driving too far away from their home charging points into regions that may have gas stations but zero charging points. Tesla has recognized this issue and has committed to building a nationwide network covering 98 percent of the population in the United States and Canada by 2015.

The best companies will understand early where bottlenecks may occur in the value chain and either design around the potential problem or build supply chains that are resilient enough to deliver at scale. Success requires having a strong supply chain to deliver a product to market at scale—as well as a Plan B for when the infrastructure comes late to the party.

THE COMMITTED CHAMPION

Getting to scale the first time isn't enough. It may take half a dozen product cycles to establish a market leadership position. Resource revolutions take time, sometimes decades, and there will be setbacks along the way, so it's crucial to live to fight another day. Most companies give up when something fails, when customers don't value a new technology or business model. So, a new mind-set needs to be cultivated, the mind-set of the revolutionary. There needs to be a committed champion inside the company who can articulate the vision, excite the talent, and develop the right innovation.

A previous McKinsey book, *In Search of Excellence*, defined champions in organizations as people who are not only determined and personally passionate but able to excite others in the cause and enlist them. The role of the champion is even more important during a resource revolution.

As we saw in chapters three and four, resource revolutions require rethinking core products and how to design, build, deliver, and reuse them. This requires an unorthodox thinker willing to challenge the status quo and, when needed, create a sense of urgency.

For many companies, resource revolutions will take them into new territory. This could mean having to learn new skills such as software or electronics, to use unfamiliar materials, or to switch to an asset-light business model. Many companies will have to make an even more basic change: learning to innovate again—the construction industry spends less on R&D than the dog food industry does. While the average amount spent on research and development across industries is 3.2 percent of sales, resource-intensive industries have spent far less. Mining spends 0.9 percent. Utilities spend 0.1 percent. The technology space—whose trappings will, as we've seen, increasingly appear in other industries—spends 10.1 percent. Champions will be required to shake resource-heavy companies out of their torpor and get them innovating.

Perhaps most importantly, to not only survive resource revolutions but to emerge as leaders, companies will have to take bold risks and shape not only their own destiny but the evolution of their industry. Problems will occur, and champions will have to rally the troops. Think of Frank Cary, the CEO of IBM in 1980. Tired of having Apple dominate the nascent market for personal computers, Cary personally sponsored the project that led to the introduction of the PC just a year later—and that let IBM dominate the market for more than a decade. Think of how Microsoft initially underestimated the effects of the Internet in the late 1990s, and of the famous memo that Bill Gates wrote that made the Internet central to strategy and, among other things, led to the dominance of Microsoft's browser. Or think of Nokia, which was a sleepy maker of rubber and forest products until it spotted an opportunity and became the leading maker of cell phones (then fell by the wayside when it failed to reinvent itself as technology progressed to smartphones).

Samsung has excelled at developing champions and shows how it's possible to do so for a few decades. Coming from behind in virtually every one of its industries, Samsung has shown dogged persistence and made bold bets, putting itself in the lead in many industries and utterly reshaping some. This company is now betting boldly on resource revolution as the path to its future—in 2010, Samsung pledged a $20.6 billion investment in five high-growth businesses, three of which are clean-tech: solar cells, rechargeable batteries for automotive applications, and LED technologies.[26] Samsung is also investing in water filtration and offshore wind even beyond the five. Samsung plans to follow its tried-and-true management philosophy, which has shown how a company can reinvent itself continuously.

Founded by Lee Byung-Chull in 1938, the Korean company started by exporting dried fish, fruit, and vegetables. Lee lost virtually everything when North Korea overran Seoul in 1950. He fled south and regrouped. After the war, he not only rebuilt his earlier business but gradually diversified into food processing, textiles, insurance, securities, and retail, becoming a partner in the government's plan to industrialize. Samsung moved into electronics in the 1960s, then into construction and shipbuilding in the 1970s. Eventually, Samsung became the largest Korean conglomerate, with global revenues that are nearly one-fifth the size of South Korea's total gross domestic product.

However, when Lee died in 1987 and was succeeded by his son, Lee Kun-Hee, Samsung was a still second-rate manufacturer in electronics—Sony and Panasonic TVs sat in store windows while Samsung equipment was buried in the back of the store. Lee did a world tour in 1993 and was stunned at Samsung's poor reputation in electronics. He reached the breaking point in Frankfurt and, on no notice, summoned his 200 top managers to the Falkenstein Grand Kempinski Hotel there. He spoke from dawn to dusk for three days straight, laying out his vision for the future. The speech

---

26   The other two are also bold moves for Samsung: building a biosimilars business and a medical-device business and exploiting a different megatrend as populations in mature markets age and need more health care.

has become legend within Samsung—one line, "Change everything except for your wife and children," has become to Samsung employees what John F. Kennedy's "Ask not what your country can do for you" is to Americans. Samsung has a Frankfurt Room at its headquarters; the company had all the furniture from the hotel conference room shipped to Seoul and arranged it precisely as it was during the chairman's speech.

In 1995, Lee sent out Samsung products as Christmas gifts and heard that many of them didn't work. He went to the main factory, in Gumi, and called all two thousand employees to a meeting in a courtyard. As they donned headbands labeled "Quality First," Lee had all the plant's inventory, valued at roughly $50 million, dumped in a pile. Lee sat below a banner that read, "Quality Is My Pride," as he had workers smash every television, every phone, every fax machine, and every other piece of inventory, then throw them on a bonfire.

Lee Kun-Hee, Samsung Group's chairman and champion.

Lee told the shocked employees that he would no longer accept poor-quality products. If the factory kept churning out inferior products, he'd come back to destroy the factory's output again. Lee reinforced the message later when someone noticed that covers for a cell phone didn't look quite like the covers that had been on the prototypes. Lee ordered that all the covers be replaced with ones that matched the original quality, even though it meant trashing more than a hundred thousand covers.

Lee realized that Samsung's future was at stake. With its home in a high-growth but, by global standards, still modest-sized economy, Samsung had to become an international player with the brand, the global reach, and the products that would allow it to be successful in much bigger markets such as the United States, Japan, and the EU. Samsung would not survive by being simply the best Korean company.

Lee's approach combined two elements. He made bold strategic moves and bets of capital on emerging parts of the electronics industry, catching up to the leader quickly and enforcing strict quality to be at parity or better in performance while being more aggressive on cost. The twenty billion to be spent over ten years in future growth businesses is not unusual for a company that has made equally big bets to establish itself in DRAMs and that bet its fortune on the transition from CRT to LCD TV by making massive capital investments with joint-venture partners Corning and Sony. In time, Samsung overtook Sony and has had major wins even against Apple.

In the late 1990s, when Korean labor became too expensive, Lee cut thousands of jobs and built factories in cheaper parts of the world. Ignoring business pundits who argued that consumer-electronics companies should outsource their components businesses and go into more profitable businesses like content, he poured billions into plants where Samsung would make its own memory chips and LCD screens. Now, his gamble is paying off as those technologies fuel a new generation of digital cell phones, video cameras, still cameras, music players, computer monitors, and high-definition TVs. As a vertically integrated, globally networked manufacturer, Samsung can produce low-cost gadgets at blistering speed. At the same time, it makes money selling components to its competitors. Whatever products consumers buy, Samsung wins.

Beyond making bold bets, Lee's approach cultivated other champions. At Samsung, the chairman's office identifies key initiatives and aggressively deploys the talent and capital to pursue them. To rise above VP rank in Samsung, one must have been a champion for a successful initiative. Samsung also realized that in a design- and innovation-driven company it needed to let go of traditional, hierarchical culture. It structured its training program to foster a culture that promotes creativity, open communication, and empowerment, even encouraging younger employees to challenge their superiors. At the same time, Samsung does not coddle entrepreneurs. If the new business has setbacks, the manager typically gets just one chance to fix it, and Samsung routinely restructures leadership for businesses that don't perform.

Samsung has an amazing track record. By 1992, Samsung had become the largest maker of memory chips in the world and the second-largest semiconductor company, after only Intel. By 2005, Samsung was the world's largest maker of liquid-crystal displays and was arguably innovating faster than Sony. In 2012, Samsung became the largest maker of mobile phones, by volume. (Rather than try to perfect products à la Apple, Samsung basically tries everything to see what works—screen size on smartphones being a notable example.) In the process, Samsung has become one of the most profitable tech enterprises on the planet, with a cool $22.5 billion in earnings last year, more even than Microsoft. And while the jury is still out on Samsung's bet on clean technologies, the company has already become one of the largest players globally in LEDs, has leveraged its expertise in lithium ion batteries for consumer mobile phones into a strong position in automotive and grid storage, and has leveraged marine experience in Samsung Heavy Industries to stake out a position for the nascent offshore wind market. It's very much Samsung's game to pick technology transition points like this to catch up to incumbents quickly. More often than not, Samsung comes out ahead.

The story of Samsung's success mirrors the findings from our research on how to succeed in resource revolutions at scale. Success requires senior commitment for bold actions from the CEO and the board: Big investments must be made, and legacy barriers within an organization need to be broken down. Success requires public, measurable goals that will be a stretch for the organization and will motivate it to break new ground and look for new ways to succeed, rather than only refine what worked in the past. This applies both to products and services and to internal processes. Samsung engineers will work through nights and weekends and, if necessary, sleep on cots at the factory when production ramps up. In semiconductors, Samsung can ramp a new chip fabrication to full production in the time it takes many American or Japanese companies to construct the building. The explicit communication of the goal is important because it aligns everyone's day-to-day priorities even many layers down and—like Lee's pyre of products—makes a clear statement about priorities. Finally, success takes committed champions leading the charge day to day. This is easy to say but hard to achieve in practice.

Finding or developing a great champion requires overcoming six common barriers:

1. Many companies have truly visionary leaders inside their organizations, but these visionaries often come from a technical background or the R&D labs and lack the business credibility or experience to make an investment case to the company. The visionary leaders may be

sitting in emerging markets or otherwise be in a position that is more on the periphery of the company, with limited access to headquarters or key investment decisions. Or, the leaders may have the right vision but not have the experience or seniority to assemble a team and deploy resources to pursue a project beyond the concept or idea stage, so they default to more of a provocateur or evangelist role. The solution is to have a process by which to pluck promising entrepreneurs with great ideas out of the line and supplement them with others who bring the rest of the required skill set. This process can be as formal as what GE calls Session C reviews or as informal as the CEO knowing who his top five creative thinkers are and having lunch with them or walking down the hall to meet them a few times a year.

2. Many people who hold significant authority are consumed by just running the current business. We see this frequently in business unit or product line leaders who have near-term financial targets, who are trying to bring out the next-generation product, and who are often involved in key customer wins. Many CEOs are scheduled in ten- to fifteen-minute intervals, with long days and packed schedules. These CEOs have very little time to step back and reflect on the overall trajectory of their business, let alone devote substantial time to an alternative technology or business model that may one day supplant their current business. This weakness can be resolved by ensuring that a few times a year the CEO and executive team have an opportunity to step back from the quarterly cycle and have a deep conversation about what assumptions, technologies, and industry conditions might change. This conversation should not be part of a normal "annual planning" cycle that typically defaults back to budgets and targets, but should be focused specifically on exploring long-shot ideas, or even some nearer-term ones that have never gotten attention.

3. Many companies make it too simple to say no. A combination of the classic "not invented here" and "we've got enough on our plate" means that even entrepreneurial leaders who are good at spotting opportunities and recruiting allies and resources may be slowed by a single person they cannot convince. Resource revolution opportunities can touch many parts of a company, so it's dangerous if someone overseeing IT resources can block a key experiment or development

step, or if an account team that doesn't want to interrupt a current sales cycle with distracting new ideas can delay critical customer feedback. There are thousands of ways for a company—sometimes with the best of intentions—to derail a capable leader trying to create a resource revolution.

4. One way around the problem is to give some emerging opportunities clear leeway to get attention and resources, perhaps through an approach like that at Google, which tells engineers to work on whatever they want for a certain percentage of their time. Another way is to help new ventures line up sponsorship at the highest levels—that's often the CEO. The final possibility is to hive off a team with explicit permission to borrow or draw on what they need from the company and with permission to break rules when they need to. This is what IBM did when it launched its original PC, what Lockheed did with Skunk Works, and what AT&T did with Bell Labs.

5. Most companies do not redeploy talent, capital spending, and R&D resources dynamically. The default position of "last year plus or minus a little" dominates in most companies, even though successful companies reallocate talent and capital rapidly toward new opportunities. Over and over again, we see that large companies correctly identified the disruptive opportunities, and even judged the magnitude of their impact correctly, but dawdled on the timeline. They never managed to shift enough resources at the speed the opportunity required or that a competitor was bringing to bear. The answer to this problem can involve tough new approaches to budgeting, including challenging existing businesses as rigorously as new ones when it comes to capital plans and deployment of talent. The answer can also be as simple as having the CEO or other senior leader carve out a portion from the annual budgeting process to invest in bold new bets.

6. Most companies attribute failures to the champion of an idea, rather than judging carefully what led to the failure of a new initiative. We have often seen examples of leading companies that, because of their insights into the market and resources, were early into a technology, before it was mature. When that first effort fails, the technology gets buried for a generation. The company then winds up being late to market, which ends up being dominated by someone who was years

behind initially. Kodak invented the sensor that made digital photography possible, yet declared bankruptcy when digital photography crushed its film, chemicals, and paper business. Other top camera makers may one day suffer the same fate: The number one camera on online photo-sharing sites is already the iPhone. The solution is not simply to add Wi-Fi or 4G to cameras but to rethink the entire experience of preserving memories and to look for ways to optimize, virtualize, to make it more convenient—and make it scale.

Even after lining up a committed champion and getting everything else about scaling right, companies in a resource revolution still have to find a new workforce. No, we aren't talking robots. But we are talking about radical changes in the skills of the people a company hires and about where to find them. We'll explain in the next chapter.

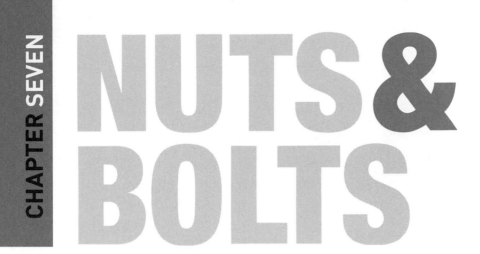

NUTS & BOLTS

GETTING TO SCALE MAY BE THE HARDEST PART of the whole resource revolution process. Success may require:

EXPERIMENTING FOR YEARS with different technologies and following a careful, disciplined process to move from pilot scale toward mass production.

SELECTING AND NURTURING THE CUSTOMERS who will let the company start to scale.

BUILDING COMMITTED CHAMPIONS who are not afraid to boldly try new approaches, learn from other industries, and toss out the old ways of doing things.

BACKWARD-COMPATIBILITY often makes customer adoption easier.

CHAPTER EIGHT

ORGANIZING FOR SUCCESS

JUST AS THE FIRST TWO INDUSTRIAL REVOLUTIONS gave us new organizational structures and management practices, the resource revolution will need to do so, as well. Those new structures will need to be filled with new types of talent, too—talent that sometimes will be found in unlikely places.

The first industrial revolution took us away from a world of guild craftsmen and gave us the limited liability corporation and the factory. Likewise, the second industrial revolution gave us the assembly line and the publicly traded corporation, leading to a command-and-control, quarterly-numbers-driven approach to management that defined the "organization man" of the twentieth century. In the resource revolution, many functions—such as the analysis of data aggregated in near real time—will need to be even more centralized, but decision making will have to happen on the front lines so that it can be fast and can fit with local conditions.

Zara,[27] the Spanish clothing retailer, shows the power of this centralized/decentralized approach, which we'll call a network organization. Zara has built a gigantic business by incorporating fast local input and decision making into the traditional, centralized model.

Historically, retailers attended fashion shows, made their best guesses about trends, ordered all the clothes for a season, and, six months later, put those clothes on sale. If items sold out, there was no way to reorder in time. When items sat on shelves, the retailer marked them down heavily,

---

27 The name doesn't mean anything in Spanish, but there is a story behind it. Initially, the first store in Galicia, Spain, was going to be Zorba, after the 1964 movie *Zorba the Greek*, but a bar around the corner already had the name, and the owner suggested there might be confusion. The molds for the letters for the store sign had already been made, and some playing around with combinations produced Zara.

then shipped anything that remained to cut-price chains that marked the items down even further. The cost of a bad guess was huge, and there were plenty of bad guesses. Amancio Ortega, however, decided he could greatly reduce waste in retailing through a concept he called "instant fashion."

Ortega, the son of a railroad worker and a housemaid, had begun his work life as an errand boy for a store chain in Galicia, a poor region in northwest Spain, so he had seen retailing waste firsthand. As he moved up in the company, he began thinking about how he could optimize design and manufacturing capabilities to turn an order into a product on the shelf in weeks rather than months. That way, he could get popular items to stores while they were still trendy. He also wouldn't need to amass so much inventory at the start of a fashion cycle, and thus wouldn't have to eat as much product when he came out with a dud.

He left the chain and started a manufacturing business, but he found that to make his "instant fashion" concept work, he needed more control over the whole process—from design through manufacturing through sales and then back through design and manufacturing. So, he decided he needed to integrate vertically (which is often necessary with resource breakthroughs). Having that control meant he could immediately learn what was selling and what wasn't, rather than wait for store owners to get around to sending him reports. Ortega could also develop systems for manufacturing and shipping that emphasized speed to market.

He opened a store in 1975 and immediately succeeded with what had begun as an idea to reduce waste but, in consumers' eyes, were fashionable items at low prices. Ortega soon began expanding and today, operating as Inditex, has more than 1,700 stores around the world.

Over time, Zara has layered technology on top of Ortega's instant fashion concept—Ortega, a tinkerer, bought his first computer in 1976, a year before Steve Jobs and Steve Wozniak introduced the Apple II, the first personal computer to generate any real sales. Initially, Ortega had sales clerks watch what people considered buying but put back. Clerks would approach the customers, ask questions, and report to the store manager, who would provide reports that would help designers tweak items and turn them into successes, even though relying solely on sales data would have meant dismissing them. As far back as 1991, Ortega outfitted clerks with custom-made mobile devices to use in interviewing and observing customers. Clerks provided the feedback straight to the designers, both increasing the speed of communication and making it more direct.

Zara has also made its operations so efficient that, while goods pass through a distribution center on their way to market, they rarely spend more than a few hours there and never stay put for more than three days.

As Zara has spread internationally, it has decentralized decision making—after all, a customer in Mexico may not have the same view on fashion as a customer in Greece or Belgium.

So, what began as an exercise in reducing waste became a vertically integrated company with a centralized/decentralized network organization and, not coincidentally, a market capitalization of more than $75 billion. Ortega, the former errand boy, passed Warren Buffett to take the third spot on the *Forbes* billionaires list in 2013.

BECOMING A NETWORK ORGANIZATION

While the assembly line gave us vertical integration—Henry Ford's ownership of everything from rubber trees to power plant to parts makers to the final assembly at his factory—a resource revolution requires a more

The integrated facilities at the Ford River Rouge factory in 1940.

flexible and robust model. In a one-size-fits-all world, a central manufacturing plant delivers a standard product at low cost. Now, flexible manufacturing enables more tailored products and can provide huge benefits that customers are coming to expect and that companies must provide. The appropriate seed and fertilizer mix for one county may be very different than for the next county, so local decision making will be required, too. The need to tailor products will be even greater in resource-intensive industries, because different local geologies, infrastructure, and environmental risk factors require local solutions.

Consolidated operations at a Dutch East India Company wharf and shipyard in Rotterdam, c. 1690.

Technological innovations, having initially driven companies to centralize decision making, will support the decentralization. In the era of the great British trading companies, businesses had to be decentralized because slow communications prevented central oversight—each local business was a separate franchise. From the advent of the telegraph on, dramatic improvements in communications technology drove centralization—the decision makers at the center had all the information and could just tell everyone what product to sell, what price to set, what deal to cut. Now, technology is allowing the best information to flow back to the front line.

The front-line employee can get great data and access to the best functional expert in the company quickly, cheaply, and easily and combine that with his local knowledge. For example, the maintenance supervisor in a remote copper mine can now see on his iPad how each of his trucks is performing compared with the rest of the company's trucks and can see his vehicles' self-diagnostics reports on engines, drive trains, and chassis. That supervisor can make his own well-informed decisions about when to pull a truck out of service for maintenance.

Komatsu and Caterpillar take this sort of approach to maintenance. Whole Foods convenes video conferences of managers at its best and worst stores, based on specific operational scorecards, so they can discover ways to improve.

DEVELOPING AN OPERATING SYSTEM

While we are recommending increased decentralization, we recognize that it presents risks. Decentralization can increase costs, as each business unit comes with the standard package of staff services and support requirements. The other major risk is entropy—if each business unit does its own thing, the rate of innovation can slow.

The way to keep costs down and everyone moving in the same direction is to create what might be envisioned as a standard operating system for the business, along the lines that Steven Johnson describes in his book *Where Good Ideas Come From*. In software, each time blocks of code are standardized into a set of simple routines that anyone can use to perform a specific function, the rate of improvement in the next generation accelerates. Similarly, a standard operating system for a corporation allows for accelerating innovation; instead of reinventing the basics, each manager can focus on innovations that matter. The companies that have a standard operating system and can integrate innovations into that system globally, quickly, and cheaply will win.

The Toyota Production System, the Alcoa Operating System, the Danaher Operating System, the ExxonMobil Operations Management System: All of these have demonstrated the power of a standard operating

Two different operating systems

Corporations have changed their management approach and operating processes over the last century.

GENERAL MOTORS CORPORATION, 1921

Coordinated control through 1) financial/operational planning, measurement, and reporting and 2) capital allocations.

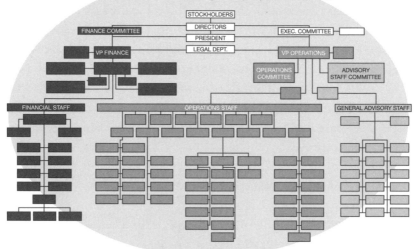

THE DANAHER BUSINESS SYSTEM, 2013

A never-ending cycle of change and improvement: exceptional people, outstanding plans, and sustainable processes that result in superior performance.

system. They provide better safety, reliability, environmental steward-ship, lower cost, higher quality, faster employee development, and more consistent results. The standard operating system builds around standard work units that can be choreographed to take out waste for maximum productivity. Combining the standard work with intensive data monitor-ing allows companies to learn, identifying the best practices globally and sharing the knowledge with the front line. The standard work also allows companies to move people around the system, confident that they will know how to do the job in the new business unit when they arrive, because their tasks follow the standard model. Now, a manager can encounter a difficult local problem and draw on all the information about how others have addressed the problem in the past.

Danaher, for one, arms its workers with systems for managing sup-ply chains. The company has leveraged its operating system to generate 50 percent more margin and nearly double the return on capital of its industrial-conglomerate peers. It has also been able to quickly tell which businesses are outperforming, doubling down on the high performers and exiting businesses that have reached their peak. It reallocates capital between two and three times as quickly and aggressively as most other companies, getting the benefits of a corporate balance sheet while nearly achieving the dynamism of a free market. This is why it has outperformed both its indus-try and the market overall by more than 40 percent in the last five years.

Standardizing work eliminates waste and helps front-line employees deliver great results consistently. Managers are better able to make quality decisions, because their data is consistent, and the decision protocols are clear and supported by all the data the company has, rather than just the personal experience of one manager. The best companies have a rigorous standard technical system (how the processes and equipment work). These compa-nies also have a simple management system that keeps everyone focused on cost, safety, reliability, margins, and growth in a consistent fashion.

If done right, a standard operating system will create opportunities for innovation.

For a century, strong functional disciplines have allowed large companies to systematically outperform smaller companies on most dimensions—but not on innovation. If the emphasis is on 100 percent compliance, and it's costly to change the system and even harder to change people's behaviors, a company can ossify. Many big companies do. With an operating system that defines ways that everyone can plug in while operating more independently, each business unit leader will be able to try new ways of improving productivity and increasing revenue. Running hundreds of well-structured experiments every year allows a company to improve at a much faster rate than ever before. Companies will be able to see what works, integrate these innovations systematically into the operating model, and have the whole organization learn rapidly.

The approach resembles what Apple has done by having thousands of independent app developers all code to a common, rapidly upgrading standard where each new release can easily and seamlessly update the user community. Apple then integrates the best capabilities into the operating system, as it has done with flashlight functionality, radio, weather, and maps. Linux has developed one of the most effective computer software programs in the world by having individuals upgrade code to a common standard. Google runs hundreds of experiments each day to improve performance of its search and advertising capabilities—and companies can do the same now with data-driven analytics supporting the performance improvement programs. Of course, resource-intensive companies aren't iPhone apps, but the techniques and approach still hold—for example, Kaggle enables natural-resource companies to publish data sets to Kaggle's website to allow the world's best data scientists and statisticians to apply their algorithms to find answers on where to drill, on a new formulation, etc.

The standard operating systems need to be widely deployed and accessible, not just to a company's direct employees but also to the supplier community, innovation partners, and customers. Each group needs to be invited to contribute to upgrading the system. These systems need to be easy to upgrade as better practices emerge and must put the power to support decisions in the hands of front-line employees. The operating system needs a webmaster who ensures that new releases are well structured and integrate seamlessly—any deviation in production performance is too expensive in low-margin markets.

It's possible to imagine extending operating systems beyond the walls of a given company. In a traditional Japanese *keiretsu*, a group of companies forms a single value chain through shared investment, collaboration, and innovation. We can imagine new forms that do so virtually, with companies forming alliances of data while collaborating as suppliers and customers rather than as owners. Companies would work together to improve product performance, reduce waste, and incorporate new technologies. Look at how Apple and Google are rolling up data providers as they compete to provide the best maps and related services. The companies own some of the data and are generating as much as they can, but they are, at least initially, mostly using a strong operating system to integrate the data and essentially form alliances among related providers. SunPower takes an operating-system approach that lets it do similar mash-ups of data to qualify potential customers—combining information about utility rates, credit scores, and satellite images that show how much sunlight is available for a lot.

LOOKING FOR TALENT FAR AFIELD

In thinking about the people who will be needed in this new organizational model and its operating system, the first thing to do is to begin to map the new skills that will be needed to pursue opportunities in resource productivity. The list will be long.

All companies will need more software talent, because software increasingly provides the operating instructions for our world. IT no longer is solely the business of managing company desktops and networks; information technology is merging with traditional engineering to create the lifeblood of the modern corporation. Those companies that can build the talent to integrate software and industrial hardware faster and more reliably than the market will win. The operating algorithms that identify which pump needs maintenance and which oil well needs more pressure will become the basis for competitive advantage, just as Amazon's book-recommendation tools and their rapid checkout management capabilities defined success in book sales. Many companies we think of as building hardware actually have more software engineers than hardware. Airplanes, automobiles, construction equipment, trains, and industrial machinery all ship with millions of lines of software code and are far more complex than the typical iPhone app.

Many companies will need more systems-integration skills, because, as we noted in chapter five, much of the power of the resource revolution will come from combining bits and pieces of disparate ideas, and most companies simply aren't very good at system integration at the moment. For companies focused on resource use, the need for specialization is high, but the scarce resources are engineers and innovators who can solve the cross-functional problems that networks of technologies create. Success will come from harnessing the rapid innovation in software and semiconductors, biotechnologies and nanotechnologies, and ubiquitous sensors and controls, then integrating them with industrial processes for the first time. While, as we've noted, emerging markets such as China and Brazil have some advantages in resource use because they're able to design networks such as electric grids from scratch, developed countries such as the United States have an advantage with the cross-functional aspects of resource productivity. The developed countries have the senior architects with thirty years' experience in designing whole systems—the kind of experience that will be needed to integrate all the technologies available.

Beyond the ability to integrate various functions, new specialty skills will come into play for the first time. For example, automotive companies in Germany have found that, while they are long on mechanical engineers, they are short on the software and chemical engineers that will be required to build electric, hybrid, and, perhaps one day, hydrogen cars. Entire components, such as transmission systems, could be eliminated with the advent of electric drivetrains, but car makers will need people who understand how to weave carbon fiber, integrate 4G communication protocols and security with the car's operating system, and deal with battery issues like heating and optimizing chemistry. Already, the electronics content in cars has hit 40 to 50 percent of their value, and this is before cars are routinely connected to the Internet. Many other industries will, like car makers, need to increase their understanding of materials science, chemistry, or biology.

Many companies will need skills at super-low-cost manufacturing, too. For years, the goal in product design was to add features and generally improve capabilities. But the ability to build high quality very inexpensively now offers the key advantage. Walmart pioneered the everyday-low-price promise and developed supply chains that could offer high-end products at very low prices. Huawei did the same with telecommunications technology. The market for high-quality, low-price goods is growing very rapidly, and all but a few companies will have to look outside their walls to find the capabilities to tap that market.

The upshot? When looking for new talent, it's no longer enough to try to raid competitors for their best people—those competitors don't have the new skills, either. The new talent needs to be found in new places.

One place to start is in neighboring industries that haven't traditionally overlapped but that have been identified as having capabilities worth borrowing. Consumer electronics will present a big opportunity. So many people have become addicted to their smartphones that they will demand that the rest of the world's interactive devices have a similarly simple, smooth interface, and, whatever the industry, companies will need to be able to provide one. Cars, for instance, are already migrating away from levers and buttons and toward iPad-like capabilities—though the switch will have to be negotiated carefully, both because of familiarity with the old ways and because drivers have to keep their eyes on the road.

The Nest thermostat provides another example. Until the Nest came along, thermostat interfaces hadn't changed much since the shift in the early 1970s from the mercury-based mechanical switch to the box with a small LCD and a bunch of buttons. The Nest now has taken on the attributes of an iPod: The thermostat, which is round again, with an interface like a trackwheel, learns users' preferences and communicates with their iPhones and other equipment in their houses over Wi-Fi. The Nest, which can adjust to the weather and can sense whether anyone is at home, takes another page from Apple in that the company sees the thermostat as just the first app for household-wide automation and convenience. Nest has already announced a smoke detector that gently announces warnings when it detects small amounts of smoke or when its battery is fading. Because the thermostat and smoke detector can already tell when someone is home, security is a natural extension. The plan is that new applications, software features, and more sensors and controls will one day allow Nest to do everything but deliver breakfast in bed.

Even though companies will need expertise on technologies such as the chips, apps, and batteries that go into consumer electronics, it won't always make sense to hire people from other industries. In some cases, it will make more sense to form partnerships with businesses in those industries that provide access to specialized expertise. For instance, rather

Natural science and engineering graduates by country

Number of doctoral graduates (thousands)

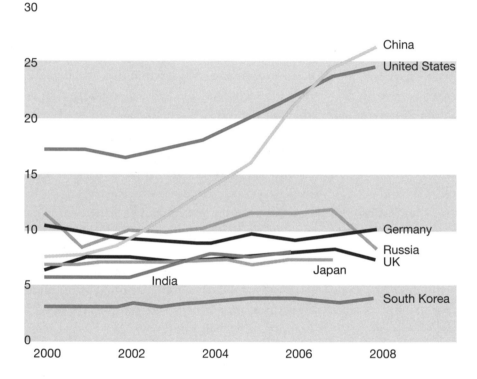

than hire all its own experts on materials science, Apple is working with Corning on glass and coatings and with Liquidmetal on casting and ductility for casing materials. To differentiate its products from competitors with similar inventions, Apple has signed extensive agreements that guarantee exclusivity and supply from its partners.

Beyond looking at new industries for talent, it will be important to look in new countries, too. When China and India are producing more advanced engineering talent than any other countries on the planet, building the leading workforce in the world requires developing a global talent-sourcing pipeline. Where companies might have traditionally recruited from the industrial engineering core in the United States' Midwest and South—the Big 10 and SEC engineering axis that powered the industrial innovations in the United States during the twentieth century—the leading companies today need to be winning on the campus of Tsinghua University in Beijing, for example. Companies need to go to Russia to find experts in algorithms, to Israel for electro-optics and water technology, to Finland for leaders in wireless technology, and so on.

Less-developed countries will be important sources of talent for low-cost manufacturing because "low cost" has a very different meaning to a street vendor in Delhi than it does to citizens of the EU. The lack of infrastructure we take for granted in the United States requires that we look at technology and design options that would never even be considered in the United States. An American-made refrigerator needs to make ice cubes, fit in with kitchen décor, and have enough storage space to hold a weekly SUV-run of groceries. For a person in the 80 percent of India's population who has no access to ice or refrigeration, there are no such

The low-cost ChotuKool refrigerator invented by Godrej in India.

expectations. That difference is why Godrej's ChotuKool, a $70 refrigerator, was developed in India and not the United States. The refrigerator, which looks like an oversized cooler and uses a battery-powered heat exchanger for its cooling technology rather than traditional compressors, comes at a price that wouldn't have even been considered possible in the developed world. Hitting that price may unlock a market for cooling in the developing world that is $108 billion today and is set to increase to

$185 billion-plus by 2018. Similarly, a low-cost sonogram machine was developed in India and is now being marketed worldwide by GE.

It isn't enough to just go looking for new talent, of course. Companies have to be able to win the competition for it. To do so, companies must first realize that they aren't just competing against traditional rivals. Companies have to win against, say, consumer electronics firms and software companies, too. Likewise, competing for talent in India, China, and Russia requires competing against local national champions and their privileged local networks.

To win, companies not only have to compete on the usual measures of compensation and responsibility but will also have to be willing to go where the talent is, whether geographically or virtually. Companies may even need to be willing to set up multiple development centers around the world to tap into those algorithm experts in Russia and the electro-optics geniuses in Israel.

DEVELOPING TALENT

In some cases, people with the skills to help companies thrive throughout the resource revolution simply don't exist, at least not in the numbers that will be needed, so companies will have to develop their own talent.

Much of the need will occur at the top of organizations, among the leaders. The leadership skills required to deliver 10 to 15 percent annual productivity gains for a decade or more are a far cry from the incremental-improvement skills that marked the generation of leaders after World War II. When technologies are largely mature in an industry, the focus on generating incremental improvement is the whole game, and we have developed a group of managers who are great at squeezing the last drop out of the radish. We developed a whole series of tools—Lean, Six Sigma, business process redesign, dispatch linear programs—all with the goal of improving productivity 1 to 2 percent annually. The idea was: Keep the process in control, squeeze the next drop out, and the company will win. But not any more.

Leaders' technology management skills will also have to improve radically. When technology is changing at a rapid pace, the ability to identify and integrate new tools to improve performance is critical.

Everyone is familiar with the difficulties of upgrading their computers to handle new software—performance is always supposed to get better, but most of the time the upgrade takes forever, and there is a great deal of lost productivity in the transition. The same can happen when a business makes a fundamental upgrade in its operating system and supporting technology. So, imagine the pressure when a manager needs to upgrade the base business technology portfolio every six to nine months and can't afford any downtime.

Even tougher, the challenge won't be just to upgrade a known form of technology; the world of resource revolutions is too cross-functional to be that simple and requires different departments, multiple suppliers, and often a customer willing to try something new. To take a simple example: It might make sense to shift from making trucks that use diesel to making trucks that use natural gas, to take advantage of low-priced, clean-burning methane. That single shift requires changes to the fuel tanks, the engine, pollution-control equipment, driver information systems, cooling systems, network fueling infrastructure, and maintenance protocols. The results can deliver a 37 percent savings in fuel costs and 9 percent savings in the total cost of ownership for the truck, but success requires taking an integrated view of the network problem. Making these integrated decisions in a world where the future differential between natural gas and diesel is highly uncertain makes the decision making even more difficult. Even within the car or truck platform, automotive companies will have to make tradeoffs that cut across software, mechanical engineering, electronics, and chemistry.

Workers will need to be developed, too, whether by schools, by the government, or by employers. The reason is that the nature of work is changing and, in many cases, becoming much more technical. Workers on a solar-panel assembly line, for instance, need to learn how to handle equipment that operates within a tolerance of a fraction of a millimeter. That doesn't require a four-year college degree but does require a great deal of training with digital process-control technologies.

Quality-control supervisors in manufacturing will have to be able to understand advanced statistical techniques and need to be able to make adjustments to process-control technology to deliver extremely tight tolerances.

Factory productivity growth

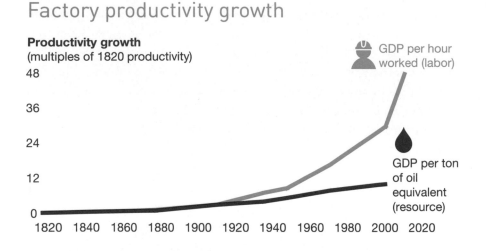

Productivity growth
(multiples of 1820 productivity)

GDP per hour worked (labor)

GDP per ton of oil equivalent (resource)

48

36

24

12

0

1820 1840 1860 1880 1900 1920 1940 1960 1980 2000 2020

Resource productivity requires front-line labor like the delivery truck drivers employed by UPS to make much more sophisticated decisions based on big data and advanced analytics. They obviously don't have the data-analysis capabilities that UPS does centrally, so UPS pushes as much information out to the drivers as possible. UPS integrates data both on actual traffic and on anticipated traffic to instruct drivers to adjust routes. Now, as drivers make their morning deliveries, UPS dynamically pulls together routes for the pickups they'll make that afternoon.[28]

Developing new talent requires a new education model, much more technically focused than the one the developed world built around German liberal education principles at the end of the nineteenth century to help people move from the farm to the city and be able to read, vote, and conduct business. The focus has been driving 90 percent of the population to have at least a high school degree. The challenge now is that a high school degree is not enough. Most countries in the developed world show 40 to 50 percent of the population having some college education, but countries will need to reach 80 to 90 percent to remain competitive with the likes

---

28 UPS is on the cutting edge in other ways, too. It is experimenting with trucks that run on natural gas, which because of shale gas breakthroughs now costs a fraction of the price of gasoline. Liquified natural gas (LNG) is also much denser than gasoline in terms of the energy it contains. UPS trucks could cross the United States from Texas to Chicago on three tanks of gas. Eventually, when enough LNG fuel stations get built, the trucks will also be able to cross east to west.

of Korea, as "knowledge worker" skills such as communications, problem solving, analyzing data, setting parameters on machines and algorithms, and collaborating globally become much more important. The German model continued to evolve after World War II to incorporate technical apprenticeships in trades like machining, carpentry, and programming, but much more is needed.

Learning will need to continue post-college, too, largely through online course work—basically, higher education will undergo its own resource revolution, delivering learning virtually rather than in classrooms and lecture halls, even though the face-to-face model has worked well for millennia. Universities like Stanford are already experimenting with a "flipped classroom" model enabled by computing technology: Students read the book and watch the video of the lectures on their own time on an iPad or laptop, and come to class (physically or virtually) to discuss, ask questions, and get a deeper understanding of the material. Once physical constraints are removed, the student can even be in a remote part of Western China and have access to the world's best professors on any topic. (A fifteen-year-old in Mongolia became one of 340 students to earn a perfect score in 2012 in MIT's Circuits and Electronics, a sophomore-level class that was the first massive open online course, or MOOC, that MIT offered. More than 150,000 students had enrolled in the course. The boy was accepted as a freshman at MIT at sixteen.)

The flipped classroom is the brainchild of companies like Udacity and Coursera that are trying to make the best courses in the world available to the masses, without requiring students to pay $50,000 a year to go to Harvard.

There also needs to be a stronger alignment between business and education, setting ever-increasing technical standards for each graduate. Students will need at least four years of mathematics plus specific technical training in statistics and data management to remain competitive during the resource revolution. Some companies are working with schools to set up feeder programs. Microsoft, for one, recently began sending engineers to high schools both to teach math skills and to generate enthusiasm that could bring more talent into software design and coding.

Businesses will need to do even more of their own training, too. There will need to be hands-on learning combined with simulations, often using the best graphics to allow hundreds of repeats on major tasks and key decisions. Businesses may want to work with universities to bring some of their experts and proven techniques to the corporate campus.

The good news is that, while the search for new organizational models and new talent in new places will be extraordinarily taxing, just about all the competition will face the same problems. That fact gives each company a bit of a grace period, but the sooner management starts confronting the gaps a company is facing, the sooner it is likely to close them—and gain a big edge on the ones who don't.

FREELANCE INNOVATION

Elance, a young company that helps organizations and freelancers find each other, illustrates smart strategies for finding, developing, and deploying talent, while also enabling other businesses to pursue free-lancers on their own. While we'd prefer to offer an example of a bigger, more established enterprise, we're in such early days when it comes to new organizational models and talent that no giant yet illustrates all the points we need to make.

Elance was inspired by a 1998 article in *Harvard Business Review* that talked about how the Internet would enable a freelance, or "e-lance," approach to hiring. The idea was catchy enough that the founders raised $66 million in venture capital, launched the business in 1999, and developed software that let corporations hire freelancers online. The company survived the bursting of the Internet bubble, then, in 2006, pivoted into a related business. Elance sold the original business and used the proceeds to relaunch itself in 2007 as an online marketplace for freelancers that enabled them to do all their work online. The hope was that they would be the eHarmony of the market for talent, letting companies post short-term or part-time jobs and instantly be matched with people who had the right skills, such as programming, marketing, or designing.

The relaunch not only took the right approach in terms of the resource revolution principles we've already laid out but also followed several of the strategies we've discussed in this chapter. The company has developed a network structure that is centralized and decentralized at the same time.

Elance, based in a two-story building nestled among numerous start-ups in Mountain View, California, has 105 full-time employees and uses about 200 freelancers that it finds through its platform. The company centralizes all data collection and analysis and has developed rigorous principles for how work should be done by the freelancers Elance hires and how decisions should be made, but it breaks work down into units that teams can handle in a decentralized way. Fabio Rosati, the CEO, describes his managers as choreographers who need new sorts of skills to bring together teams with such different talents and in varied locations.

Elance has also, quite explicitly, developed an operating system that both workers and companies can plug into. An organization specifies work and payment in terms that the Elance system accepts. Freelancers not only describe themselves but take tests that help rate their skills and collect feedback from Elance customers as they complete work. Freelancers also provide feedback on employers. Once work is posted, the system automatically generates candidates for the employer and facilitates the communication that quickly leads to someone's being hired.

Importantly, the operating system can be upgraded quickly, without disrupting the business, as Elance learns more. For instance, Rosati says the company has learned that it's actually providing a workplace, not a marketplace. The same freelancers may get hired at Google or Facebook, but they will need to be able to act differently depending on the culture and the rules that govern how work is done in a particular company. So, Elance is going beyond presenting a temp for hire and helping those who hire them integrate them quickly into the workflow.

Because the Internet reaches just about everywhere, Elance is also following a key personnel strategy and finding talent in new places, from Costa Rica to the Costa del Sol, from Peru to Pakistan. While the credentials may sometimes be unconventional by the standards of American businesses, the talent is there—for example, while a website design job could cost tens of thousands of dollars from a traditional agency in the United States, a freelancer with a strong reputation online could do the work for a few hundred dollars.

By setting up the right structure and operating system and assembling considerable talent, Elance has had more than 500,000 businesses hire people through it—345,000 in 2012 alone. People hired via Elance billed more than $200 million for their services in 2012, bringing the total to $730 million since the company relaunched in 2007.

By providing such flexible access to skills, Elance (along with its main competitor, oDesk) is helping other companies with their own transition into new organizational models for a resource revolution. For instance, Johnson & Johnson now does much of its marketing work using a network model. While the company defines messages and goals centrally, it uses Elance to find talent for specific projects. J&J managers then choreograph the work in teams on a decentralized basis. Rosati says the company is finding that it can do the marketing work in about a tenth of the normal time and at much lower cost. As a bonus, he says, J&J is finding that the new structure produces better quality because the creative people are working directly with the manager responsible; in the hierarchical structure used in the past, middle managers would take ideas from the senior leader and define a set of requirements for the creative talent, but something was inevitably lost in translation.

Change will take time. Elance's $200 million of billings in 2012 mean it is about the equivalent of one Walmart. But the change is coming.

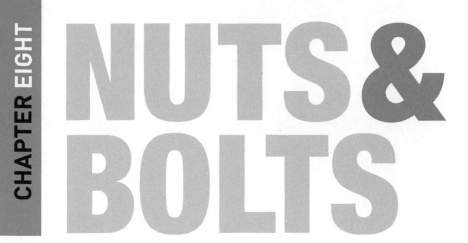

CHAPTER EIGHT

NUTS&BOLTS

To attract the right talent and organize it effectively in a resource revolution, it is necessary to:

BECOME A NETWORK ORGANIZATION.

DEVELOP A STANDARD "OPERATING SYSTEM" to speed decisions and innovation.

LOOK FOR TALENT FAR AFIELD, in other industries and developing markets.

DEVELOP THAT TALENT starting on day one.

FREELANCE INNOVATION, leveraging broad external networks to accelerate success.

CHAPTER NINE

GO BIG OR GO HOME

Often, when people think about what they see as the coming resource crisis, they focus on the need for conservation. When companies enter the conversation, it's often because they face a threat. For instance, investors note that, as newspaper readership moves online and use of paper generally declines, the traditional model for pulp and paper companies is threatened: No longer will companies plant forests, cut them down, and turn them into paper with very water- and chemicals-intensive processes.[29]

But some companies are making lots of money on paper. The reason is Yan Cheung—and hers is the kind of story that should be told more often, about the grand successes that will be possible in the resource revolution.

Yan is the eldest of eight children of an army officer and grew up in China during the Cultural Revolution. She began her career in a textile mill and then worked in a paper trading company in Shenzhen when Deng Xiaoping declared Shenzhen a special economic zone. She moved to Hong Kong in 1985 to set up her own paper trading company, Nine Dragons, and then to Los Angeles in 1990 to open the U.S. subsidiary. Her insight? China was critically short of paper and didn't have trees to cut down to make more. All this in a country that was on the cusp of becoming the manufacturing hub of the world, and nearly everything people buy from China involves paper in some form—wrapping, packaging, instructions.

Her business model: Buy waste paper in the United States for less than $100 a ton (compared with more than $500 a ton for virgin paper from trees), then buy capacity in shipping containers, which would otherwise have returned empty to China after having unloaded goods in the United States and which were available for pennies on the dollar, because almost

---

29   A decade ago, 40% of the garbage dumped in landfill was paper, and half of that was newspaper.

no one was competing for return-trip capacity. She then reprocessed the pulp into packaging material (mainly cardboard) and sold it in a market where paper is chronically in short supply.

As Yan's business grew, she invested in techniques to reprocess paper with drastically lower water usage. She also set up her plants in parts of China that are not suffering from the water shortages that Beijing or parts of Western China face.

With margins of more than 12 percent, Nine Dragons is 50 percent more profitable than International Paper. Boise Cascade, which has transformed itself into OfficeMax, an office products company, makes just above 1 percent margins.

Yan Cheung is now China's richest woman and the wealthiest woman in the world who made, rather than inherited, her fortune.

The point is that the talk of "less" is generally misguided. People talk of doing "less with less," à la the traditional paper companies and their declining fortunes. People worry that we may actually face a future of "less with more," à la conventional oil companies that have been spending more on exploration and development while finding smaller fields. In fact, as we have shown throughout this book and as Yan shows dramatically, many companies will find ways to do "more with less."

These opportunities don't just lie in the future—though we'll get to that in a minute, sketching out some possibilities that could be huge winners—but include plenty of people and companies that are prospering right now as part of the resource revolution and that can serve as exemplars for those thinking about getting into the game.

We've already covered some of this revolution's heroes, including: George Mitchell, the pioneer of fracking; Elon Musk of Tesla; Cree, the lighting pioneer led by Chuck Swoboda, and founded by Calvin Carter, John Edmond, and Neal Hunter; Samsung and its chairman, Lee Kun-Hee; Dan Yates and Alex Laskey, cofounders of Opower; and Nest and its founder, iPod designer Tony Fadell. But that's just the start of the list.

Big companies, which sometimes resist innovation, are leading the way in many cases. GE, while it missed the move to LEDs, has made a big push for resource productivity through what it calls ecoimagination. GE has also made a major bet on the Internet of Things, which will lead to lots of opportunities to do more with less both for GE and for other companies

Automotive shakeout

Number of U.S. automobile manufacturing firms (year founded)

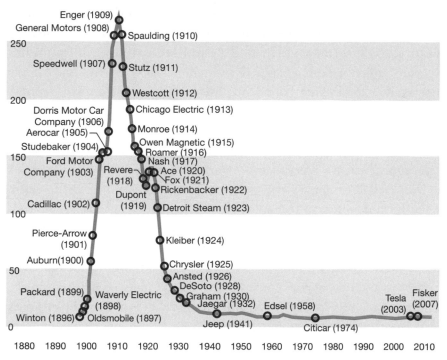

that can capitalize on the spreading network of devices that can sense and communicate with each other, without human intervention. IBM has its Smarter Planet initiative. Philips Electronics, like Cree, is leading the way to LEDs and much more efficient lighting. Sharp is innovating in solar. United Technologies is pushing large-scale storage of electricity, which could play a major role in taking grid technology from the nineteenth century well into the twenty-first. The State Grid Corporation in China is pioneering an architecture and techniques that could become the model for the rest of the world: building a system of high-voltage direct-current links from inland hydropower and renewable sources out to the coastal cities, the centers of population and economic activity. Singapore Water is doing the same with desalination and treatment of water for reuse, issues that will become increasingly important for the rest of us.

Venture capitalists are pushing even harder, though their efforts have achieved scale only in limited areas thus far, such as solar. There are John Doerr, Michael Linse, and John Denniston at Kleiner Perkins, many of whose companies we interviewed and used as examples. For instance, Kaiima, the company that is trying to reengineer crops to greatly increase yield, is a Kleiner company. There is Vinod Khosla, who is perhaps the one venture capitalist most identified with the resource revolution. Khosla, not known for lacking confidence, disdains investments that promise incremental improvement, investing instead in projects that he figures have only a 10 percent chance of success but that will transform markets if they succeed. Some investments are so far out there that he calls them "imprudent science experiments." Alan Salzman and Stephan Dolezalek at VantagePoint Capital Partners have about $1 billion invested in clean-tech. Ira Ehrenpreis at Technology Partners was an early backer of Tesla and a number of solar companies with disruptive technologies. Foundation Capital also has a major clean tech investing practice, led by Paul Holland, Steve Vassallo, and Warren "Bunny" Weiss, but took a different approach, largely focused on energy conservation and business model innovation. Holland and his wife have built a home in the hills above Silicon Valley that is not only beautiful but has been called the most energy-efficient house in the world. It is a showcase for others—visitors just need to watch their step if Holland lets the chickens into the house while they're there.

The pantheon wouldn't be complete without the individual innovators who have driven so much of the progress, among them Alan Mulally, who showed the way on system integration while at Boeing and does so now as CEO of Ford; Yet-Ming Chan of A123, a leader in battery innovation; Shuji Nakamura and Eric Kim, pioneers in lighting; Don Sadoway, an important figure in grid storage; and Arun Majumdar, the initial director of ARPA-E, the research branch of the Department of Energy that aspires to do for energy what DARPA did in other spheres. (Think Internet, GPS, and more.)

REVOLUTIONARY POSSIBILITIES

When we revisit the issue in twenty years, who will the giant successes be, the companies that become for the next century what Siemens, IBM,

Ford, and others have been to the past century? It's obviously too early to tell, because resource revolutions will play out through a lot of hard thinking by a lot of smart and creative people. But, to provide inspiration, here are twelve companies that could be shaped in the coming two decades and that could dominate for decades beyond:

1. **MAXIMUM OIL** RECOVERY ENTERPRISE Maximum Oil Recovery Enterprise (MORE)—An oil company will decrease the rate at which production from a well declines. Traditionally between 6 and 8 percent a year, the rate will drop to between 1 and 2 percent annually. MORE will use advanced sensor networks as well as newer operating techniques, such as steam injection, to recover between 60 and 70 percent of the oil in a field, up from the traditional 20 to 30 percent, all while avoiding the need to drill in remote, environmentally sensitive areas. These changes may seem to be just traditional improvements, not game-changers, but they would double the value of existing fields and existing companies. Remarkably, today, oil company valuations pay only for reserves valued at current production capabilities and rates, placing almost no value on these untapped resources, so the opportunity for value creation is massive. We saw what happened when George Mitchell and his work on fracking unlocked the potential of shale gas and then shale oil. The world is full of these opportunities.

2. **ERGO** EFFICIENT RESILIENT GRID OPERATOR Efficient Resilient Grid Operator (ERGO)— The power grid will shift away from an analog, hub-and-spoke system and become a digital, real-time network. The change will be on the order of the switch from the early phone system, where armies of operators manually connected calls, to the Internet. The new grid will connect multiple, distributed power generators rather than treat each generating plant as a largely discrete entity. The new grid will incorporate massive amounts of storage, so power can be generated whenever that would be most efficient, can flow in both directions, and be rerouted to make up for faults or shortages. Digital transformers and other developments will sharply reduce the loss of power in transit. Advanced building controls will let users be incorporated into the management of the grid—rather

than balance the grid just by adding excess power, as happens today, the grid will be balanced dynamically based on either additions of supply or reductions of demand in real time. Again, this new company we envision may seem to embody just an increase in complexity rather than something wholly new, but the effects of ERGO would be extraordinary. By managing the interconnection of hundreds of thousands of distributed generation sites and loads, ERGO would increase the efficiency of electricity generation and distribution by more than 50 percent. Instead of the myriad local networks we have today, the minimum efficient scale will suggest the nation should have three or four utilities rather than a hundred.

3. **Home Unified Services** HOme Unified SErvices (HOUSE)— This company will reach into our homes more completely than security, electric utility, and media and content companies do today, providing customized personal services that anticipate a person's actions and preferences to provide greater comfort and convenience. Based on individuals' mobile devices, HOUSE will recognize preferences for light, temperature, music, photographs, and the like and reflect those in the settings of the home (or hotel room, office, or hospital room) over the course of the day as individuals move from room to room. Imagine your car GPS not only checking you in to a hotel and setting the thermostat but downloading your favorite family photos and TV programs to your room before you arrive. Today, the average home each year wastes the energy equivalent of an entire refrigerator, running full-time, just from having TVs, furnaces, air conditioners, and the like ready to provide service or comfort whenever an individual wants. By making homes smarter about when services will actually be required, HOUSE will reduce energy requirements for the average home 20 to 30 percent and increase available services.[30] On the hottest summer days, HOUSE may even send you a movie ticket or gift certificate to the shopping mall so you'll leave and let HOUSE shut

---

30 Turntoo in the Netherlands is an early example of what HOUSE might be. It contracts with homes and businesses, taking over ownership of furnaces, lightbulbs, and so on and providing their use as a service. Having ownership means Turntoo keeps upgrading to whatever is the most efficient technology and delivers savings to its customers.

your home systems down for the early afternoon. The opportunities for similar companies to serve businesses are even larger.

4.  Convenient Organizer Service for Travel (COST)—This company will handle all details for travel with radically better efficiency, providing rides, rooms, tickets to events, and any other required services. It will have optimized routing and inventory—a user will just type in where he or she wants to go, and when, and COST will handle the rest, choosing among cars, trains, planes, and more. It will be as flexible as Zipcar and Airbnb, coordinate trips for family and friends, and organize adventures. COST will put together recommended offers for birthdays, reunions, honeymoons, and more. In the process, COST will reduce the capital requirements for travel by 95 percent and drastically increase the amount of travel that people can do economically. COST could lead to a major reduction in road building and new car sales globally, as well as higher occupancy rates for hotels and planes.

5.  Global Recovery Of Waste (GROW)— The most profitable miner in the world may be recovering high-value products from the waste streams around the world: gold and silver from consumer electronics, lithium from geothermal effluent, and high-value rare earth metals from electronics, using new microfluidic technologies. GLOW will also provide heat, power, and fertilizer from neighborhoods' organic waste. Our total material resource footprint will shrink from 86 metric tons per person annually to a little more than our body weight.

6.  WAter DElight (WADE)—The company will deliver the best drinking water in the world, through nonchemical purification techniques and mineralization technologies that provide the freshest taste. WADE will also provide high-quality agricultural irrigation water. Through strong partnerships with agriculture to reduce waste, closed-loop treatment systems, and network-wide leak detection and management

in cities, WADE will ensure that a system only needs 20 percent new water annually. The health benefits from expanding access to freshwater will more than pay for the new infrastructure requirements.

7.  Fresh Organic Opportunities Delivered (FOOD)—The global, integrated company will produce high-quality food locally using one-tenth the water and energy of existing methods and deliver the food to consumers with less than 20 percent waste. FOOD will also customize each person's food with nutraceuticals and tailor diets based on genetic fingerprints to maximize longevity and reduce the risk of disease. As with WADE, FOOD has the potential to increase the availability of food and reduce the volatility of prices.

8.  Lightweight Innovation Technology Engineering (LITE)—The global company will deliver carbon fiber at a cost per pound below that of aluminum.[31] Cars, trucks, ships, planes, and buildings will all become safer and more efficient. The human world will no longer be rectilinear but full of the pleasing, sculpted, aerodynamic, and comfortable shapes that can be made from carbon fiber. Additive, or 3-D, manufacturing will make it possible to replace parts in a matter of moments anywhere on the planet. The carbon-fiber recycling system will close the loop and allow for true circularity.

9. Government Operations Verified (GOV)—This low-cost service provider will let governments use a technology platform, standardized online globally, to deliver services tailored to each citizen, issuing passports, drivers' licenses, health care, retirement plans, and tailored career training and advice. "Government service" will no longer be an oxymoron, and many private companies will deliver efficient,

---

31 If this sounds implausible, given the high cost of carbon fiber today, consider what it was like to attend a banquet hosted by Napoleon. Those in the lowest rank used utensils made of silver. Those of higher rank had utensils made of gold. Those at Napoleon's table used . . . aluminum. The metal was that hard to produce from ore and that scarce—until it wasn't, at which point objects made of aluminum became everyday items rather than rarities to adorn an emperor's table.

innovative services over the GOV platform, much like apps on our iPhones do today. GOV will have figured out how to keep information private for taxpayers and patients while supporting fast, low-cost service and using big-data analytics to reduce waste, fraud, and abuse.

10. SEnsor Network SOlutions (SENSO)—This global technology leader will deliver trillion-point, integrated sensor networks for companies and provide access to a marketplace of algorithm-based analysis of the sensor data. Much as Google search terms create a whole new field of research, SENSO will give small companies access to big data and the tools to make real-time business decisions based on it. The impact on competitiveness for countries that have a broad SENSO network in place will be dramatic.

11. Equipment as Service for You (EASY)—The world became quite comfortable with software as a service, and now we will see the development of equipment as a service. Rental companies already provide this at small scale, and GE provides engines as power by the hour. Soon every major equipment supplier will begin to deliver machine-by-the-hour services to complement equipment sales.

12.  Basics All Supplied in Container (BASIC)—This company will serve emerging markets, such as villages, delivering essential infrastructure in rugged containers: solar power, electrical storage, cell tower, phone charging and service, water pumping and purification, LED lamps, and Internet access with a dedicated channel for information and services. This channel would also offer large global companies access to the bottom of the pyramid. It's the grid-plus-information network for emerging markets.

These twelve examples are just the beginning. The actual possibilities are far, far broader. As we've shown throughout the book, the real benefits come not just from using less but from the fact that managers actually can build whole new classes of capabilities. When a manager does away with CDs and switches to digital music files, that leader doesn't just do away with packaging and unsold merchandise; the change opens the way for the iPod and the iTunes store; then the iPhone; personal radio; compositions that go viral; and more apps than anyone could have imagined. Stefan learned to knit from his grandmother; his daughter is learning from a twelve-year-old girl in Kansas who loves to make YouTube instruction videos. In the future, even wilder combinations of people and capabilities will be knit together, and those who figure out how to invent the future will ride the resource revolution to unprecedented success.

It's time to define your destiny.

CONCLUSION

BROADER IMPLICATIONS

As we hope we've demonstrated thoroughly by now, we are standing before the biggest opportunity in a century. Just as during prior industrial revolutions, this is a time for extraordinary wealth creation as dominant new positions and new business models are established. But this is also a time of creative destruction as old paradigms are supplanted. The integration of 2.5 billion more people into the urban middle class represents a historic economic and social opportunity. However, building the cities to house those 2.5 billion, constructing the transportation networks to connect home and work, and providing the energy, water, and food to support a middle-class lifestyle in the next two decades also represents one of the greatest challenges ever. The global economy is trying to do in two decades for emerging markets what it took the whole twentieth century to accomplish for the OECD countries.

Across the last century, the developed world and the world's leading companies got used to commodity prices that remained relatively stable (outside of shocks such as those that sometimes hit oil) or even bene-fited from real declines—metals prices declined 0.2 percent annually, and prices of agricultural commodities fell 0.7 percent per year between 1900 and 2000. As a result, while good managerial leadership improved labor productivity and capital productivity at more than 3 percent a year, gains in resource productivity have languished at less than 1 percent a year for the last twenty years. Meeting the needs of the new urban 2.5 billion will require companies and countries to improve resource productivity at closer to 3 percent a year for the next twenty years—triple recent levels.

Less is more

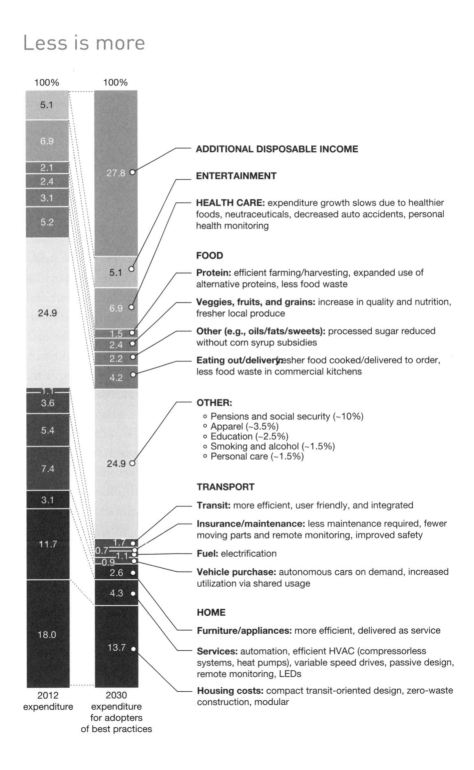

ADDITIONAL DISPOSABLE INCOME

ENTERTAINMENT

HEALTH CARE: expenditure growth slows due to healthier foods, neutraceuticals, decreased auto accidents, personal health monitoring

FOOD

Protein: efficient farming/harvesting, expanded use of alternative proteins, less food waste

Veggies, fruits, and grains: increase in quality and nutrition, fresher local produce

Other (e.g., oils/fats/sweets): processed sugar reduced without corn syrup subsidies

Eating out/delivery: fresher food cooked/delivered to order, less food waste in commercial kitchens

OTHER:
- Pensions and social security (~10%)
- Apparel (~3.5%)
- Education (~2.5%)
- Smoking and alcohol (~1.5%)
- Personal care (~1.5%)

TRANSPORT

Transit: more efficient, user friendly, and integrated

Insurance/maintenance: less maintenance required, fewer moving parts and remote monitoring, improved safety

Fuel: electrification

Vehicle purchase: autonomous cars on demand, increased utilization via shared usage

HOME

Furniture/appliances: more efficient, delivered as service

Services: automation, efficient HVAC (compressorless systems, heat pumps), variable speed drives, passive design, remote monitoring, LEDs

Housing costs: compact transit-oriented design, zero-waste construction, modular

2012 expenditure

2030 expenditure for adopters of best practices

We know how to innovate at these rates—managerial focus has improved labor and capital productivity at these rates consistently. In addition, incentives for rapid innovation on resources have been piling up. Since 2000, commodity prices have surged—a 225 percent increase for energy, 275 percent for metals, 125 percent for agricultural products. Resource prices have become more volatile and are increasingly linked—in 1970, the correlation between food commodities and oil prices generally ranged from the negative to less than 0.36 (out of a possible 1.0), but the correlation today exceeds 0.8 for most food commodities. The immediate implication is that any surge in oil prices will lead, more than before, to surges in food prices. The broader point is that all commodities are more linked than in the past, so almost any shock wave will spread further these days.

Yet, the convergence of industrial technologies and information technologies, biology, and nanoscale material science is creating remarkable opportunities. We can already point to some sustained examples of much greater resource productivity. Between 1950 and 2000, U.S. corn productivity improved almost 3 percent each year. For the better part of the last decade, shale oil and gas have delivered productivity improvements of around 22 percent a year, laying the foundation for a restructuring of the U.S. energy sector. The new American fuel economy standards and European CO_2 requirements enabled by dramatic improvements in engine technologies will drive a 5 percent per year improvement in automobile fuel productivity across the next decade and save consumers $8,200 a year in fuel spending per household.

There are plenty more opportunities where those came from. Half of all food production is not consumed in both the developed and the developing world—in the developing world, more than half the food spoils in the fields or on the way to market while, in developed markets, close to half the food spoils or is thrown out at the point of consumption. Oil and gas production processes recover 20 to 40 percent of the resource in place. Only 14 to 26 percent of the energy in the fuel in a car's tank actually gets used to move the car down the road. In many cities around the world, a third to half of the water is wasted. The same is true in agriculture because of the evaporation of irrigation water. In the power sector, even the most efficient central station plants convert only about 60 percent of the fuel

Resource productivity—past and future

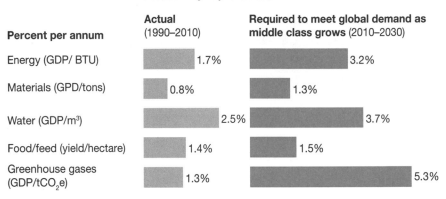

Productivity improvement

Percent per annum	Actual (1990–2010)	Required to meet global demand as middle class grows (2010–2030)
Energy (GDP/ BTU)	1.7%	3.2%
Materials (GPD/tons)	0.8%	1.3%
Water (GDP/m³)	2.5%	3.7%
Food/feed (yield/hectare)	1.4%	1.5%
Greenhouse gases (GDP/tCO₂e)	1.3%	5.3%

into power. Many of our capital assets have average utilization rates in the teens or single-digit percentages—roads, office buildings, cars, transmission lines. And on and on and on.

We also see vastly different rates of productivity between companies and countries, demonstrating that a step up in performance is possible. For instance, LED penetration is one-third higher in China than in the EU, and both are far ahead of the United States. Phnom Penh has a lower water leakage rate than London, thanks to a reform plan initiated by Ek Sonn Chan, the director general of the Water Supply Authority in the 1990s. Singapore and Israel lead the world in water reuse and reclamation. Latvia is the EU leader in building-efficiency improvement due to a concerted campaign that included new mandates, audits, information campaigns, financing, and application of new technologies.

Success depends on changing the fundamental rules of business, focusing managerial innovation on improving resource productivity at 3 percent–plus a year. Improvements in labor and capital productivity won't be enough anymore. Nor will incremental improvement in resource productivity.

As we've shown throughout the book, it's imperative to think big and drive the pace of innovation. The energy, water, and food systems around the world are mature global businesses at a massive scale—tinkering around the edges, while romantic, won't drive the productivity improvement required.

WHAT COMPANIES SHOULD FOCUS ON

To succeed in the coming decades, companies must systematically look at resource opportunities to drive growth and profits. Can a new material substitute for one that has been used historically? What science-inspired ideas to self-assemble, to design new structures, or to boost performance of substances derived from biological organisms can generate surges in productivity? Where can waste be eliminated by applying the growing body of so-called lean operating principles to energy, water, and materials? What would it take to increase upgrades, reuse or recycling, making a process circular? What opportunities are there to optimize some inefficient process for the company, its suppliers, or its customers, when looking across the integrated supply chain? What would it take to move something out of the physical realm and into the virtual?

After raising the initial questions about opportunities to save resources, companies must focus on integrating seamlessly all the capabilities of new offerings, while adding software and other information-technology capabilities. Even while innovating, companies need to ensure compatibility and integration into existing infrastructure. Companies must also investigate new business models to enable adoption and capture all the potential benefits. Naively adding something new to existing systems often reduces system performance. To succeed in the long term, companies have to understand the workings of the whole system into which an offering fits.

A result will be that companies will sell more services and integrated solutions, not just equipment. That shift will put new strains on business models but create significant opportunities for those companies that have the organizational capabilities to deliver software and systems in an industrial context at scale, along with the ability to innovate in their financing.

Once a company has decided what to bring to market, it needs to carefully consider when the timing will be right, both for the technology and for the customer. Then come the tough issues involved with getting production to full scale and with preparing the market. Given the rapid rate of change in industry cost structures, the question of timing will be essential—too early and a company ends up like lightbulb inventor Joseph Swan (forgotten because of Thomas Edison's improvements a decade later);

too late and a company ends up like Kodak (behind in the market it created in the 1970s when a Kodak researcher invented the digital camera sensor).

Finally, companies will have to change their organizational structures and rethink their operating processes while training workers to do very different tasks and finding new types of workers for the skills needed in the transformation from leathernecks to automation and optimization. The new era will be defined by an organizational structure that can work with digital natives, driving great data and decision-support tools to the front line and building the networked organization.

IMPLICATIONS FOR GOVERNMENTS

Throughout this book, we have focused primarily on the management toolkit and principles that allow companies to not only survive resource revolutions but to capture the business opportunities they create. Clearly, the dynamics we have described will also unleash structural transformations of entire industries, even countries and continents. The dynamics will change trade flows as substitutions or new technologies give newfound advantage to different resources or allow new reserves to be exploited. This resource revolution also represents a structural transformation of the entire economy, one that offers an opportunity for countries to leapfrog into middle-income levels and potentially even allows resource-poor countries to reach economic prosperity at OECD levels. (The macroeconomic perspectives and performance gaps between countries have been discussed in detail in the resource revolution reports published by the McKinsey Sustainability and Resource Productivity Practice and McKinsey Global Institute.)

This resource revolution represents an enormous challenge for governments. Governments have a large role to play, including funding basic research on materials, biology, and systems performance as well as on new energy, transport, and agricultural technologies. It is also essential for governments to ensure a level playing field that minimizes subsidies to legacy industries. In addition, governments must avoid the temptation to write codes and laws that require specific technologies; instead, governments should set bold, long-term performance standards, while leaving it to the market to determine how to lock in those improvements. For example, governments should just require that storage of pollutants be permanent, not necessarily "geologic"; that there should be energy storage but not necessarily "battery" storage; that transportation should meet efficiency standards, but not mandate specific fuel types or mixtures.

Governments also need to recognize that technologies have vastly different learning curves that drive cost reduction and different scaling potential. If a technology's potential is large and transformative, and the cost reduction rapid, it deserves a much more aggressive adoption than technologies that are improving slowly and incrementally and have no foreseeable way to get to commercial viability, or have only limited deployment potential. The former are going to save households and companies money and transform the economy, while the latter are subsidies for (most likely) regional pet projects or special interests. It is possible to invest government spending, provide incentives, and even apply mandates—as controversial as they are in the United States—to boost economic performance without picking specific companies or products as winners. Setting an aggressive vehicle mileage standard or tightening efficiency standards for appliances, lightbulbs, buildings, and the like allows multiple technologies and business models to compete, allows private capital to invest in innovation over years, and yields savings for companies and households that can be reinvested in other areas for GDP growth.

As knowledge workers, software skills, and techonology-enabled services become more important, governments will need to ensure that workforces have the proper skills and education to participate in new business models and evolving sectors. Over time, governments may want to shift tax bases from labor and residency to value creation, intellectual property, and resource consumption.

Government has a substantial role to play in broader macroeconomic measurements, too—those that drive behavior, policies, and investment flows. We take current government statistics—GDP, unemployment, Treasury interest rates, and so on—as the right measures, as though they're written in stone. But they are outcomes from the second industrial revolution. Each was an innovation and designed for a specific purpose. For instance, the notion of gross domestic product was developed by Simon Kuznets at the National Bureau of Economic Research in 1934 specifically to drive growth in the midst of the Great Depression. GDP became broadly adopted as a way to maximize war production during

World War II. Ten years later, GDP was used to measure the progress of countries under the Bretton Woods system of financial management and eventually was adopted by the United Nations and the World Bank. Kuznets won the Nobel Prize in Economics in 1971 for his innovation. But in his first report to Congress in 1934, Kuznets warned that "the welfare of a nation can scarcely be inferred from a measure of national income" and that GDP and GNP oversimplify the real health of a country because they do not reflect income distribution or the "intensity and unpleasantness of effort going into the earning of income." We also know that GDP does not measure quality-of-life drivers such as education, medical care, raising children, the recreational benefits of nature, undeveloped natural resources, and even what has more recently become known as "ecosystem services"—the benefits that nature provides to companies in the form of coastal protection, stability of ecosystems, and so forth.

It's important to recognize that our most common measurements still focus predominantly on capital flows (capital accounts, market cap, trade flows, foreign direct investments, and the like) and on labor productivity (unemployment and GDP per capita). We do not have an equivalent set of national accounting standards for how efficient we are in our use of land, water, metals, and other natural resources. We don't speak in terms of GDP per acre, or GDP per mineral reserves depleted or "invested." It is fascinating that, prior to the second industrial revolution, measurements such as land holdings, the number of boxcars, or fur trade rights defined prosperity. Even beyond tracking resource productivity directly, the shift from products to services and, beyond that, to convenience and service quality, raises the issue of whether a country's welfare should be measured primarily in material output. This is actually not a new idea: When Thomas Jefferson wrote the Declaration of Independence, he borrowed John Locke's original declaration of fundamental rights, keeping the words "life" and "liberty" but substituting "property" with "happiness." Bhutan employs a very literal (and sometimes ridiculed) measure of gross national happiness. Yet the American notion that "equal opportunity" enables the "pursuit of happiness" echoes the caveats, raised by Kuznets in his GDP reports, that income distribution is as important for a country's welfare as GDP. The

fundamental adage that each generation needs to leave both growing prosperity and a growing resource endowment to the next generation is at the
heart of the resource revolution.

Nicolas Sarkozy established a commission of Nobel laureates to begin
to develop more comprehensive alternative measures that would include
not only measures of output but other measures of performance and productivity. In simple terms, we need to move from just "bigger" to "better."
While this is clearly not a simple issue to resolve, we see the effort by the
Sustainability Accounting Standards Board (SASB) to define materiality
of different aspects of sustainability as a good step in the right direction,
because it enables companies and investors to begin to understand the
resource productivity of companies in each industry and to compare
them. The effort will also help reveal the risks embedded in exposure to
resource supply, price shocks, and the externalities that are not adequately
priced into company valuations.

IMPLICATIONS FOR NON-GOVERNMENTAL ORGANIZATIONS

The disruptive nature of the changes underway in resource revolutions
will also change the work of NGOs. Historically, many NGOs have
focused on a primary issue: preserving land, fighting air pollution,
ensuring clean water, and so forth. Given the tighter connection between
resources, and the substitution dynamics and introduction of disruptive
technologies, many NGOs will have to broaden their scope of issues.
It will not work to solve a water shortage with a lens on only water,
for example, because some solutions such as desalination essentially shift
the problem to energy, while changes in agriculture will have an impact
on soils and food production. Yet others, like changes in river flow, will
affect energy generation that depends on hydro or even simply cooling
water. (Globally, 8 percent of water is used for energy production.)
The desired changes cannot be brought about simply through lawsuits
or compliance actions. They require collaborative approaches such as
those being pioneered now by the Environmental Defense Fund and the
Nature Conservancy, working together with companies and governments
to define new best practices.

INVESTING IN RESOURCE REVOLUTIONS

Resource revolutions combine commodity price volatility, creative destruction of companies, and industries and new business models and technologies interacting to create disproportionate wealth. We have seen how much shareholder value was created by software and IT in the enterprise, consumer device and entertainment, and Internet realms. These industries are still small compared with the global energy, materials, transportation, infrastructure, and industrial sectors, where these IT technologies are now unleashing productivity. It is easy to see why this is fertile ground for the savvy investor looking for alpha growth.

But getting investing right over the next few decades will not be easy. More than half the value of most natural-resources companies (oil, mining, etc.) is in the proven reserves, not in operating cash flows. As demand grows and the marginal producer has to extract lower-grade resources in tougher conditions, prices can rise steeply. But a doubling of economically viable reserves in existing wells, as we are now seeing in U.S. shale and light tight oil, can also drastically lower prices—gas dropped from $11 per million BTUs to around $2 before recovering.

Even beyond the direct resources and these relatively short-term effects, investors face challenges. Pension funds and other long-term investors are typically overweighted in their allocation to energy and infrastructure companies; the majority of them are centered on current technology. While their valuations will be governed in the near term by earnings performance, they are vulnerable to substantial declines in market capitalization, as replacement technologies and business models emerge. For instance, we looked at the exposure of a large utility's earnings to the penetration of solar-distributed generation and energy-efficiency technologies for buildings. A conservative analysis of technological progress showed that, instead of 4 percent annual earnings growth, the utility would experience a 10 percent decline in earnings over ten years. A more aggressive penetration of these technologies would reduce earnings by 35 percent. Once the market becomes aware of this dynamic, market caps will reset to reflect the new expectations. Similarly, used-SUV prices declined substantially in 2008 when gas prices rose above $4 per gallon and American car buyers switched to smaller, more efficient cars and upgraded less frequently. If even just a portion of buyers are only interested in hybrid or electric cars, the entire car-financing market will be in trouble, because its economics rely on the value of the car at the end of the lease.

Smart investors such as Harvard's endowment and Singapore's sovereign wealth funds have made long-term bets on rising resource prices and on shifts between asset types. Even commodities like water, while hard to invest in directly, can be accessed indirectly by buying water rights or products that represent large amounts of water embedded in a product or invested in the production of the product. A firm financed by eBay's cofounder Jeff Skoll, Capricorn Investment Group, has even combined strategies: It has bought farmland in the portions of California that are also highly suitable for solar—investing near-term in rising agricultural commodities with a steady cash flow while placing a long-term bet on water rights and solar potential. If one thinks of the water and solar potential as upside option bets, this example makes clear that investing in resource revolutions is quite different from exclusionary screens based on social-impact criteria, which have long been derided by "purist" investors looking only for good returns. The revolutionary part here is the additional alpha from a long-term secular trend, driven by urbanization, and the rise of the middle class in emerging markets, but manifested in very specific additional option value above market expectations—pure alpha.

A FINAL NOTE FOR CONSUMERS

If you've gotten this far in the book, you may be wondering what all this means for each of us as a citizen, consumer, and parent. We began this book with a dedication to our children, because we both believe we are talking about a generational change. The world we live in today will be as different from the one our children will inherit as the Victorian era of mansions, servants, and tenements in the 1880s was different from the Golden Age in the 1920s, with electric appliances and lighting, motor cars, skyscrapers, radio, indoor plumbing, multinationals, stock markets, public libraries, and concert halls funded by the wealth the age created. We can guess at cleaner cities that combine autonomous electric vehicles and mass transit, that reclaim road space for urban green space and agriculture, that reuse nearly all materials for new production and energy generation. But before we get beyond guessing, each of us has hard work to do, just like the companies we profile.

We need to ensure our government shapes this transformation, and use our votes to counteract the influence of incumbents vested in locking in an unsustainable status quo. We can make informed choices in the products we select, beginning with our own measurement of resource productivity in the food, cars, and homes we buy, even before governments change GDP metrics. We can educate our children to be ready for a world where understanding software, having the ability to work in a networked global organization, and being able to integrate systems across disciplines matter more than ever before. Then our children will enjoy the fruits of our labor, our capital, and our resources.

We wish you the best, not the biggest!

ABOUT THE AUTHORS

In many ways, this book began in the late 1970s in Saalfelden, Austria. Nestled in a valley near Salzburg at the foot of the Sea of Stones Mountains, the town contains a Gothic chapel from the 1600s and is surrounded by several castles. Stefan's maternal grandfather, Peter Stautzebach, had retired to Saalfelden after a career as a welder, and he was thinking not about the picture-postcard past, but about the future.

Stautzebach, a tinkerer who held numerous patents, had become intrigued by the possibilities of solar power and enlisted the help of then-seven-year-old Stefan to build a solar system to heat his house. The system worked so well that the furnace stayed off on most winter days. The allure of solar energy stayed with Stefan and, years later, as a Stanford University freshman, he heard about a competition for solar-powered cars. He formed a group for the national competition—a race from Florida to Detroit sponsored by General Motors. Stefan's group finished fifth; they later went to a track and got their car up to 75 mph, powered by solar panels that produced about as much electricity as that needed to power a hair dryer.

At McKinsey, Stefan served the semiconductor industry. Working with companies that were making Moore's Law happen, he became immersed in technologies that power exponential change. He also saw how semiconductor technologies could drive radical improvements in other fields, including clean energy—letting them benefit from the plunging cost curves that Moore's Law has defined in the computer industry. While old-line industries such as electricity and lighting had seen only incremental improvement for a century, they are now benefiting from the kind of disruptive progress that has taken a gigabyte of storage from costing $300,000 in 1980 to about a dime today.

In 2006, Stefan stepped aside as the head of the McKinsey Semiconductor Practice to return to the interest in clean energy that his grandfather had kindled in the Alps decades earlier. He wanted to add "a second bottom line," not only to help companies grow faster and make more profit but also to have a bigger impact on society and contribute to the quality of life of future generations.

Matt was arriving at the same ideas, but from a very different direction: the heavy-industry world of oil and gas companies, utilities, and aerospace. Matt had spent twenty years consulting in the industrial world and led McKinsey's power and oil and gas practices in the Americas. He helped improve refining performance in the United States, Australia, Japan, Korea, and Wales; set up gasoline retailing ventures in the United Kingdom and Thailand; optimized oil tanker movements in the Gulf of Mexico; assessed pathways to enter the Russian oil sector and the Brazilian power sector; helped set up one of the first smart-grid networks in the United States; and reduced the costs of building some of the world's largest airplanes. Over time, Matt served clients on every continent except Antarctica.

Our joint work took a detour when Matt agreed to run the team at the Department of Energy that allocated the $36.5 billion of funds that the DOE controlled as part of the Recovery Act. The goal of the eighteen-month position was to get money out the door quickly—to stimulate the flailing economy—but it was also to find as many opportunities as possible that could lead to breakthroughs in clean-energy production and in energy efficiency across the United States. The position provided an extraordinarily broad look at everything energy, including the innovations being fostered at the DOE's National Labs and in the newly formed Advanced Research Projects Agency–Energy (ARPA–E), which broadened Matt's view of what was possible.

Matt returned to McKinsey in October 2010 and soon flew to Boston for a meeting of senior partners. At the meeting, Stefan had been talking about a book that would look broadly at what he saw as a coming revolution in the use of all resources, not just those used to generate energy. When Matt arrived at the meeting, he began describing the outlines of a book very similar to this one that would draw on his experiences at DOE.

It didn't take us long to find each other and agree to work together on what you now hold in your hands.

NOTES

INTRODUCTION
Page

4   **a major McKinsey Global Institute Report:** McKinsey Global Institute, *Curbing Global Energy-Demand Growth: The Energy Productivity Opportunity*, May 2007, www.mckinsey.com/insights/energy_resources_materials/curbing_global_energy_demand_growth.

4   **the seminal report on the resource revolution:** McKinsey Global Institute, *Resource Revolution: Meeting the World's Energy, Materials, Food and Water Needs*, November 2011, www.mckinsey.com/insights/energy_resources_materials/resource_revolution.

7   **the average European was only about two times as well off as a Roman:** Maddison, Angus. *Contours of the World Economy 1–2030 AD: Essays in Macro-Economic History*, Oxford: Oxford University Press, 2007.

7   **the average European today is some thirteen times as well off:** Ibid.

7   **Boeing has the potential to reduce:** R. R. Boyer, "Attributes, Characteristics, and Applications of Titanium and its Alloys," *Journal of Materials*, Vol. 62, No. 5.

7   **use 20 to 30 percent less energy than their competitors:** Bill Trout, "Energy Intensity Index," Solomon Associates, 2012.

8   **capital requirements for our transportation systems:** Paul Barter, "'Cars Are Parked 95% of the Time.' Let's Check!" *Reinventing Parking* (blog), February 22, 2013, www.reinventingparking.org/2013/02/cars-are-parked-95-of-time-lets-check.html.

CHAPTER ONE

11   **China alone will build two and a half cities the size of Chicago:** McKinsey Global Institute, *Urban World: Cities and the Rise of the Consuming Class*, June 2012, www.mckinsey.com/insights/urbanization/urban_world_cities_and_the_rise_of_the_consuming_class.

12   **55 percent of the copper supply comes from recycled sources:** "Copper in the USA: Bright Future Glorious Past," Copper Development Association Inc., 2013, www.copper.org/education/history/us-history/g_fact_producers.html.

13   **13 percent of the world's population industrialized:** Jeremy Grantham, "Resource Limitations 2: Separating the Dangerous from the Merely Serious," *GMO Quarterly Letter,* July 2011.

13   **16 percent of the world industrialized for the first time:** Ibid.

13   **37 percent of the world's population:** *Urban World*, McKinsey Global Institute.

13   **the daily energy usage of someone in the middle class:** Morgan Kelly and Cormac Ó Gráda, "Agricultural Output: Calories and Living Standards in England Before and During the Industrial Revolution," University College Dublin Centre for Economic Research, April 2012, www.ucd.ie/t4cms/WP12_12.pdf.

13   **a member of the middle class uses more than 200,000 kcalories:** U.S. Energy Information Administration, *Annual Energy Review 2011*, September 2012, www.eia.doe.gov/emeu/aer/eh/intro.html.

14   **the demand for steel is expected to rise 80 percent by 2030:** *Resource Revolution*, McKinsey Global Institute.

14   **The need for energy will climb by a third:** Ibid.

14   **a third of the world's arable land:** "World Development Indicators: Agricultural inputs," The World Bank, 2013, wdi.worldbank.org/table/3.2.

15   **a pound of beef takes fifteen times as much water:** World Economic Forum App, 2013.

15   **A calorie of beef requires 160 times more energy:** David Pimental and Marcia Pimentel, "Sustainability of Meat-Based and Plant-Based Diets and the Environment," *American Journal of Clinical Nutrition*, Vol. 78, No. 3, ajcn.nutrition.org/content/78/3/660S.abstract.

15   **Animal protein requires:** Lucas Reijnders and Sam Soret, "Quantification of the Environmental Impact of Different Dietary Protein Choices," *American Journal of Clinical Nutrition*, September 2003, Vol. 78, No. 3, ajcn.nutrition.org/content/78/3/664S.full.

        H. L. Tuomisto, "Food Security and Protein Supply—Cultured Meat a Solution?" Wildlife Conservation Research Unit University of Oxford, 2010, www.new-harvest.org/wp-content/uploads/2013/07/AAB-food-security-conf_Tuomisto-2010.doc-Compatibility-Mode.pdf.

15   **The first well struck oil at sixty-nine feet:** "The Energy Report," Texas Comptroller of Public Accounts, May 2008, www.window.state.tx.us/specialrpt/energy/pdf/96-1266EnergyReport.pdf.

15   **The cost of bringing each new oil well online:** "U.S. Nominal Cost per Crude Oil Well Drilled," U.S. Energy Information Administration, May 31, 2013, www.eia.gov/dnav/pet/hist/LeafHandler .ashx?n=PET&s=E_ERTWO_XWWN_NUS_MDW&f=A.

16   **Those nuggets were 95 percent pure:** Richard Schodde, "The Key Drivers Behind Resource Growth: An Analysis of the Copper Industry Over the Last 100 Years," Presentation at the 2012 MEMS Conference Mineral and Markets over the Long Term, Phoenix, March 3, 2010, www .slideshare.net/RichardSchodde/growth-factors-for-copper-schodde-sme-mems-march2010-final. Kevin M. Cullen, "Old Copper Culture," Milwaukee Public Museum, 2006, www.mpm.edu/research-collections/anthropology/online-collections-research/old-copper-culture.

16   **Singapore already gets 25 percent of its water:** "The Singapore Water Story," Public Utilities Board, www.pub.gov.sg/water/pages/singaporewaterstory.aspx.

16   **In San Diego, a $1 billion desalination plant:** Felicity Barringer, "In California, What Price Water?" *New York Times*, February 28, 2013, www.nytimes.com/2013/03/01/business/energy-environment/a-costly-california-desalination-plant-bets-on-future-affordability.html.

16   **the water level fell by a full meter:** *Resource Revolution*, McKinsey Global Institute.

23   **Animal power was so scarce:** Braudel, Fernand. *Civilization and Capitalism, 15th–18th Century: The Wheels of Commerce*. Berkeley: University of California Press, 1982.

24   **seventy-five steam engines were in operation:** Rolt, L.T.C. and John Scott Allen. *The Steam Engine of Thomas Newcomen*, Moorland Publishing Company, 1977.

24   **generated a tenfold increase in productivity:** *Countours of the World Economy 1–2030 AD*, Maddison.

        "The Industrial Revolution 1780–1860: a survey," *The Economic History of Britain since 1700*, Roderick Floud and Donald McCloskey, eds., Cambridge University Press, 1981, www .deirdremccloskey.com/docs/pdf/Article_62.pdf.

25   **It took Watt more than ten years to perfect his design:** Carl Lira, "Biography of James Watt," Michigan State University College of Engineering, May 21, 2013, www.egr.msu.edu/~lira/supp/steam/wattbio.html.

25   **Watt had to give up two-thirds of his business:** Arago, François. *Historical Eloge of James Watt*. John Murray, 1839. Accessed December 9, 2013, books.google.com/books?id=3lUEAAA AMAAJ.

25   **a thirty-year surge in prices for commodities:** "U.S. Crude Oil First Purchase Price," U.S. Energy Information Administration, www.eia.gov/dnav/pet/hist/leafhandler.ashx?n=PET&s= F000000__3&f=A.

        "Historical Gold Prices—1833 to Present," National Mining Association, www.nma.org/pdf/gold/his_gold_prices.pdf.

"Retail Prices of Selected Foods in U.S. Cities, 1890–2011," Pearson Education, www.infoplease .com/ipa/A0873707.html.

28 **the *Times* of London estimated that horse manure:** Owen, David. *Green Metropolis: Why Living Smaller, Living Closer, and Driving Less Are the Keys to Sustainability*, New York: Penguin, 2010.

32 **Railroad builders received 127 million acres of land:** Opie, John. *The Law of the Land: Two Hundred Years of American Farmland Policy*, University of Nebraska Press, 1987.
Richard Sylla and Robert E. Wright, "Early Corporate America: The Largest Industries and Companies Before 1860," *Finance Professionals' Post*, September 27, 2012, post.nyssa .org/nyssa-news/2012/09/early-corporate-america-the-largest-industries-and-companies-before-1860.html.

33 **consumes 1 percent of the world's electricity:** Hager, Thomas. *The Alchemy of Air: A Jewish Genius, a Doomed Tycoon, and the Scientific Discovery that Fed the World but Fueled the Rise of Hitler*, New York: Random House, 2008.

34 **another thirty-year rise in commodity prices:** "U.S. Crude Oil First Purchase Price," U.S. Energy Information Administration.
"Historical Gold Prices—1833 to Present," National Mining Association.
"Retail Prices of Selected Foods in U.S. Cities, 1890–2011," Pearson Education.

35 **the Club of Rome returned to the Malthusian thesis:** Graham Turner, "A Comparison of the Limits to Growth with Thirty Years of Reality," CSIRO Working Paper Series, June 2008, www .csiro.au/files/files/plje.pdf.

36 **world GDP per person is more than double:** "GDP per capita (current US$)," The World Bank, 2013, data.worldbank.org/indicator/NY.GDP.PCAP.CD/countries.

36 **Prices for oil and energy have more than quintupled:** "World Bank Commodity Price Data (The Pink Sheet): annual prices, 1960 to present, nominal US dollars," The World Bank, November 05, 2013, siteresources.worldbank.org/INTPROSPECTS/Resources/3349341304428586133/ pink_data_a.xlsx.

37 **the IT industry as a whole:** Forrest, William, James M. Kaplan, and Noah Kindler, "Data centers: how to cut carbon emissions and costs," *McKinsey on Business Technology*, Vol. 14, No. 6, 2008.

38 **an opinion piece in the Wall Street Journal:** Robert J. Gordon, "Why Innovation Won't Save Us," *Wall Street Journal*, December 21, 2012, online.wsj.com/article/SB1000142412788732446 1604578191781756437940.html.

CHAPTER TWO

43 **Texas oilman George Mitchell:** George Mitchell, interview by Jim Barlow, *Houston Oral History Project*, Houston Public Library, November 20, 2007, digital.houstonlibrary.org/oral-history/ george-mitchell.php.

50 **gas from shale accounting for more than 20 percent:** "Technically Recoverable Shale Oil and Shale Gas Resources: An Assessment of 137 Shale Formations in 41 Countries Outside the United States," U.S. Energy Information Administration, June 10, 2013, www.eia.gov/analysis/ studies/worldshalegas.

51 **The United States is now producing:** U.S. Energy Information Administration, *Annual Energy Outlook 2014*, early release reference case, December 16, 2013, www.eia.gov/forecasts/aeo/er/ pdf/0383er(2014).pdf.

51 **The United States is on a path to pass Saudi Arabia:** Ibid.

51 **the United States is on pace to export:** Ibid.

51 **60 percent of the U.S. trade deficit is oil imports:** Robert E. Scott, "U.S. trade deficit up in 2011; China accounted for three-fourths of rise in non-oil goods trade deficit," Economic Policy Institute, February 10, 2012, www.epi.org/publication/trade-deficit-2011-china-accounted-fourths.

51 **gas prices in the United States have dropped 66 percent:** "Natural Gas Market Overview: U.S. v. European Prices," Federal Energy Regulatory Commission (FERC), Market Oversight, September 2013.

52   **The sheer volume of water used in fracking:** "Water Usage," Chesapeake Energy, www .hydraulicfracturing.com/water-usage/pages/information.aspx.

56   **OPower now reports on electricity usage:** Alex Laskey (Founder, Opower) and Ogi Kavazovic (Vice President of Strategy & Marketing, Opower), in discussion with the authors, February 1, 2013.

CHAPTER **THREE**

62   **average occupancy has dropped:** U.S. Department of Transportation Federal Highway Administration, *Summary of Travel Trends: 2009 National Household Travel Survey,* June 2011, nhts.ornl.gov/2009/pub/stt.pdf.

62   **Amory Lovins has pointed out:** Lovins, Amory. *Reinventing Fire: Bold Business Solutions for the New Energy Era,* White River Junction, Vermont: Chelsea Green Publishing Company, 2011.

62   **own a car mainly to park it:** "'Cars are parked 95% of the time.' Let's check!", Barter.

62   **Americans devote 17% of their annual spending:** "Average Annual Expenditures and Characteristics of All Consumer Units, Consumer Expenditure Survey, 2006–2012," U.S. Department of Labor Bureau of Labor Statistics, September 10, 2013, www.bls.gov/cex/2012/ standard/multiyr.pdf.

62   **lose $1,522 per person annually to traffic accidents:** "AAA Study Finds Costs Associated with Traffic Crashes Are More than Three Times Greater than Congestion Costs," AAA Newsroom, November 3, 2011, newsroom.aaa.com/2011/11/aaa-study-finds-costs-associated-with-traffic- crashes-are-more-than-three-times-greater-than-congestion-costs.

62   **the ninth leading cause of death:** "The Top 10 Causes of Death," World Health Organization, July 2013, www.who.int/mediacentre/factsheets/fs310/en.

62   **A freeway operating at peak throughput:** John van Rijn, "Road Capacities," Indevelopment, 2004, www.indevelopment.nl/PDFfiles/CapacityOfRroads.pdf.

63   **Pilot tests by the Department of Transportation:** "Applications for the Environment: Real-Time Information Synthesis (AERIS)," U.S. Department of Transportation Intelligent Transportation Systems Joint Program Office, August 16, 2012, www.its.dot.gov/aeris/world_congress/aeris_ ecodrive_applications.htm.

64   **30 percent of the emissions from cars:** John Markoff, "Can't Find a Parking Spot? Check Smartphone," *New York Times,* July 12, 2008, www.nytimes.com/2008/07/12/business/12new park.html.

64   **Inrix gathers location information:** Bryan Mistele (President & CEO, INRIX), in discussion with the authors, February 4, 2013.

65   **9.4 million cars a year are involved in accidents:** "Fatality Analysis Reporting System General Estimates System: 2011 Data Summary," U.S. Department of Transportation National Highway Traffic Safety Administration, April 2013, www-nrd.nhtsa.dot.gov/Pubs/811755DS.pdf.

65   **getting adaptive cruise control into 20 percent of the cars:** George Arnaout and Shannon Bowling, "Towards Reducing Traffic Congestion Using Cooperative Adaptive Cruise Control on a Freeway with a Ramp," *Journal of Industrial Engineering and Management,* September 2011, dx.doi.org/10.3926/jiem.344.

65   **33 percent of drivers didn't even touch the brakes:** Joseph B. White, "The Future, Coming Soon: Self-Driving Cars Mainstream by 2025," *Corporate Intelligence (blog), Wall Street Journal,* April 17, 2013, blogs.wsj.com/corporate-intelligence/2013/04/17/the-future-coming-soon-self -driving-cars-mainstream-by-2025.

68   **Platooning increases gas mileage by 30 to 40 percent:** Erik Larsson, Gustav Sennton, and Jeffrey Larson, "Computational Complexity and Heuristic Solvers for Maximizing Platooning Fuel Savings," *Optimization Online,* August 22, 2013, www.optimization-online.org/DB_ FILE/2013/09/4030.pdf.

68   **more than 30,000 lives would be saved:** "Early Estimate of Motor Vehicle Traffic Fatalities for the First Half (January–September) of 2013," U.S. Department of Transportation National Highway Traffic Safety Administration, October 2013, www-nrd.nhtsa.dot.gov/Pubs/811845.pdf.

68   **More than 2 million people:** Lan Zhao, Jennifer Lucado, and Carol Stocks, "Emergency Department Visits Associated with Motor Vehicle Accidents, 2006," *Healthcare Cost and Utilization Project,* Agency for Healthcare Research and Quality, January 2010, www.hcup-us .ahrq.gov/reports/statbriefs/sb84.pdf.

68   **$260 billion would be saved:** "AAA Study Finds Costs Associated with Traffic Crashes Are More than Three Times Greater than Congestion Costs," AAA Newsroom.

68   **optimal capacity on a freeway:** David Levinson, "Highway Capacity and Level of Service," University of Minnesota, 2007, nexus.umn.edu/Courses/ce3201/CE3201-L2-04.pdf.

69   **a company might offer consumers transportation:** Lawrence D. Burns, William C. Jordan, and Bonnie A. Scarborough, "Transforming Personal Mobility," The Earth Institute, Columbia University, January 27, 2013, sustainablemobility.ei.columbia.edu/files/2012/12/Transforming-Personal-Mobility-Jan-27-20132.pdf.

69   **telecom companies make 8.5 percent net margins:** "Industry Summary," Yahoo! Finance, November 14, 2013, biz.yahoo.com/p/840conamed.html.

71   **the cost to operate an electric car:** Don Anair and Amine Mahmassani, "State of Charge: Electric Vehicles' Global Warming Emissions and Fuel-Cost Savings across the United States," Union of Concerned Scientists, June 2012, www.ucsusa.org/assets/documents/clean_vehicles/ electric-car-global-warming-emissions-report.pdf.

71   **Porsche has built two electric motors:** Jens Meiners, "Porsche 918 Spyder Priced, Matching 911 Turbo S Will Be Optional," *Car and Driver,* March 2011, www.caranddriver.com/ news/2014-porsche-918-spyder-pricing-news.

72   **Electric motors are 95 percent efficient:** Anup Bandivadekar, et al, "On the Road to 2035: Reducing Transportation Petroleum Consumption and GHG Emissions," MIT Laboratory for Energy and the Environment, July 2008, web.mit.edu/sloan-auto-lab/research/beforeh2/otr2035/ On%20the%20Road%20in%202035_MIT_July%202008.pdf.

73   **the *Wall Street Journal* review of the Model S:** Dan Neil, "I Am Silent, Hear Me Roar," *Rumble Seat* (blog), *Wall Street Journal,* July 6, 2012, online.wsj.com/news/articles/SB10001424052702 3042118045775046322387409666.

75   **batteries take far longer to recharge:** "Global EV Outlook: Understanding the Electric Vehicle Landscape to 2020," International Energy Agency, April 2013, www.iea.org/topics/transport/ electricvehiclesinitiative/EVI_GEO_2013_FullReport.pdf.

80   **Some 1.7 trillion hens' eggs are laid every year:** Josh Tetrick (CEO & Founder, Hampton Creek Foods), in discussion with the authors, March 25, 2012.

80   **about 70 percent of the cost of an egg is corn:** Ibid.

80   **the Proterra bus is five times more fuel efficient:** Marc Gottschalk (Chief of Business Development, Proterra), in discussion with the authors, February 4, 2013.

82   **manufacturers have the opportunity to reduce energy usage:** Ken Sommers, "Perspectives on Energy and Optimization," McKinsey and Company working paper 774797, February 2010.

84   **the prospect for a 20 to 50 percent increase in fuel efficiency:** Don Runkle (CEO, EcoMotors International), in discussion with the authors, June 27, 2013.

84   **implementation of tighter corporate average fuel economy (CAFE) standards:** "Obama Administration Finalizes Historic 54.5 mpg Fuel Efficiency Standards," National Highway Traffic Safety Administration, August 28, 2012, www.nhtsa.gov/About+NHTSA/Press+Releases/2012/ Obama+Administration+Finalizes+Historic+54.5+mpg+Fuel+Efficiency+Standards.

84   **Kaiima is going even further:** Doran Gal (CEO, Kaiima), in discussion with the authors, March 4, 2013.

84   **60 percent of the packaged foods in grocery stores:** Pollan, Michael. *The Omnivore's Dilemma: A Natural History of Four Meals.* New York: Penguin, 2006.

84   **EIA estimates are about $3,000 per car:** "State of Charge: Electric Vehicles' Global Warming Emissions and Fuel-Cost Savings across the United States," Union of Concerned Scientists.

86   **the industry went from using 20 percent recycled material:** Diamandis, Peter H., and Steven Kotler. *Abundance: The Future is Better Than You Think.* New York: Simon and Schuster, 2012.

86   **saves 95 percent of the energy required:** Ibid.

88   **Americans buy 150 million cell phones a year:** Kelly Carnago (Senior Vice President, Marketing, eRecyclingCorps), in discussion with the authors, February 6, 2013.
Mary Bristow (Vice President, Marketing & Communications, eRecyclingCorps), in discussion with the authors, February 6, 2013.

88   **$90 billion could be generated each year:** Ellen MacArthur Foundation, *Towards the Circular Economy Volume 2: Opportunities for the Consumer Goods Sector,* January 2013, www.mckinsey .com/~/media/mckinsey/dotcom/client_service/sustainability/pdfs/towards_the_circular_ economy_emf_report.ashx.

88   **e-waste contains 100 times as much gold:** "There is Gold in that Garbage!" McKinsey Institute, April 2012.

88   **we are throwing away about 35 percent of the metal:** Sibley, Scott F. *Flow Studies for Recycling Metal Commodities in the United States,* U.S. Geological Survey, 2004, pubs.usgs .gov/circ/2004/1196am/c1196a-m_v2.pdf.

89   **ATMI grew about twice as fast as the semiconductor industry:** "SEC Filings," ATMI, accessed December 9, 2013, investor.atmi.com/sec.cfm.

89   **biology-inspired manufacturing:** Benyus, Janine M. *Biomimicry: Innovation Inspired by Nature.* New York: William Morrow, 1997.

90   **The giant American waste company Waste Management:** Zain Shauk, "Houston Waste Company Turning Trash Into Treasure," Fuel Fix, December 31, 2012, www.fuelfix.com/ blog/2012/12/31/houston-waste-company-turning-trash-into-treasure.

92   **the new patterns . . . save 20 percent on fuel:** Clay Dillow, "To Increase Passenger Jet Fuel Efficiency, Airlines Look to Nature's Flying Formations," *Popular Science*, December 8, 2009, www.popsci.com/technology/article/2009-12/increase-aircraft-efficiency-researchers-look -natures-flying-formations.

93   **get about 16 percent of the revenue from a digital ad:** Rick Edmonds, Emily Guskin, Tom Rosenstiel, and Amy Mitchell, "Newspapers: Building Digital Revenues Proves Painfully Slow," *The State of the News Media 2012*, Pew Research Center Project for Excellence in Journalism, February 11, 2013, stateofthemedia.org/2012/newspapers-building-digital-revenues-proves-pain fully-slow.

96   **The Pentagon figures it will spend:** U.S. Department of Defense, Fiscal Year (FY) 2013 President's Budget Submission: Air Force Justification Book Volume 1, Aircraft Procurement, February 2012, www.saffm.hq.af.mil/shared/media/document/AFD-120210-115.pdf.

CHAPTER **FOUR**

101   **Between 10 and 15 percent of all material:** Dan Burgoyne, "Construction & Demolition (C&D) Waste Diversion in California," State of California Department of General Services, 2003, www .calrecycle.ca.gov/condemo/CaseStudies/DGSDiversion.pdf.

101   **36 percent of all residential and commercial waste:** Humes, Edward. *Garbology: Our Dirty Love Affair with Trash.* New York: Penguin, 2012.

112   **In China, Zhang Yue:** Keith Bradsher, "Across China, Skyscrapers Brush the Heavens," *New York Times,* August 27, 2013, www.nytimes.com/2013/08/28/realestate/commercial/across-china-skyscrapers-brush-the-heavens.html.

118   **reduces the power requirements for a plane by some 40 percent:** "SiC Power Module: 2009 R&D 100 Entry," Sandia National Laboratories, February 9, 2009, www.sandia.gov/research/ research_development_100_awards/_assets/documents/2009_winners/SIC_Power_Module_ SAND2009-1903P.pdf.

CHAPTER **FIVE**

123   **Paul Krugman wrote:** Paul Krugman, "Why Most Economists' Predictions Are Wrong," *New York Times*, June 1998, web.archive.org/web/19980610100009/www.redherring.com/mag/ issue55/economics.html.

124   **50 billion devices will be connected to the Internet:** Kevin J. O'Brien, "Talk to Me, One Machine Said to the Other," *New York Times*, July 29, 2012, www.nytimes.com/2012/07/30/technology/talk-to-me-one-machine-said-to-the-other.html?pagewanted=all.

129   **only 20 to 40 percent of the transmission and distribution capacity:** Peter Mark Jansson and John Schmalzel, "Increasing Utilization of US Electric Grids via Smart Technologies: Integration of Load Management, Real Time Pricing, Renewables, EVs, and Smart Grid Sensors," *International Journal of Technology, Knowledge, and Society*, Vol. 7, No. 5, January 2012, ijt.cgpublisher.com/product/pub.42/prod.802.

134   **Renewable generation such as solar or wind power:** "Net Generation by Energy Source: Total (All Sectors), 2003–August 2013," U.S. Energy information Administration, October 24, 2013, www.eia.gov/electricity/monthly/epm_table_grapher.cfm?t=epmt_1_01.
        "Electric Power Monthly June 1996," U.S. Energy information Administration, June 1996, www.eia.gov/electricity/monthly/archive/pdf/02269606.pdf.

134   **American utilities could learn from Germany:** Eric Wesoff, "Germany Hits 59 Percent Renewable Peak, Grid Does Not Explode," The Energy Collective, November 2, 2013, theenergycollective.com/stephenlacey/294991/germany-hits-59-renewable-peak-grid-does-not-explode.

137   **Otis has developed a highly integrated approach:** Goodwin, Jason. *Otis: Giving Rise to the Modern City*. Landham Maryland: Ivan R. Dee, 2001.

138   **the time from factory to warehouse is thirty minutes:** Charles Fishman, "The Insourcing Boom," *The Atlantic*, November 28, 2012, www.theatlantic.com/magazine/archive/2012/12/the-insourcing-boom/309166.

139   **GE reduced materials costs by 25 percent:** Ibid.

139   **the water heater made in the United States:** Ibid.

139   **Workers were able to reduce the amount of steel:** John W. Miller, "Indiana Steel Mill Revived with Lessons from Abroad," *Wall Street Journal,* May 21, 2012, online.wsj.com/article/SB10001424052702304444604577340053191940814.html.

140   **the innovator's dilemma described by Clayton Christensen:** Christensen, Clayton M. *The Innovator's Dilemma: When Technologies Cause Great Firms to Fail*, Boston: Harvard Business School Press, 1997.

140   **Silver Spring Networks:** Eric Dresselhuys (Executive Vice President, Global Development, Silver Spring Networks), in discussion with the authors, February 5, 2013.

141   **Another start-up, AutoGrid:** Amit Narayan (CEO, AutoGrid), in discussion with the authors, April 24, 2013.

141   **C3 Energy takes the insights one step further:** www.C3energy.com.

CHAPTER SIX

148   **electricity cost some $5 per kilowatt hour:** Seth Blumsack, "How the Free Market Rocked the Grid," Institute of Electrical and Electronics Engineers, November 22, 2010, spectrum.ieee.org/energy/policy/how-the-free-market-rocked-the-grid.

150   **it takes 2,000 gallons of water and fifteen pounds of feed:** World Economic Forum App. Elizabeth Weise, "Eating can be energy-efficient, too," *USA Today*, April 21, 2009, usatoday30.usatoday.com/news/nation/environment/2009-04-21-carbon-diet_N.htm.

150   **Beyond Meat and other start-ups:** www.beyondmeat.com

151   **electricity from solar cost:** Ridley, Matt. *The Rational Optimist: How Prosperity Evolves*, New York: Harper, 2010.

153   **it took 160 days of work to buy an hour of light:** Ibid.

153   **an hour of light at night cost two days of labor:** Ibid.

153   **two hours of daylight work could buy one hour of light:** Ibid.

153   **eight seconds of work could buy an hour of light at night:** Ibid.

153   **today it costs only half a second of work:** Ibid.

154   **Some 300,000 lamps were sold in 1885:** Kane, Raymond and Heinz Sell. *Revolution in Lamps: A Chronicle of 50 Years of Progress*, Lilburn, Georgia: The Fairmont Press, 2001.

154   **roughly 1.5 billion bulbs were sold in 2011:** "Incandescent Bulbs Still Play a Role in the Future of Lighting," Energy Information Administration, March 23, 2011, www.eia.gov/todayinenergy/detail .cfm?id=630.

154   **95 percent of the electricity that goes into a bulb:** "Smart Lighting," Fraunhofer-Gesellschaft, January 2013, www.fraunhofer.de/en/publications/fraunhofer-magazine/magazine _2013/Fraunhofer-magazine_1-2013/magazine_1-2013_36.html.

154   **a commercial building devotes some 5 percent of its energy:** "Energy Star® Building Upgrade Manual," United States Environmental Protection Agency Office of Air and Radiation, 2008, www .energystar.gov/buildings/sites/default/uploads/tools/EPA_BUM_Full.pdf?4bac-ce19.

154   **lighting consumes 12 percent of the electricity used:** "How Much Electricity Is Used for Lighting in the United States?" U.S. Energy Information Administration, January 9, 2013, www. eia.gov/tools/faqs/faq.cfm?id=99&t=3.

154   **greater energy efficiency in buildings that could save:** McKinsey & Company, *Unlocking Energy Efficiency in the U.S. Economy,* July 2009, www.mckinsey.com/client_service/ electric_power_and_natural_gas/latest_thinking/unlocking_energy_efficiency_in_the _us_economy.
Diana Farrell and Jaana Remes, "Promoting Energy Efficiency in the Developing World," *McKinsey Quarterly,* February 2009, www.mckinsey.com/insights/economic_studies/promoting _energy_efficiency_in_the_developing_world.

158   **Cree seized the opportunity:** Chuck Swoboda (Chief Executive Officer, Cree), in discussion with the authors, July 9, 2013.

CHAPTER SEVEN

165   **The world consumes roughly 1.3 trillion gallons of oil:** U.S. Energy Information Administration, *International Energy Outlook 2013,* July 25, 2013, www.eia.gov/forecasts/ieo.

168   **the cost of solar power has fallen:** Krister Aanesen, Stefan Heck, and Dickon Pinner, "Solar Power: Darkest before Dawn," McKinsey & Company, April 2012, www.mckinsey.com/ client_service/sustainability/latest_thinking/solar_powers_next_shining.

170   **"Customers are used to buying power, not a power plant":** Edward Fenster (CEO, SunRun), in discussion with the authors, May 31, 2013.

172   **The term, coined by author and consultant Geoff Moore:** Moore, Geoffrey A. *Crossing the Chasm: Marketing and Selling Disruptive Products to Mainstream Customers.* New York: HarperCollins, 2002.

173   **Rene White and Steve Kimball of Moore's Chasm Group:** Renee White (Managing Director, Chasm Group), and Steve Kimball (Principal, Chasm Group), in discussion with the authors, June 6, 2013.

175   **CalStar, a Wisconsin-based building-products manufacturer:** Joel Rood (Chief Executive Officer, CalStar), in discussion with the authors, May 10, 2013.

177   **FirstSolar, arguably the most successful new solar technology start-up:** www.firstsolar.com.

177   **Stion, a leading thin-film solar panel manufacturer:** Chet Farris (CEO, Stion), in discussion with the authors, May 1, 2013.

177   **LanzaTech produces:** Prabhakar Nair (Executive Vice President of Business Development Asia, LanzaTech), in discussion with the authors, April 24, 2013.

179   **As ethanol made from corn reached scale:** Randy Schnepf, "Agriculture-Based Biofuels: Overview and Emerging Issues," Congressional Research Service, May 1, 2013, www.fas.org/ sgp/crs/misc/R41282.pdf.

179   **ethanol consumed more than 40 percent:** "Corn-Based Ethanol Production Should Cease," National Center for Policy Analysis, January 24, 2013, www.ncpa.org/sub/dpd/index .php?Article_ID=22773.

179   **The complexity of this temporary supply chain:** Platts, *New Crudes, New Markets,* March 2013, www.platts.com/IM.Platts.Content/InsightAnalysisIndustrySolutionPapersNewCrudesNew Markets.pdf.

181   **A previous McKinsey book, *In Search of Excellence*:** Peters, Thomas J., and Robert H. Waterman, Jr. *In Search of Excellence: Lessons from America's Best-Run Companies.* New York: HarperCollins, 2012.

181   **the average amount spent on research and development:** National Science Foundation, "Business R&D Performance in the United States Increased in 2011," September 2013, www .nsf.gov/statistics/infbrief/nsf13335.

         "Research and Development: National Trends and International Linkages," *Science and Engineering Indicators 2010,* National Science Foundation, January 2010, www.nsf.gov/stat istics/seind10/c4/c4s3.htm.

182   **Samsung has excelled at developing champions:** Chris Velazco, "How Samsung Got Big," Techcrunch, June 1, 2013, www.techcrunch.com/2013/06/01/how-samsung-got-big.

CHAPTER **EIGHT**

195   **Steven Johnson describes in his book:** Johnson, Steven. *Where Good Ideas Come from: The Seven Patterns of Innovation.* New York: Penguin, 2011.

200   **the electronics content in cars has hit 25 percent of their value:** "Automotive Technology: Greener Vehicles, Changing Skills," Center for Automotive Research, May 2011, www .drivingworkforcechange.org/reports/electronics.pdf.

203   **Hitting that price may unlock a market for cooling:** "Commercial Refrigeration Equipment Market: Global Industry Size, Market Share, Trends, Analysis and Forecast, 2012–2018," Transparency Market Research, October 22, 2012, www.transparencymarketresearch.com/ commercial-refrigeration-equipment-market.html.

         "HVAC Equipment Market: Global Industry Analysis, Size, Share, Growth, Trends, and Forecast, 2012–2018," Transparency Market Research, August 23, 2013, www.transparencymarketresearch .com/hvac-equipment-market.html.

         Prahalad, C. K. *The Fortune at the Bottom of the Pyramid: Eradicating Poverty through Profits.* New Jersey: Pearson Education, 2005.

205   **The results can deliver 25 to 35 percent-plus savings:** "Natural Gas Fleet Savings Calculator," America's Natural Gas Alliance, 2013, http://anga.us/issues-and-policy/ transportation#.UqCZLGRDseZ.

208   **Elance, a young company:** Fabio Rosati (Chief Executive Officer, Elance), in discussion with the authors, April 16, 2013.

         Elance, *Work Differently: Annual Impact Report,* June 2013, www.elance.com/q/sites/default/ files/docs/AIR/AnnualImpactReport.pdf.html.

CHAPTER **NINE**

213   **The reason is Yan Cheung:** Evan Osnos, "Wastepaper Queen: She's China's Horatio Alger Hero. Will Her Fortune Survive?" *The New Yorker,* March 30, 2009, www.newyorker.com/ reporting/2009/03/30/090330fa_fact_osnos.

213   **40% of the garbage:** *Garbology,* Humes.

214   **ecoimagination:** Deborah Frodl (Global Executive Director, GE), in discussion with the authors, July 9, 2013.

CONCLUSION

223   **metals prices declined 0.2 percent annually:** McKinsey Global Institute, Sustainability & Resource Productivity Practice. *Resource Revolution: Tracking Global Commodity Markets.* McKinsey, 2013.

223   **gains in resource productivity languished:** "Average Annual Expenditures and Characteristics of All Consumer Units, Consumer Expenditure Survey, 2006–2012," U.S. Department of Labor Bureau of Labor Statistics.

225 **Since 2000, commodity prices have surged:** "Commodity Prices and Price Forecast in Nominal U.S. Dollars," The World Bank, January 15, 2013, siteresources.worldbank.org/INTPROSPECTS/Resources/334934-1304428586133/Price_Forecast.pdf.

225 **the correlation between food commodities and oil prices:** *Resource Revolution: Tracking Global Commodity Markets*, McKinsey Global Institute.

225 **U.S. corn productivity improved almost 3 percent each year:** "Quick Stats: National, Corn, Grain—Yield, Measured in Bu/Acre, 1866–2013," U.S. Department of Agriculture National Agricultural Statistics Service, Accessed December 5, 2013, quickstats.nass.usda.gov/results/0CAFB589-05CE-365D-A219-03030420CDB3.

225 **shale oil and gas have delivered:** "Drilling Productivity Report: For key tight oil and shale gas regions," U.S. Energy Information Administration, December 2013, www.eia.gov/petroleum/drilling/pdf/dpr-full.pdf.

225 **a 5 percent per year improvement:** "A Review of Consumer Benefits from Corporate Average Fuel Economy (CAFE) Standards," *Consumer Reports*, June 2013, consumersunion.org/wp-content/uploads/2013/06/FuelEconomyStandards.pdf.
"Fuel Economy Basics," Union of Concerned Scientists, August 23, 2012, www.ucsusa.org/clean_vehicles/smart-transportation-solutions/better-fuel-efficiency/fuel-economy-basics.html.

225 **Half of all food production is not consumed:** Institute of Mechanical Engineers, *Global Food: Waste Not, Want Not,* January 2013, www.imeche.org/docs/default-source/reports/Global_Food_Report.pdf.

225 **Oil and gas production processes recover:** "Enhanced Oil Recovery," U.S. Department of Energy Office of Fossil Energy, energy.gov/fe/science-innovation/oil-gas/enhanced-oil-recovery.

225 **Only 14 to 26 percent of the energy in the fuel:** "Fuel Economy: Where the Energy Goes," U.S. Department of Energy, www.fueleconomy.gov/feg/atv.shtml.

225 **a third to half of the water is wasted:** "Threats: Water Scarcity," World Wildlife Fund, 2013, worldwildlife.org/threats/water-scarcity.
McKinsey Global Institute, 2030 Water Resources Group, *Charting Our Water Future: Economic frameworks to inform decision-making.* McKinsey, 2009.

225 **even the most efficient central station plants:** Sonal Patel, "Pushing the 60% Efficiency Gas Turbine Barrier," *Power Magazine*, July 1, 2011, www.powermag.com pushing-the-60-efficiency-gas-turbine-barrier.

226 **LED penetration is one-third higher in China than in the EU:** McKinsey & Company, *Lighting the way: Perspectives on the global lighting market*, July 2011, img.ledsmagazine.com/pdf/LightingtheWay.pdf.

228 **Governments have a large role to play:** Mazzucato, Mariana. *The Entrepreneurial State: Debunking Public vs. Private Sector Myths.* New York: Anthem Press, 2013.

231 **Globally, 8 percent of water is used for energy production:** "Water," Food and Agriculture Organization of the United Nations, February 5, 2013, www.fao.org/energy/81341/en.

EXHIBITS

12 **Accelerated expansion of the middle class:** Angus Maddison; University of Groningen; McKinsey & Company analysis.

14 **The land, water, and energy content of food:** USDA, Morrison; Heitschmidt et al, Waterfootprint.org.

17 **Reserves are getting more expensive to extract:** USDA, Morrison; Heitschmidt et al, Waterfootprint.org.

20 **Wealth creation in industrial revolutions:** *Fortune* magazine; press search.

37 **Commodity price evolution during industrial revolutions:** U.S. wholesale commodity price indices, anchored on Warren and Pearson index values from 1779 onwards.

46 **Hydraulic fracturing:** National Energy Board of Canada, *Tight Oil Developments in the Western Canada Sedimentary Basin,* December 2011, www.neb-one.gc.ca/clf-nsi/rnrgynfmtn/nrgyrprt/l/tghtdvlpmntwcsb2011/tghtdvlpmntwcsb2011-eng.pdf.

50   **North American unconventional oil and gas reserves:** Drilling Info; Energy Insights (a McKinsey Solution); EIA; Deutsche Bank; Shale Gas.com; USGS; NPC; company announcements; McKinsey analysis.

63   **Waste in fuel, cars, and roads caused by automobile transportation:** Rocky Mountain Institute.

72   **Tesla performance, fuel economy, and safety data:** Motor Trends; NHTSA.

75   **95 percent improvement cost and range of electric vehicles over 25 years:** Buchman 2005; GreenCarReports.com; IEK; DOE.

78   **Possible resource shortages:** U.S. Geological Survey (USGS); McKinsey analysis.

82   **Fuel efficiency by country:** International Council on Clean Transportation (ICCT).

90   **Annual resource consumption in America:** "Materials Flows in the United States Economy: A Phyical Accounting of the U.S. Industrial Economy," World Resources Institute, 2008.

113   **China is building the equivalent of 100 New Yorks:** Kathryn Blaze Carlson, "Above the world in 90 days: China building world's tallest skyscraper—220 storeys—in just three months," *National Post*, November 24, 2012, news.nationalpost.com/2012/11/22/above-the-world-in-90-days-china-building-worlds-tallest-skyscraper-220-storeys-in-just-three-months.

114   **Building modular skyscrapers:** Ibid.

119   **Rise of computing power compared to evolution of animal brains:** Kurzweil, Ray. *The Singularity Is Near.* New York: Penguin, 2005.

130   **Telecom subscribers and data traffic:** Kleiner Perkins; Cisco; OECD.

132   **The smart grid:** "Can the Smart Grid live up to its expectations?" McKinsey & Company, 2010, www.mckinsey.com/client_service/electric_powerand_natural_gas/latest_thinking/mckinsey_on_smart_grid.

136   **Growth of new data generated by the smart grid:** Brian Bohan, Vitria Technology, and Bret Farrar and Mark Luigs, Sendero Business Services, 2011.

149   **Speed of market penetration for new innovations:** McKinsey/PTW-HAWK Survey.

151   **Protein prices:** IMF, World Bank, Index Mundi, USDA, Nutrition data, IGD.com.

152   **Pace of new technology adoption:** Michael Cox and Richard Alm, "You are what you spend," *New York Times*, February 10, 2008, www.nytimes.com/2008/02/10/opinion/10cox.

155   **Making light affordable:** Eco-Efficiency Action Project; *Journal of Physics* "Solid-state lighting an energy-economics."

165   **Learning curve for solar innovation:** Paul Maycock, Bloomberg New Energy Finance.

169   **Retail grid parity is here:** Enerdata; EIA; PV Watts; SERC; India Central Electricity Authority; Utility publications; IEA; McKinsey Global Solar Initiative.

196   **Two different operating systems:** "Danaher Business System," Danaher, 2013, www.danaher.com/danaher-business-system.
        "General Motors: A Century of Innovation and Leadership," GM Heritage Center, history.gmheritagecenter.com/wiki/index.php/General_Motors:_A_Century_of_Innovation_and_Leadership.

202   **Natural science and engineering graduates by country:** National Science Foundation, 2012.

206   **Factory productivity growth:** Angus Maddison.

215   **Automotive shakeout:** Steven Klepper, "The Evolution of the U.S. Automobile Industry and Detroit as its Capital," Carnegie Mellon University, November 2001, www.druid.dk/uploads/tx_pictureedb/dw2002-440.pdf.
        "List of automobile manufacturers of the United States," Wikipedia, December 10, 2013, en.wikipedia.org/wiki/List_of_automobile_manufacturers_of_the_United_States.

224   **Less is more:** U.S. Bureau of Labor Statistics' Consumer Expenditure Survey, 2013.

226   **Resource productivity—past and future:** GDP: Global Insight; Water: McK global supply-demand model; GHGs: IPCC; Oil: IEA WEO 2008 reference scenario; Power: IEA WEO 2008 (historic) and McKinsey Global Abatement Cost Curve v2.0(2030); Food/feed: FAO 2008.

BIBLIOGRAPHY

Anderson, Chris. *Makers: The New Industrial Revolution.* New York: Random House, 2012.

Brand, Stewart. *Whole Earth Discipline: Why Dense Cities, Nuclear Power, Transgenic Crops, Restored Wildlands, and Geoengineering Are Necessary.* New York: Penguin, 2010.

Braungart, Michael, and William McDonough. *Cradle to Cradle: Remaking the Way We Make Things.* New York: North Point Press, 2010.

Brynjolfsson, Erik, and Andrew McAfee. *The Race Against the Machine: How the Digital Revolution is Accelerating Innovation, Driving Productivity, and Irreversibly Transforming Employment and the Economy.* Digital Frontier Press, 2011.

Carnegie, Andrew. *James Watt.* New York: Doubleday, Page & Company, 1905.

Fletcher, Seth. *Bottled Lightning: Superbatteries, Electric Cars, and the New Lithium Economy.* New York: Hill and Wang, 2012.

Govindarajan, Vijay, and Chris Trimble. *The Other Side of Innovation: Solving the Execution Challenge.* Harvard Business Review Press. First eBook edition, September 2010.

Malthus, Thomas. *An Essay on the Principle of Population.* Oxford: Oxford University Press, 1993.

McKinsey Global Institute, Sustainability & Resource Productivity Practice. *Resource Revolution: Tracking Global Commodity Markets.* McKinsey, 2013.

——. *Resource Revolution: Understanding and Accelerating Progress.* McKinsey, 2013.

McKinsey Global Institute, 2030 Water Resources Group. *Charting Our Water Future: Economic Frameworks to Inform Decision-Making.* McKinsey, 2009.

Porter, Michael E. *Competitive Strategy: Techniques for Analyzing Industries and Competitors.* New York: Free Press, 2003.

Smith, Adam. *The Wealth of Nations.* Oxford: Oxford University Press, 2003.

Smolan, Rick, and Jennifer Erwitt. *Blue Planet Run: The Race to Provide Safe Drinking Water to the World.* Earth Aware Editions, 2007.

Yergin, Daniel. *The Quest: Energy, Security, and the Remaking of the Modern World.* 2nd Ed. New York: Penguin Books, 2012.

CREDITS

INDEX